Mechanisms
of Cognitive Development

A series of books in psychology

Editors: Richard C. Atkinson
           Gardner Lindzey
           Richard F. Thompson

Mechanisms
of Cognitive Development

ROBERT J. STERNBERG, Editor

W. H. Freeman and Company
New York

Library of Congress Cataloging in Publication Data
Main entry under title:

Mechanisms of cognitive development.

  (A Series of books in psychology)
  Bibliography: p.
  Includes index.
  1. Cognitive.   2. Developmental psychology.
I. Sternberg, Robert J.   II. Series.
BF311.M433   1984   153.4   84-4038
ISBN 0-7167-1596-1
ISBN 0-7167-1597-X (pbk.)

Printed in the United States of America.

1 2 3 4 5 6 7 8 9   MP   2 1 0 8 9 8 7 6 5 4

Contents

Preface   vii
ROBERT J. STERNBERG

1   Introduction: The End of the Age of Development   1
WILLIAM KESSEN

2   The Process of Stage Transition: A Neo-Piagetian View   19
ROBBIE CASE

3   Processes of Cognitive Development: Optimal Level and
Skill Acquisition   45
KURT W. FISCHER, SANDRA L. PIPP

4   Mechanisms in Cognitive Development and the Structure
of Knowledge   81
FRANK C. KEIL

5   Transition Processes in Quantitative Development   101
DAVID KLAHR

6   Mechanisms of Cognitive Growth: Variation and Selection   141
ROBERT S. SIEGLER

7   Mechanisms of Cognitive Development: A Componential
Approach   163
ROBERT J. STERNBERG

8   Discussion   187
JOHN H. FLAVELL

Index   211

250256

Preface

One might argue that there are two fundamental questions in developmental psychology: First, what are the psychological states individuals pass through at different points in their development? Second, what are the mechanisms of development by which individuals pass from one state to another? A strong case could be made that the second question is the more fundamental one, as the states are in large part outcomes of the developmental mechanisms. In a sense, then, the developmental mechanisms are more basic. Yet, even a cursory review of the literature in developmental psychology would reveal that a far larger amount of theory and data address the former question than the latter. Indeed, I doubt that as much as 1 percent of our developmental literature addresses the question of the mechanisms by which developmental changes are effected. If one examines some of the traditional and modern approaches to developmental psychology, one can begin to see why this is so. Consider four such approaches: the psychometric, the behavioristic, the Piagetian, and information processing.

The psychometric approach, which in the second half of the twentieth century has lost much of the popularity it enjoyed in the first half, is essentially a structural approach. Its main tool, factor analysis, yields a set of static, structural factors. These factors can provide useful maps of cognitive, affective, and possibly motivational structures at different points in development. The formalism provides no way, however, of characterizing—much less of explaining—transitions from one structure to another. As a result, a strictly factorial account of mechanisms of cognitive development appears to be logically impossible. Certainly, no such account has ever been provided. Psychometric accounts of psychological structures at different points in development would have to be supplemented by accounts of another kind in order to explain, or even describe, how changes in states come about.

The behavioristic approach to cognitive development clearly can provide an account of developmental change: indeed, this approach has worked best when applied to phenomena of learning. What is less clear is whether it can provide an account of the mechanisms by which change takes place. In traditional behavioristic accounts, description is at the level of the chain of successive stimulus inputs and response outputs; accounts of mental events mediating between these two end states are omitted, and even eschewed. Yet it is precisely in the interval between stimulus and response that mental mechanisms must act. "Revisionistic" accounts have allowed the specification of organismic variables between stimulus and response. But behaviorism does not seem to have—within the S–R formalism—the theoretical apparatus for describing just what mental mechanisms operate between the stimulus and response. Rather, to provide genuine mediational accounts, behaviorism, like psychometrics, needs to borrow from another approach some kind of mechanistic formalism that can explain, or at least describe, change. Thus, both behavioristic and psychometric accounts seem not so much wrong as incomplete. Psychometric accounts provide structural description but no means of accounting for change. Behavioristic accounts provide descriptions of change (especially through learning) at the level of stimulus and response, but little or no means of describing the mechanisms that mediate the mental events that occupy the time between stimulus and response.

The Piagetian approach to cognitive development is certainly the most nearly complete systematization we have of how individuals develop, especially in the cognitive domain. Moreover, the approach does have two processes of equilibration that most definitely can describe how change takes place—namely, assimilation and accommodation. Even as parts of the Piagetian edifice have seemed to crumble in recent years, these two mechanisms of equilibration have managed to hold their own. If they are to be criticized at all, it might be in terms of their having more heuristic than detailed explanatory value. If we accept these two processes as bases for mental development, then one might ask for a more detailed specification of just what happens—at the level of mental mechanisms—when assimilation and accommodation take place. For example, what is the mental control system that initiates and guides these processes, and what mental events take place when assimilation and accommodation occur? The Piagetian view, then, like the others, seems not be incorrect but incomplete. It is in need of more microscopic psychological analysis to supplement its useful macroscopic description of cognitive development.

The information-processing approach provides the microscopic level of analysis that I believe fills in the details that the Piagetian approach does not provide. It contains within it a variety of formalisms that can describe the nature of the mechanisms of cognitive development. Chapters 2 to 7 in this book represent six attempts to specify just how subsets of these formalisms can be used to provide such description. Indeed, I believe the book is unique in bringing together in one place alternative accounts of just how information-processing psychology (or any form of psychology!) can illuminate the mechanisms of cognitive development. Although all six contributors share their information-processing orientation, they differ widely in their views as to how the orientation should be applied to understanding cognitive development. For example, they differ in their ideas regarding the respective roles of knowledge versus process, of executive versus nonexecutive processes, and of the extent to which a wholly general account is even possible. It is important to add as well that their theories, like any accounts within a single approach, must necessarily be incomplete. Moreover, these accounts must be viewed as preliminary: despite the age of the question they address (indeed, the question is as old as developmental psychology), the question of the mechanisms of cognitive development has received relatively little attention, and thus attempts to answer it must, regrettably, be viewed as still in their infancy. Certainly, they cannot be expected to draw upon the detailed data bases available for questions regarding the states of development that children are in at various ages in their cognitive growth.

To conclude, I believe that these accounts provide exciting and innovative early passes addressed to the question of how cognitive development takes place. I hope the accounts will stimulate further thinking along these (or more advanced) lines, and that they will encourage others to pay more attention to the fundamental but neglected question of just what mechanisms underlie cognitive development.

Mechanisms
of Cognitive Development

1 | Introduction: The End of the Age of Development

William Kessen

Those who assert that a blind fatality
produced the various effects we behold in this
world talk very absurdly; for can any thing be
more unreasonable than to pretend that a
blind fatality could be productive of
intelligent beings?

Montesquieu, The spirit of laws, 1748

Psychology is always in crisis (Willy, 1899). The looping repetition of the theme that we are going to hell in a handbasket may give comfort to the skeptics and reassurance to the fearful, but there is an urgency and a uniformity in the current crisis that may mark it as unique (Kessen, 1981). Particularly for the psychologists who built their hopes for a science of mind on positivism and physics, the news that we are in a post-positivistic age where biological images command attention and applause must arrive as heavy and unwelcome. More locally relevant to the book you now read, the greatest weight may fall on the developmental psychologist, who, already in trouble with the general deconstruction of psychology, must face the frightening prospect that we are at a turning point—the end?—of the Age of Development.

The notion of development as a generative force permitting, even demanding, the continual improvement of mankind was latent in the secular humanism of the late Renaissance, and came to its first flower in the obsession with machinery and technology that characterized Western European intellectuals in the eighteenth and early nineteenth centuries. Steam engines, railroad trains, geographical exploration and colonization, scientific achievement, political revolution: all were seen as representative of the inevitable upward march of the species. *Development as Progress* lay hold of Western imagination in ways that we can begin to detect only now, as we near the end of the Age of Development. From Goethe's prescient ambivalence about development (Berman, 1982) to Kipling's crude celebrations of Victorian perfection, there runs a steady stream of poetic praise for the wonders of progressive development. Poets echoed scientists and entrepreneurs in depicting most of the last two centuries as a time of perfecting transformation when, through knowledge and industry, we came closer and closer to the ultimate goals of truth and efficiency (Mandelbaum, 1971). There were hold-outs to the dream, of course: the anti-modernists from Blake to Pound (and their scarcer allies in politics) called for a return to community, simplicity, and the countryside. But, amid the cheers that went up for development, progress, and perfectibility, the voices of doubt sounded vague and quaint (Lears, 1981; White, 1962).

Emily Cahan, Carol Feldman, Thomas Gamble, and Mark Lipian have talked with me through the past year about the issues raised in the present paper. I thank them heartily but I cannot hold them responsible for my interpretations. Research for the paper was generously supported by the Carnegie Corporation of New York.

Thus, the West was well prepared—preadapted, if you like—for the intellectual events that brought all living beings, even children, into the encompassing domain of Development as Progress: the publication of *The origin of species* (1859) and *The descent of man* (1871). Darwin was, as usual, closely guarded in his personal convictions about the progressive character of evolutionary change, and the human machine for assembling facts did not commit himself to evolutionary perfectibility. This Darwin of the texts—whom I will call the Darwin of the First Kind—pronounced a gradualist theory of phylogenetic transformation, but he did not use the theory as a political or ethical platform; nor did he see phylogenetic changes as inevitably pointed toward progress.

The Darwin of the Second Kind—the Darwin of interpretation, misreading, and extension—was a creation of the earlier commitment to Development as Progress. It was this Second Darwin who so profoundly influenced developmental psychology. The thinkers who tied evolutionary concepts to child development (Spencer, Romanes, Hall, Baldwin, and Piaget, among the crowd) were convinced that the development of the child is a progressive transformation from the less good to the better. Haeckel's (1874) analogy between evolution and embryology was expanded to an analogy among evolution, embryology, and the development of children. And developmental psychologists borrowed more from readings and misreadings of evolutionary theory and its precursors in eighteenth-century thought than from ideas about the succession of human improvement (the most un-Darwinian "stages" of development). Progressive development was seen to possess a kind of inevitability, a life force, an innate press that would carry the child forward. Further, and in peculiar tension with the premise of inevitability, progressive development was seen to require active manipulation and transformation of the child. Just as forests had to be cleared for cities to be built, and tribal natives had to be converted to Christianity, so the child, to reach "full potential," had to be restrained and instructed. In short, the ambiguity about the inevitability and uniformity of progressive development that runs through the progressivist treatises of the eighteenth and nineteenth centuries was transferred unresolved to the study of children. By the mid-twentieth century, the developing child, along with the developing country, had become the primary image of human progress and perfectibility.

Why, then, is developmental psychology in crisis; on what grounds can we suspect that we are near the end of the Age of Development? For one, many Western institutions seem less secure in their hopes for ameliorative change than they did a few decades back. The wings of enthusiasm that carried us from 1946 to 1976 have lost their loft: in political and literary criticism, in education, in economic forecasts, in discussions of energy and the environment, we hear doubts being expressed about Development as Progress; the anti-modernists are feeling their oats. It is not surprising that technical developmental psychology now reflects, as it always has to some extent, the spirit of the times.

But there are grounds more closely relevant than the dank infectious cultural surroundings for the contemporary uneasiness among child psychologists. First of all is the sharpened recognition that the analogy between progressive evolutionism and child development is *only* an analogy; it has logical force no greater than the comparison of a child to a flower. Whatever utility the evolutionary analogy has depends on its provocation of empirical testing *within* the domain of child development. Second, the foundation (the evolutionary analogy) upon which we have erected the house of child development is in poor repair; classical neo-Darwinian interpretations of evolution—emphasizing, as they do, random variation, selection by consequences, and relatively slight incremental change— are under close critical examination by evolutionary biologists (Gould, 1977; Gould and Lewontin, 1979). We face the chilling possibility that we are resting our discipline on analogies with biological principles that are being abandoned by the legitimate heirs of the principles![1] Third, and most particularly, students of cognitive development are in retreat from Piaget's theoretical simplicities and from the sensitivity of his observations. The king is dead and all the provincial governors are laying claim to his crown.

At this moment of doubt and indecision, Sternberg and his colleagues have taken on a strangely neglected problem in child psychology: the mechanisms of transition in cognitive development. They have bent their several generous talents to the task, and the result, as you will see, is a display of the hesitations, the strengths, and the likely futures of research on the development of mind. My task is to provide a reader's guide to the essays. I propose to do so by using the problem of cognitive transitions as a vehicle for a limited disquisition on the present moment in developmental psychology. At varying length and in varying depth, I will address the following four themes: the ends of development; mechanisms of transition, directive and open; research domains and their boundaries; and history, context, and essential messiness.

THE ENDS OF DEVELOPMENT

The idea of development entails the existence of an endpoint: the child moves, steadily or erratically, toward a goal (Kaplan, 1967;

Kessen, 1966). Of course, not all theorists are explicit in specifying where their particular form of the developmental race will end, but the problem of goals hovers over all attempts to understand human development:

> The specification of the dimensions of the developmental goal limits the relevant evidence; only some parts of the observational range are seen as part of appropriate inquiry; even before a single datum is collected or a single measure taken, there is reduction of the possibilities of answer. The reduction is unavoidable, certainly, but it need not be unconscious. (Kessen, 1966), p. 63f.

A further distinction is necessary. In the *strong* form of the end-point argument, development is measured as a discrepancy from the values of the goal; thus, the development of problem-solving skill is measured by its approach to (or its distance from) adult or ideal forms. All observations and evidence are gathered with an eye on the horizon that represents finished forms. In the *weak* form of the argument, the endpoint is used only to specify a domain of investigation (personality development or moral development, for example), and age-local studies are made of the domain. Thus, the moral principles of the 6-year-old can conceivably be studied without attention to the discrepancy of those principles from adult morality. Piaget has tried mightily to comprehend cognitive development in such an age-local fashion, but even for him the pull of the finished forms in discussing the unfinished forms has been almost irresistible (see Piaget, 1980). Weak-form goal systems tend to become strong-form systems. It should be emphasized as well that, in both the strong and the weak forms of the argument, there is an explicit or implicit setting of boundaries on the domain under study. I will return to the question of domains and their boundaries shortly.

We should remember at this point that there have been child psychologies for whom the notion of development is not a key, or even a necessary, part of describing and discussing change over age. For the most radical of these psychologists (Watson and his dozen infants leap to mind, but Watson has had successors), it has not been necessary to specify endpoints toward which "development" tends. Each change in the child's behavior is the consequence of a complex set of environmental contingencies that can vary over an enormous range. Changes with age must be organized and understood not in terms of endpoints, but rather in terms of a succession of arranged or adventitious circumstances. Although such explanations were held in generally low regard during the domination of Piaget over the study of cognitive development, they are making a reappearance in two forms that differ markedly in their ancestry. The first is the reappearance of discussions of learning; the second is in the current zest for explanations of children's cognition as influenced largely by culture and context. The heirs of Watson and the heirs of Vygotsky are strangely allied in their attempt to build child psychologies that escape the specification of species-general developmental goals. But take care, Reader! Even those theories of development that attempt to avoid the statement of species-general goals do, in fact, point the child toward some endpoint, some adult condition. As we shall see, the variation in endpoints implied by such theories poses interesting moral and political questions.

As you read the essays that follow, you should keep in mind a query about each scholar's position on developmental goals. Are these goals explicitly stated? Is the argument strong-form or weak-form? Are the goals, stated or implied, meant to be species-general or conditional? If developmental endpoints are not specified, can you detect evidence for implicit goals in the essay? Are goals colored by perceptible ethical or political principles?

Mechanisms of Transition, Directive and Open

One can imagine a child psychology that consists of a conglomerate of domains of discourse, each telling the story of how some aspect of children's minds changes over time. There would be disagreements about the interest or centrality of a particular domain, and arguments about whether or not the changes move toward some fixed goals, but in this imagined world there would be no discussions of the modes and mechanisms of transition, no treatment of the question of how the child gets from one condition in time to another. Not only can one imagine such a state of affairs; much of child psychology, in demonstrable fact, ignores or lightly touches on the issues that define the intention of this book. The rapidity and complexity of children's development has made it possible to tell interesting stories about change without explaining them. However, in cycles of undetermined periodicity, child psychologists return sooner or later to the mechanisms of change in their attempts to understand and to organize the sometimes bewildering multiplicity of the child's mind.

Mechanisms of transition and developmental end states must occupy the same conceptual space because, at least historically, there is so intimate a relation between a commentator's vision of where development is going, on the one hand, and how it gets there, on the other. One of the engaging problems of explanation in child psychology is the degree to which developmental ends and means can be disaggregated. I will sketch out some of the issues raised by a consideration of transitional mechanisms in five bins, bins with walls that are somewhat permeable: *pseudomechanisms, directive mechanisms, constrained mechanisms, open mechanisms,* and *the curious problem of motivation.*

Pseudomechanisms. The differentiation of description and explanation that sounds so elegant and so conclusive in elementary textbooks becomes fluid and shifting when it is applied to current candidates for mechanisms of cognitive development. Nonetheless, as witness to our good intentions, the reader should look at Chapters 2 to 7 with the following question in mind: to what extent are the proposed mechanisms *elaborated descriptions* (more or less successful) of the phenomena under discussion, and to what extent do they take us beyond the observations? I suggest two general criteria to use in addressing this question, which will, in any case, not be given a clear-cut answer. Criterion A: is the proposed mechanism *generative*? That is, will it tell us something we did not know from looking at the observations themselves, and, in particular, does it produce a prediction that can be tested in the domain? Criterion B: is the mechanism bounded? Criterion B is complementary to criterion A and could be loosely rephrased as: does the mechanism explain everything? A persistent difficulty in developmental psychology has been the giddy oscillation between mere reformulations of observations, on one side, and unbounded universal "explanations," on the other. We are well acquainted with single ideas filled beyond their capacity ("equilibrium" and "reinforcement" are perhaps the most problematic of a numerous set), but there is another form of empty or inclusive explanation that the reader should be alert to. If the scholar uses seven propositions to "explain" a limited domain of phenomena, it is proper to ask if the seven propositions define any boundaries whatsoever. Archimedes would not be remembered if he had postulated twenty levers and a hydraulic jack to move the world. The scholars who have written chapters for the present book have chosen somewhat limited domains of discourse; therefore, the reader is presented with an unusual opportunity to measure the generativity and the boundedness of the mechanisms proposed.

Directive Mechanisms. The oldest and most persistent mechanism of development has been a ballistic, biological or pseudobiological force usually called *maturation.* Marked by species generality and by relatively little variation in timing from child to child, maturation has been called on to "explain" locomotor development, the onset of speech, and (sometimes) the regularities of sensorimotor cognitive development. I haul out this poor weary horse once more to make two points that are often neglected.

First, naked evocation of maturation is either a stand-in for description ("children walk near the end of the first year") or a synonym for age with no leftover meaning, except, perhaps, an implication such as, "the appearance of these acts is hard to influence under ordinary circumstances." Although we have learned a great deal about mechanisms of maturational change in some animals, our conceptual apparatus for talking about tissue-driven processes in human beings is wobbly and uncertain.

Second, and of more consequence for the present book, one cannot escape the problem of quasidescription or pseudomechanisms by dressing developmental mechanisms in nonbiological language. To assert that the child's memory space increases with age or that there is a developmental shift in rule- systems is to go not much beyond Gesell. *Dei ex machina* wear different costumes in different plays, but the costumes cannot hide the failure to present *ways of understanding* human development that will permit interesting new observations and that will generate provocative new conclusions.

Constrained Mechanisms.   The most popular mechanisms on the cognitive market these days are those based on the idea that development occurs when a system of knowledge (a structured mind) encounters some event, presentation, stimulus, or problem that is, to some degree, new to the existing system. This epigenetic proposal has been set forth by Baldwin, by Piaget, by Vygotsky, and by Waddington, among others. The position if attractive because it seems so balanced: change takes place because of encounters of mind and world, but the change is constrained by the child's response capabilities, characteristics of memory, earlier history, and so on. Certainly, the epigenetic proposals are both more plausible and have a firmer epistemological base than directive mechanisms and open mechanisms, but, as the authors of this book recognize, the proposals pose a set of problems that will have to be dealt with eventually. The central problems with which any theory of epigenetic transition must deal are the problem of *specification of structure* and the problem of *measurement of cognitive distance.* If we continue to be fond of structuralist or constructionist theories of cognitive development, then we will have to state the *specific* terms, dimensions, and linking relations of structures. In parallel, if we are committed to notions like "the zone of proximal development" or "re-equilibration," some persuasive measure or index of cognitive distance must be proposed. (For example: What makes a problem a problem? What gets inside and what lies outside the zone of proximal development?) Because the scholars whose essays follow are all in one corner or another of the structuralist-discrepancy camp, the reader will want to know, at least programmatically, how each scholar handles the two linked problems. These chapters tell us both (1) that the right questions about constrained mechanisms are beginning to be asked with some concreteness, and (2) that we have a long way to go yet for a full statement. The tasks are inordinately difficult, and it is easy to understand how developmental psychologists might tend to turn back, toward the solace (often misplaced) of directive mechanisms (Chomsky may owe much of his appeal to such an escape), or toward the nonstructuralist conceptions of open mechanisms.

Open mechanisms.   From Taine (1888) to Skinner (1938), there have been thinkers who have used the least-bounded mechanism of development ever proposed: selection by consequences, a notion congenial to the First Darwin. The position, unconstrained by particular *contents* of behaviors and depending almost entirely on transition rules, is—despite its poor reputation among the writers and doubtless among the readers of this book—the most fully worked out, detailed, and empirically supported mechanism of change (development?) that we know. There are signs, here and elsewhere, that cognitive psychologists are revisiting some old haunts of learning theory for help in specifying mechanisms of change.

Another form of open mechanism besides the reinforcement-contingency model was presented by Dewey (1920), perhaps under James' influence. This mechanism, which has sometimes been revived in recent writings of the neo-Vygotskians (Cole and Scribner, 1974), may be called *local adaptation*. Children are seen as solving problems or constructing new rule systems in a fashion quite like that suggested by the constrained mechanists. The difference lies in the absence of any normal or expected ultimate outcome; change takes place, to be sure, but the change has neither *necessary* nor predetermined end states.

We can now see how the question of developmental endpoints enters into our discussion of transition. For the Piagetians and their allies (including many of the information-processing theorists), there is an expectation that children will get to, or at least systematically approach, some common end state—an end state that bears a strong resemblance to the adult cognitions of developmental psychologists! There is no such expectation for the scholars committed to learning and to local adaptation. The child is not approaching *anything*; the child only learns more responses and their relations, or solves more and more local problems. Taken seriously, these latter positions are truly *open* and require, in sharply distinct ways, the abandonment of the idea of Development as Progress. The logical successors to the First Darwin—the Darwin of directionless change—turn out to be the least *developmental* of all theorists of child psychology.

The Curious Problem of Motivation.   Just as developmental psychologists' intense affair with learning theories went out with short hair and saddleshoes, so did our rapture with the issue of motivation. The problem was not solved: most cognitive developmental psychologists simply ignored it. One reading of the turning away may be that the ghost in the machine was exorcised; another may be that ideas of energy, push, drive, or need are fundamentally ill suited to contemporary ways of talking about mind. There is no space here to revive and rework the problem of the motivation for cognitive development, but the reader may want to ask each of the theorists who appear in this book: "What makes the system run? What turns it on, stops it, amplifies it, possibly directs it?" The default answer to these questions—that cognitive development is a characteristic of human tissue—seems intellectually insufficient. Whether cast in traditional or in novel forms, the problem of the motivation of cognitive development transitions must be faced by our thoughtful authors.

Domains of Discourse and Their Boundaries

Any field of knowledge that is worth our serious attention must eventually be segmented and subdivided; it is vainglorious to speak of "the whole child" except for rhetorical purposes. The subdivision of developmental psychology has not been closely studied, but there is suggestive evidence that it moves with the tides of politics, academic organization, personal interest, and available technology, as well as with the thoughtful analysis of observation and theory. The title of this book, *Mechanisms of cognitive development*, reflects the segmentation of the field in two ways: first, by coming to grips with *cognitive* development rather than reaching across a wider stretch of phenomena; and second, by specifying the crucial plural form "mechanisms." We have come a good distance from the days when a single correct theory of developmental psychology was sought, or when we would speak unthinkingly of "the" concept of development (Harris, 1957; and others). The sophistication of the authors has made this book an unusually focused set of documents that provide ideas about what *kinds* of domains of discourse exist in developmental psychology, and how they are joined (or not joined) to one another. The loose-jointed typology that I propose here carries little epistemological weight; it is, rather, a possible framework for talking about the modes of question-posing and the grounds for the selection of particular patterns of research in developmental psychology. The order in which I mention the types does not have any significance, nor do I maintain that the groupings are independent of one another.

Domains of Theory.   Freud, Baldwin, Koffka, Werner, and Piaget may be suspected of having thought across the entire range of human development, but the rest of us can unhesitatingly plead "not guilty." It is an irony of scientific change that the more we learn, the less well our knowledge can be made to hang together; the more we know in the small, the less we know in the large. Psychologists often make obeisance toward the notion of a summary integration, a grand synthesis that will gather all the particles into a single pattern. But the historical fact is that analysis begets further analysis, and, at least in developmental psychology, *the process has never been reversed.* I suspect, however, that our affection for analysis and reduction is driven by more than empirical advances; the ancestor of all cognitive psychology, William James, presented us as model and message a *gatherum omnium* of all the observations and ideas he found interesting. The zest for analysis and for particulars may lie close to the center of American psychology's unspoken creed.

In short, whatever our protestations, the chances for a rational or theoretical division of cognitive developmental psychology seem slight.

Domains of Method.   No one has attempted to characterize the domains of developmental psychology in regression analysis or in terms of factor analysis, but a good hunch might be that the most variance in our system of subdivisions would be carried by method. So much has been written on the theme of the methodolatry of psychologists—from Wundt's reaction-time devices to Sternberg's—that the point need not detain us here. Still, the generality of our observation that our domains of study are often organized about variation in method, technological or mathematical, should not dim our appreciation of how important the observation is. In the best of cases, the organization of the field by method represents a more profound organization around an empirical or theoretical question of some consequence. But, again, I suggest that the reader maintain an enquiring spirit in examining the chapters ahead, to determine the degree to which the method is driven by the problem, and the degree to which the problem (and its permitted answers) is driven by the method.

Domains of Affiliation.   Closely tied to subdivision by method is subdivision by affiliation, by the (often personal) bonds of respect and interest that are shared by small or large groups of developmental psychologists. As the domains of our interest become smaller in scope and more highly specialized, the affiliative criterion for the formation of audiences, critics, and intellectual caretakers will become more obvious and, perhaps, more inhibiting of cross-domain communication (Kessen, 1981).

Borrowed Domains.   Just for the record, it should be noted that many of our most active research areas in cognitive development have borrowed their methods and their guiding ideas from other parts of psychology or from outside the field. Language development remains the most telling example, but script formation, infant perception, and learning studies have also used children to try out ideas that were first proposed elsewhere.

Domains of Content.   If one asks cognitive developmental psychologists these days to place themselves in the entire space of their field of study, they are likely to answer by designating some particular content of developmental psychology: early memory, color perception, semantic development, metacognition, or the like. It would be fascinating and important to launch a study of the origin of these subdivisions; we can guess that they are tied in complicated ways to the subdivisions by method and affiliation. But I would like to suggest that the contemporary structuring of domains in developmental psychology in general, and in cognitive development in particular, is based on a largely unexamined and messy theory of *natural kinds*. That is, we all possess a vernacular theory of what children are about, what is important in their lives, what touches us as parents or citizens, and, by no means least, what the endpoints of development are. At first glance, a field of study divided and organized by a vernacular theory of natural kinds may seem both unsystematic and pedestrian. It may be agitating to accept that we study language, at least in part, because language is a significant part of a child's life, or that we study attachment at least partly because of our conviction that early affiliations are important to our children. Such a recognition puts us at a far remove from our myth of the nature of real science.

But adherence to a theory of natural kinds can also cheer us. In the absence of a persuasive rational or theoretical basis for subdividing and organizing the field, the safest and most productive way for us to proceed is to stay close to the ordinary, commonly accepted dimensions of the child's life and to make as much systematic, verifiable good sense as we can of the resulting domains. The justification by natural kinds may not have the encompassing power of a theory of birth trauma or selection by consequences, but it may provide information and ideas that will withstand better the winds of historical change.

Domains of History and Politics.   The last of the provisional types of domains I want to propose is the counterweight to the domains defined by content and natural kinds. With historical change, whether sudden or slow, there are changes in our conceptions of children and of child psychology (Kessel and Siegel, 1983). To make the point in baldest form, *historical change revises our theories of natural kinds.*

It is possible that some of our most heavily engaged research issues in cognitive development nowadays derive directly or indirectly from problems posed by political issues or historical shifts. The nature of intelligence, of reading skills, and of script formation are among the problems in cognitive development that are influenced by changes that are, in the narrow sense, outside developmental psychology. Perhaps the most dramatic instance is our interest in the cognitive consequences of day care, an important problem that would probably never have received the attention it has recently gotten from fine scholars and researchers if the patterns of American family structure had not changed in the late twentieth century.

The unmistakable message of my review of the domains of developmental study is the presence of *variety.* No universal principle seems safe; no single set of explanatory principles will gather together all the diversity; rather, we see a family of limited descriptive and explanatory schemes. As you approach the chapters just ahead, there are, therefore, another group of questions to carry with you. Across what domain of phenomena does the essayist cast his explanatory net? Do his organizing ideas arise chiefly from concerns with theory, method, affiliation, content, or politics?

It is especially important for the reader to be sensitive to the distinction between an author's claim and his achievement. Throughout Western science, but particularly in behavioral studies, there has been a tendency to universalize relatively small domains of interest. That is, a scholar establishes a favorite research preparation, draws some persuasive findings from it, and moves to a universal statement of the principles underlying broad areas of human development. If it is correct that developmental psychology is a family of explanatory schemes, then such universalization, accomplished more or less by authorial proclamation, should be met with some skepticism.

History, Context, and Essential Messiness

In the twentieth century many developmental psychologists, and not they alone among scientists, have grown up with a vision of a science of simplicity and completeness moving slowly but steadily toward truth. The dreams of Carnap (1967) and his colleagues in philosophy, and of Hull (1952) and his colleagues in experimental psychology, were imbued with an optimism and a confidence that were widely shared by child psychologists. Now, we confront at least three invasions of our hope: the threats of essential messiness, essential incompleteness, and essential moral choice.

Essential Messiness.   Our hopes for a philosophy of science that would be both directive and complete have been eroded; radical critics like Feyerabend (1975) have vividly articulated a reluctance among philosophers of science to seek first principles and simplicities. Correspondingly, the grand plans made a few decades back for full explanations in psychology, hypothetical-deductive or not, have melted into obscurity. In their places are active discussions of the context-contingent character of much psychological knowledge (Bronfenbrenner, 1979), and proposals about the modular character of the human mind (Chomsky, 1972). It is not critical to the present argument whether the claims for context and the claims for modularity represent new, useful scientific insights or whether they are rather rationalizations of social changes in the scientific community. What is of primary importance is that we have entered an age of scientific explanation that accepts, and sometimes applauds, diversity, competing explanations in a single domain, open systems, and a multiplicity of method.

Essential Incompleteness.   Developmental psychologists, who are participating in the changes that are listed in the foregoing paragraph, face at least one problem that is more specifically their own. If, as has been maintained here, significant parts of human development represent the shaping of historical circumstances, then we must give over our expectations for a fully normative and complete developmental psychology. Parts of the story of human development will be forever subject to the sometimes slow, sometimes rapid transformations of human history. Developmental psychology, then, cannot be fully normative and must be continuously revamped, in some of its most interesting parts, with the changing times.

Essential Moral Choice.   If evolutionary biology had prescribed the mechanisms of cognitive development in full and thereby shaped its ends, or if human beings and the world were so constituted that our developmental endpoints, although not *forced* by biology, were specifiable, then the tasks of the developmental psychologist could be nonevaluative and nonprescriptive. If, however, the end states of human growth are not considered fully specifiable and open mechanisms are at work, then the task of the developmental psychologist becomes shaped in part by considerations of ethical choice. Kohlberg (1971) and White (1983) have written wisely about the dilemma thereby posed to students of children, but the traditional construal of our scientific reponsibilities has not prepared developmental psychologists well for the moral interpretation of development.

The proper answer to Montesquieu—an answer the First Darwin would have approved—may well be:

> Yes, blind fatality produced intelligent beings; we cannot call on wise planning by Providence (McCosh, 1883) or by Evolution (Spencer, 1899) to account for progress in the formation of the species.

For developmental psychologists, the message of the analysis displayed in these pages may turn out to be similar:

> An undetermined part of human change is under strong influence by ancient phylogenetic selection, however blind. The residuals—the fascinating variety of behaviors that define many individual differences and all cultural variation, and that select paths for change within cultures—are all under the strong influence of historical and political tides. Much of human change escapes the comforting protection of Development as Progress. We may have to accept the end of the Age of Development and deal in part with uncertain unprescribed change in children.

No message of despair is contained in these words, no despair that pushes developmental psychologists toward muteness and immobility; rather, the questions raised in these pages are congenial to a vigorous and transforming study of the child. To be sure, we might well pay close attention to the mapping of the territory our theories are meant to encompass, we must tolerate irreducible ambiguity and diversity, and we should accept the moral responsibility put on us as expert witnesses to human change.

The book before you illustrates the new hopes and the new responsibilities. The thoughtful scholars whose work you read here are sensitive to the issues of domain, multiplicity, and moral choice. They are also sensitive to the injunction this book obeys: to engage in intellectual sharing and in conversations across the fences that separate our domains of professional interest, for only then will a new developmental psychology be constructed.

Read on!

NOTE

[1] Ironically, some of the revisionist proposals make our misreadings more plausible; the best case is the analogical support given the notion of developmental stages by evidence for saltatory evolutionary change. What cannot be misunderstood, however, is that the newer evolutionary biology is based solidly on the Darwin of the First Kind, not on the Darwin who inhabits developmental psychology. Lewontin (1983) discusses the condition of evolutionary biology in an accessible way.

REFERENCES

Berman, M. *All that is solid melts into air*. New York: Simon and Schuster, 1982.

Bronfenbrenner, U. *The ecology of human development*. Cambridge, Mass.: Harvard University Press, 1979.

Carnap, R. *The logical structure of the world: Pseudoproblems in philosophy*. Berkeley, Calif.: University of California Press, 1967.

Chomsky, N. *Language and mind* (Enlarged ed.). New York: Harcourt Brace Jovanovich, 1972.

Cole, M., and Scribner, S. *Culture and thought: A psychological introduction*. New York: Wiley, 1974.

Darwin, C. *The origin of species*. London: Murray, 1859.

Darwin, C. *The descent of man*. London: Murray, 1871.

Dewey, J. *Reconstruction in philosophy*. New York: Holt, 1920.

Feyerabend, P. *Against method*. London: Verso, 1975.

Gould, S. J. *Ever since Darwin: Reflections in natural history*. New York: Norton, 1977.

Gould, S.J., and Lewontin, R.C. The spandrells of San Marco and the Panglossian paradigm: A critique of the adaptationist programme. *Proceedings of the Royal Society of London*, 1979, B205, 581–598.

Haeckel, E. H. P. A. *Anthropogenie, oder Entwickelungsgeschichte des Menschen*. Leipzig: Engelmann, 1874.

Harris, D. *The concept of development: An issue in the study of human behavior*. Minneapolis: University of Minnesota Press, 1957.

Hull, C. L. *A behavior system*. New Haven: Yale University Press, 1952.

Kaplan, B. Meditations on genesis. *Human Development*, 1967, *10*, 65–87.

Kessel, F., and Siegel, A. *The child and other cultural inventions*. New York: Praeger, 1983.

Kessen, W. Questions for a theory of cognitive development. *Monographs of the Society for Research in Child Development*, 1966, *31*, 55–70.

Kessen, W. Early settlements in New Cognition. *Cognition*, 1981, *10*, 167–171.

Kohlberg, L. From is to ought: How to commit the naturalistic fallacy and get away with it in the study of moral development. In T. Mischel, (Ed.), *Cognitive development and epistemology*. New York: Academic Press, 1971.

Lears, J. *No place of grace*. New York: Pantheon, 1981.

Lewontin, R. C. Darwin's revolution. *New York Review of Books*, June 16, 1983, *30*, 21–27.

Mandelbaum, M. *History, man, and reason: A study in nineteenth-century thought*. Baltimore: Johns Hopkins University Press, 1971.

McCosh, J. *Development: What is can and what it cannot do*. New York: Scribner's, 1883.

Montesquieu, C.-L. *The spirit of laws*. Paris, 1748.

Piaget, J. *Adaptation and intelligence: Organic selection and phenocopy*. Chicago: University of Chicago Press, 1980.

Skinner, B. F. *The behavior of organisms: An experimental analysis*. New York: Appleton-Century-Crofts, 1938.

Spencer, H. *Principles of psychology*. New York: Appleton, 1899.

Taine, H. A. *De l'intelligence*, 5th ed. Paris: Hachette, 1888.

White, M. G. *The intellectual versus the city, from Thomas Jefferson to Frank Lloyd Wright*. Cambridge, Mass.: Harvard University Press, 1962.

White, S. H. Psychology as moral science. In F. Kessel and A. Siegel (Eds.), *The child and other cultural inventions*. New York: Praeger, 1983.

Willy, R. *Die Krisis in der Psychologie*. Leipzig: Reisland, 1899.

2 The Process of Stage Transition: A Neo-Piagetian View

Robbie Case

[T]he two classic questions in the field of intellectual development are how best to characterize children's intellectual functioning at different stages of development, and how best to describe the transition from one of these stages to the next. These two questions are, of course, closely related. It is not a coincidence that Piaget conceptualized the process of stage transition as one of equilibration, whereas behaviorists conceptualized it as one of modeling and reinforcement. The former notion fits well with the idea that development can best be characterized as a sequence of increasingly sophisticated logical structures, each of which has a broad domain of application. The latter notion agrees well with the idea that development may most profitably be viewed as a sequence of increasingly well adapted intellectual skills, each of which has a relatively local domain of application.

My own position with regard to the first question can best be labeled "neo-Piagetian." Like Piaget, I believe that children's intellectual functioning at different stages of development is most usefully depicted as a sequence of increasingly sophisticated mental structures. Also like Piaget, I believe that the underlying form and complexity of these structures at any age is constant across a wide variety of content domains (providing that children are exposed to the appropriate opportunities for learning). Unlike Piaget, however, I believe that children's mental structures can best be modeled by using the sorts of concepts developed in the field of information processing and computer simulation, rather than those developed in the field of symbolic logic. And this difference in the way children's mental structures are conceptualized leads to a difference in the way in which the stage-transition process is conceptualized as well.

In the present chapter, I shall first provide an illustration of the way in which I would model children's intellectual functioning at two successive stages of development. I shall then describe the underlying processes I would postulate, in order to explain the transition from one of these stages to the next.

The work on which this article is based was supported by grants from the Spencer Foundation, the Canadian Social Sciences and Humanities Research Council, and the Guggenheim Foundation, whose assistance is gratefully acknowledged. Thanks are also extended to Dr. Nancy Link, for her comments on a draft of the manuscript.

INTELLECTUAL FUNCTIONING AT DIFFERENT STAGES OF DEVELOPMENT

One of the major changes that takes place with development—if not *the* major change—is in the child's ability to assemble executive control structures for solving different classes of problems. An executive control structure is defined as a mental blueprint or plan for solving a class of problems. All executive control structures are presumed to have at least three components:

1. A representation of the problem *situation*; that is, of the conditions for which the plan is appropriate, and under which it may be applied.

2. A representation of the problem *objectives*; that is, the conditions that are desired, and toward which the plan is directed.

3. A representation of the problem *strategy*; that is, the procedure for going from the problem situation to the objectives via a set of mental and/or physical steps.

To illustrate how children's control structures would be characterized at two successive stages of development, consider several sets of data:

The first set is drawn from the recent literature on preschool cognition, and concerns children's problem-solving abilities from the ages of 4 to 5. During these years, children typically solve the following three tasks for the first time.

Task 1.   In the first task, children are exposed to a warm-up period in which they are presented with a balance beam and a set of weights, and are encouraged to put weights of various sizes on each side of the balance arm and watch what happens. After this warm-up, they are presented with a locked balance beam that has a large, heavy weight resting on one side and a small, light weight resting on the other. When they are asked which side of the beam they think will go down when the lock is removed, the children respond (correctly) by pointing to the side with the large weight, and justify their choice by saying that it is "big" and/or "heavy" (Liu, 1981).

Task 2.   In the second task, children are first exposed to a warm-up period in which various combinations of small cups of juice and of water—all the same size—are dumped into large empty pitchers that are also the same size. Children are asked to observe the resultant mixtures, and are told that some will taste "juicier" than others. They are then shown two new sets of juice and water cups; each arranged in an equally spaced line. One line has a large number of juice cups and a few water cups. The other has a small number of juice cups and the same number of water cups as the first. When they are asked which mixture they think will taste juicier, children respond (correctly) by pointing to the array with the long line of juice cups. Their justifications include such comments as "there's a lot there" (Noelting, 1975).

Task 3.   In the third task, children are first exposed to a warm-up period in which they are asked to count a variety of objects around the room. They are then presented with two small arrays of approximately the same size, each containing a number of discrete objects. When they are asked which array has the greater number of objects in it, they respond (correctly) by counting the objects in each array and picking the one with the greater number (Bryant, 1972; Saxe, 1975). In a recent study, Siegler and Robinson (1981) have shown that children think about numbers in the same way they think about other dimensions, as being "big" or "little." Also, children's answers are accurate only when the numbers are drawn from classes they see as being different in absolute magnitude (for example, 1, 2-3-4, 5 +).

In the context of my theory, children's intellectual functioning on the first task would be represented as follows:

PROBLEM SITUATION   OBJECTIVE

• Two objects, each on a differ-   • Determine the object with the
ent side of the balance beam.   heavy weight.

STRATEGY
• Scan each object. Pick the one
that is big.

Their intellectual functioning on the second task would be represented as follows:

PROBLEM SITUATION   OBJECTIVE

• Two sets of cups, each set   • Determine the set with a lot
with some juice cups and   of juice.
some water cups.

STRATEGY
• Scan each line of juice cups.
Pick the set where the line of
juice cups is long.

Their intellectual functioning on the third task would be represented as follows:

PROBLEM SITUATION

OBJECTIVE

- Two sets of objects, each set of roughly the same size.

- Determine the set with the large number of objects.

STRATEGY

- Count each set. Pick the set with the big number.

The above characterizations are not meant to *explain* children's intellectual functioning, but merely to describe, as succinctly as possible, the mental representations on which this functioning must logically depend. Of course, like any descriptions, these descriptions are not theoretically neutral. One assumption on which they are based has already been mentioned: that children's intellectual functioning on tasks of this sort may be parsed into at least three components—a representation of the current situation, a representation of the desired situation, and a representation of the operations that will lead from the first situation to the second. Another assumption is that these control structures are either assembled or applied in real time, in the order specified by the arrows. For each task, it is assumed that the child first focuses on the array and problem as it is explained. The child then converts the question the experimenter asks into an objective that makes sense within this problem representation. Finally, the child assembles or applies a strategy that will result in movement from the problem situation to the goal. Each of these component processes may take some time. It may also involve some request for further clarification, some trial and error, or some "doubling back." However, the general flow of the child's thinking is presumed to be in the direction indicated by the arrows.

In the present article, I shall make no attempt to justify the above assumptions. I shall simply invite the reader to suspend judgment, and to note the conclusions that follow once these assumptions are made. One such conclusion is that the control structures for solving apparently dissimilar problems are, in fact, very similar in their underlying form. In the above example, all three of the control structures relate to a problem situation that includes a statement about two different arrays. All three have an objective that requires a decision between two polar possibilities (heavy/light, a lot/a little, large/small). Finally, all three utilize a strategy that entails focusing on one dimension (size in the first case, length in the second, number in the third) and making a judgment in terms of a polar category either closely related to or identical to the possibilities in the objective (big/small, long/short, and so on).

Of course, the three tasks that I have used as illustrations represent no more than a tiny fraction of the total repertoire of competencies that 4- and 5-year-olds possess. Nevertheless, when a much wider range of tasks is modeled in this fashion, the same conclusion appears to hold up. Providing that children are presented with the appropriate experience, they will apply a control structure that is very similar to those indicated above, across a broad range of content domains including language, social interaction, spatial reasoning, and scientific reasoning.[1]

I turn now to a second set of illustrative data, this time gathered on children who are 1 or 2 years older.

Task 1.   At 6 years of age children become capable of solving balance-beam problems in which a stack of weights is placed on one side of the balance and a stack of similar size is placed on the other. Children solve such problems by counting the weights in each stack and picking the side that has the greater number (Siegler, 1976).

Task 2.   At 6 years of age, children also become capable of solving a new class of juice problems. In these problems, the line of juice beakers is made approximately the same length on each side, and children are asked which will taste jucier. They respond (correctly) by counting the number of juice beakers in each line and picking the side with the greater number (Noelting, 1975).

The executive control structure for solving the first problem may be represented as follows:

PROBLEM SITUATION

- Two stack of weights, each on a different side of the balance beam.
- Each stack is approximately the same size.

OBJECTIVES

- Determine the stack with the greater weight.
- Determine the stack with the greater number of units.

STRATEGY

1. Count each weight stack. Note the one with the bigger number.
2. Assume that the set with the bigger number is heavier. Pick it.

The executive control structure for solving the second problem may be represented as follows:

PROBLEM SITUATION   OBJECTIVES

- Two sets of cups, each set   • Determine the set with the
  with some juice cups and ——→ greater juiciness.
  some water cups.

- Each line of juice cups is ap-   • Determine the set with the
  proximately the same length. ——→ greater number of juice cups.

STRATEGY

1. Count each line of juice cups. Note the line with the bigger number.

2. Assume that the line with the bigger number will taste juicier. Pick it.

Once again, the above descriptions are not theoretically neutral. However, once the assumptions on which they are based are accepted, several interesting conclusions follow. One is that, again, the two different control structures are extremely similar in their underlying form. A second conclusion is that both of the new control structures are in fact "superstructures" which are composed of two structures, each of the sort that the children could have assembled at the age of 4 or 5. In the first task, the superstructure comprises the 4-year-old's structure for weight determination plus his structure for number determination. In the second task the superstructure comprises the 4-year-old's structure for juiciness determination plus his structure for number determination.

A third conclusion is that the way in which the various dimensions are represented has changed. They are no longer encoded in absolute, polar terms (such as big/little). Rather, they are encoded in relative, more "fine-grained" terms (bigger/smaller). Finally, a fourth conclusion is that the two more elementary structures are integrated in a nested fashion: that is, the structure for number determination in each case serves as a subordinate routine that must be executed as a subgoal if the objective specified by the other structure is to be attained. For the balance of the paper, I shall refer to two structures that are related to each other in this way as being "hierarchically integrated" (cf. Flavell, 1972).

In most theories of intellectual development, the transition from 4 to 6 years of age is viewed as a major one. In Piaget's theory, for example, this is the time when the first "functional logic" emerges: the logic from which the full concrete-operational structure will ultimately be assembled (Piaget and Fot, 1977). In Bruner's theory, this is the period when children's symbolic processes first become capable of overriding their iconic processes (Bruner, 1964). In Siegler's (1976) theory, this is the age when the child's first quantitative "rules" appear. In Halford's (1980) theory, this is the period during which the first "second-order symbols" emerge. In my own theory the transition from 4 to 6 is also viewed as a major one, in that it divides the period of "relational" thought from the period of "dimensional" thought (Case, in press). As may be seen, the main characteristics of this transition are (1) that children coordinate two control structures, each of which was already in their repertoire, (2) that the coordination involves the hierarchical integration of these two structures, (3) that some sort of differentiation takes place simultaneously, and (4) that the result is the emergence of a new type of unit in the child's thought: the "variable" or the "quantitative dimension."

Of course, further developments take place from ages 6 to 8, and from ages 8 to 10. However, these developments do not involve a new level in the control structure, nor do they require the emergence of a new unit of thought. For example, on the balance beam, children move to a consideration of distance from the fulcrum, as well as weight. In the juice problem, they begin to consider the number of water cups as well as the number of juice cups. In neither task do they look at the second dimension as a means to drawing a conclusion about the first. Rather, the new dimension is simply "added" to the first, as another factor to be considered in drawing a conclusion about the outcome in question. Also, neither task leads to a new type of operation (for example, ratio) that can act directly on the products of other operations. In my system, then, the changes in functioning that take place from ages 6 to 10 are not seen as involving a major qualitative change, but rather a series of minor qualitative changes. In effect, they constitute a progressive elaboration of the more fundamental change that takes place between the ages of 4 and 6.

Were this sort of "hierarchical integration" followed by a period of "progressive elaboration" typical only of the period from 4 to 10 years of age, it might be of relatively limited interest—even though it does occur across a wide variety of content domains at the same time. I believe it can be shown, however, that this is not the case: that the same sort of progression that is observed from ages 4 to 10 characterizes all the other major stages of development as well. At the beginning of each stage, two formerly discrete and qualitatively distinct control structures are hierarchically integrated, thus giving rise to a new unit of thought. After this initial transition is made, there is a further progression through a sequence of substages, with the number of such units that can be considered increasing, and the overall complexity of children's mental representations increasing with it (Case, in press).

Because I believe that the changes that take place on the balance-beam or juice-cup problems between ages 4 and 6 are typical of the changes that take place at all major stage transitions, in the remainder of this article I shall reformulate the stage-transition question as follows: "What sort of underlying process is responsible for producing the hierarchical integration of two executive control structures, each of which existed previously in the child's repertoire in an isolated and less differentiated form?" For the sake of exposition, I shall break this general question down into two subquestions, namely:

1. What capabilities or processes does the organism come equipped with at birth, in order to insure that this sort of hierarchical integration and differentiation will take place?

2. What capabilities does the organism *not* come equipped with; that is, which ones does it develop only gradually, thus delaying particular hierarchical integrations until particular periods in time (such as from ages 4 to 6)?

THE PROCESS OF STAGE TRANSITION

Functions That Do Not Vary In Human Development

The term "functional invariant" is one that was coined by Piaget, in order to refer to a process or function that does not change with development but that is at least partially responsible for producing the changes that do. In Piaget's system, processes such as assimilation, accommodation, and equilibration are accorded this status. If one assumes that stage transition entails the hierarchical integration of functionally discrete control structures, what sorts of functional invariants might one postulate in the human psychological system? As a minimum, it seems to me that the following capabilities would have to be postulated:

a. The capability for setting goals.

b. The capability for activating existing schemes in novel sequences, in the pursuit of these goals.

c. The capability for evaluating the results of these novel scheme-sequences in the light of the current situation and the goals.

d. The capability for reworking or "retagging" sequences that are evaluated positively, in such a way that they can be generated intentionally in the future.

e. The capability for recalling these reworked structures on future occasions, and consolidating them so that they form smoothly functioning executive structures.

In addition to the above capabilities, it seems to me that the system would also have to possess a set of more global cognitive and affective processes that would enable it to draw on these basic capabilities and orchestrate them appropriately. At least four such global processes appear to be present from an early age.

1. The first of these is *problem solving*. As will no doubt be apparent, infants are preprogrammed to find certain states inherently pleasant and others inherently unpleasant. The sensation of a nipple or a thumb in the mouth, for example, is an inherently pleasant one. The sensation of a face at a distance of less than an inch is inherently unpleasant. What may be less obvious, and what is often left out of behaviorist accounts of learning, is that infants are also preprogrammed with certain basic problem-solving processes that permit them to work toward the attainment of states they find inherently pleasant, and toward the elimination of states they find inherently unpleasant. The 2-month-old baby who has just experienced the sensation of having his finger in his mouth, for example, will actively work towards reinstating this sensation, by experimenting with various arm movements that may enable him to do so (Piaget, 1952/ 1936). Similarly, the 2-month-old who is experiencing a face approaching her too closely will actively work at escaping from the sensation being produced, by experimenting with various head and eye movements (Stern, 1977). Although the problems children can solve become more complex with age, the basic processes on which all problem solving depends must be present from a very early age. Note that these processes draw on all five of the systemic capabilities mentioned above:

a. Problem solving begins, by definition, with the setting of a goal, a state that is different from the state currently being experienced.

b. The next phase of problem solving, the trial-and-error component, draws on the systemic capability for activating familiar schemes in a novel sequence. When children are blocked from achieving the current goal via a familiar operation, they actively search for other operations, often ones they have never used in this context or sequence before.

c. In trying each new operation, children also evaluate its effectiveness. They do not normally persevere with operations that do not bring the goal any closer, nor do they abandon ones that do.

Thus, problem solving also draws on the systemic capability for *evaluation*.

d. At some point after a problem is solved—or perhaps during the process—some retagging or restructuring appears to take place. Even young infants, when they are placed in a problem situation that they have encountered a few seconds earlier, do not simply repeat their earlier problem-solving activities. Rather, they select the actions that were successful, and execute them in an intentional rather than trial-and-error fashion. This implies that some retagging of the component schemes has taken place.[2]

e. On successive encounters with a problem situation, shorter reaction times and increased integration of component schemes are observed. This indicates that some sort of *consolidation* is taking place as well.

Returning to the tasks described in the first section, then, one could suggest that one way in which subjects might come to integrate the 4-year-old's structures for numerical quantification and weight estimation would be by attempting to solve the sorts of problems that a balance beam can present. The most likely timing for this integration would be in the course of the testing itself. After the experimenter posed the first question, the subjects would first try to apply the weight-estimation structure they had developed during the warm-up period. In doing so, they would discover that the size of each weight stack was about the same, and that this structure could therefore not be applied. This would, in effect, pose a new problem for them. Consequently, they would search for some other way of determining the weight or size. Either by trial and error, or by rapid access of a structure that was already in their repertoires and that was suited for this purpose, they would then proceed to count the weights in the two stacks and determine their relative number. Once the subjects realized that this procedure solved the original problem— that is, gave them an estimate of relative weight and size—they would review the sequence that led to success, restructuring or retagging it in the process. Finally, on subsequent exposures to the problem, this new structure would be recalled and gradually consolidated.

2. There is a second organized activity in which children engage virtually from birth, and that is *exploration*. As observers of infant behavior have often noted, infants are not motivated solely by a desire to reinstate pleasant sensations or to eliminate unpleasant ones. They are also motivated by curiosity; that is, by a desire for exploration. In the first few months of life, the most obvious form of exploration is visual. The infant will scan any new environment in

which he is placed with great interest, until he notices all the salient features in it. If a new object is introduced, or if he is placed in a different position, he will re-initiate the scanning process. By the age of 4 to 8 months, exploration is extended to include manual and oral activity as well. Any time a novel object is placed within an infant's reach, she will explore its properties in a variety of ways: picking it up, putting it in her mouth, shaking it, and so on. Moreover, she will repeat these various actions—either within or across encounters with an object—until she appears to know "in advance" what operation will lead to what consequence. At this point, she will lose interest in it (Biemiller, 1966).

Although it may not be obvious at first glance, exploration draws on the same five systemic capabilities as does problem solving, and in the same order:

a. Although exploration does not begin with the setting of a specific objective, it does begin with the setting of a general objective: the discovery of new outcomes.

b. The experimental or "try-and-see" component of exploration draws on the system's capability of applying pre-existing schemes in a novel sequence.

c. Just as children monitor their progress toward a specific goal in problem solving, so they monitor their progress toward their general goal in exploration. This implies that the systemic capability for novel-sequence evaluation is being drawn upon.

d. Executive restructuring begins as soon as a new outcome or operation is discovered. At that point children immediately set themselves the goal of reproducing the interesting event or operation. And this necessitates some restructuring of their internal record, from the form "operations XY happened to be followed by (novel) state Z" to the form "when Z is my goal, I shall try to execute XY."

e. Children's criterion for continuing to explore an object or an operation on subsequent trials appears to be the predictability of the result and/or the smoothness of the operation itself (Biemiller, 1966). In effect, then, the children repeat a new executive sequence until some sort of consolidation has been achieved, and then lose interest in it unless some specific need for it arises.

Returning again to the tasks described in the first section, one could suggest that exploration would be a second way in which 4-year-olds might come to integrate their structure for weight determination with their structure for enumeration. During the warm-up period, some children might set a certain number of weights on one side of the balance beam and a slightly different number of weights on the other, counting them as they did so.[3] Having noted that one side had more weights than the other, it would be difficult for them *not* to notice that—in spite of the apparent equality in the size of the stacks—one side of the balance beam went down. Children intrigued by this phenomenon might try out a few more examples to see if the side with the greater number of weights always went down. This sort of "scientific" repetition is often observed in young children of this age, and would presumably lead to the sort of executive restructuring described above. Subsequent application would then lead to further consolidation.

3. There is a third type of activity that could lead to the hierarchical integration of previously existing structures. That is the *observation* of other humans, followed by *imitation*. The processes of observation and imitation are particularly well suited for the task of assembling operational structures that are the product of the organism's cultural evolution—such as those involved in counting—rather than of its biological evolution. The processes also emerge at a very early age. Although there is some controversy as to whether imitation can be observed in the first week of life (Meltzoff, 1981), it can certainly be observed as early as 7 months. Although imitation is superficially quite different from exploration, it may actually be considered a socially facilitated form of the same process. Children do not imitate everything their parents or older siblings do, but merely those actions that have familiar elements, but whose overall configuration is novel. What this implies, then, is that children's observation of others is motivated by the same goal as is their exploration: namely, discovering "what leads to what." It also implies that they evaluate particular action sequences, and attempt to restructure each sequence that meets this criterion (of linking familiar actions with novel consequences), until the new action sequence can be generated intentionally. Finally, children's criterion for *stopping* a recently imitated behaviour appears to be the same as in exploration: successful assembly of the pre-existing elements into a smoothly functioning new structure. This implies that the systemic capability for consolidation is drawn upon.

Returning once again to the balance-beam example, then, one could suggest that a third way in which a child could come to assemble the 6-year-old's control structure, given that he or she had both of the appropriate 4-year-old's control structures, would be via observation and imitation. Such a process could take place outside the laboratory, if the child lived in an environment where balance beams or seesaws were present. However, it could also take place inside the laboratory in the course of the testing session itself. The

subject could note that the experimenter counts out a different number of weights on each trial (albeit covertly), and could decide to
imitate this and observe (or guess at) the consequences.

4. There is one final type of activity that could lead to hierarchical integration, and that is *mutual regulation*. By mutual regulation, I mean social regulation in which, unlike imitation, the influence of the two actors is bidirectional: at the same time as the
child is affected by some other person, the child also exerts a direct
effect on that person.

Like problem solving and exploration, mutual regulation is a
process that emerges at a very early age. By 1 or 2 months, for example, infants and their mothers engage in a pattern of interaction
that has been called "protocommunication." The mother smiles and
coos at the baby, and the baby smiles and coos at the mother in return,
with each partner actively working to sustain and regulate the pattern of interaction so that it meets their basic needs (Stern, 1977).

This early protocommunication gradually expands to include a
variety of more complex interactions. For the present purposes, however, the most interesting of these are those in which the child solicits
the adult's cooperation in approaching a task in which the child is
presently engaged. In effect, this form of "assistance seeking" may
be thought of as socially facilitated problem solving, just as imitation
may be thought of as socially facilitated exploration. And, as might
be expected, it draws on the same systemic capabilities. The process
begins when the child sets himself a top level goal, and solicits the
adult's assistance. It continues while he watches or listens to the
adult, using the adult's behavior as a cue to what schemes to activate,
and in what (novel) sequence. As these schemes are activated, they
are evaluated with regard to their success. Finally, the child gradually takes over the executive function himself, thus restructuring
his internal record and consolidating a new structure in the process.

Returning one last time to the balance-beam example, one could
suggest that still another way children could come to assemble the
6-year-old's control structures, given that they had the appropriate
4-year-old's control structures, would be via mutual regulation. For
example, having seen several students taken out of class by an experimenter, a child might ask one of them what had happened. On
being told that they had been shown a balance toy and asked which
side went down, she might ask, "How do you know?" The answer
might be, "It's easy, you just count the weights!" Such an interchange
would of course be quite meaningless if the child did not possess a
counting executive already. If she did, however, it could form the
basis of a successful response. When the child's turn came to be
tested, she could listen to the experimenter's question about weight,

realize that the two weights looked about the same size, and then utilize her friend's suggestion as to how to come up with an answer under these circumstances. Similar sorts of interchanges could also take place in an on-line fashion in the classroom, rather than in testing situations. The new structures to which they would lead would then be consolidated with practice.

In summary, it may be said that although the processes of problem solving, exploration, imitation, and mutual regulation appear to be quite different on the surface, they are quite similar at a deeper level. They all involve a sequence of basic subprocesses that entail (1) goal setting, (2) experimenting with novel scheme-sequences, (3) evaluating the consequences of those sequences, (4) restructuring valuable sequences so that they can be used intentionally in the future, and (5) practicing these new structures until they become consolidated. The differences among the various processes lie in the degree to which the child must set a specific, as opposed to a general, goal, and the degree to which the activation of particular schemes is socially facilitated.

Given that the above processes could be expected to contribute to the process of stage transition on *logical* grounds, are there any *empirical* grounds for coming to a similar conclusion? There are two kinds of evidence that are relevant to this question. The first comes from naturalistic studies. In one such study using 21-month-old children as subjects, White (1975) found that the children spent 88 percent of their time in some sort of clearly identifiable activity, and only 12 percent in a process that appeared to be either undirected or unclassifiable. Of the various activities White described, the majority could be classified as being an integral part of one of the above four processes (Case, in press, Chapter 12). It does seem clear, then, that children at least *engage* in these four processes with a high degree of frequency and from an early age.

What about the *results* of such activity? In studies done in our own laboratory, we have engaged 4- and 6-year-olds in each of these processes, and assessed the consequences. What we have found is that—at least for the 6-year-old population—all four processes appear to be capable of leading to hierarchical integration (Case, in press). On empirical as well as logical grounds, then, it appears reasonable to suggest that the above processes and subprocesses must play an important role in the stage-transition process.

Capabilities That Are Not Present From Birth

The model of stage transition that I have advanced so far—although somewhat global—is capable of explaining why it is that hierarchical integration takes place whether or not there is any direct attempt on the part of an adult to produce it. There are two phenomena that the model cannot explain, however:

1. The fact that there is a 2-year lag between the emergence of the 4-year-old's control structures and their integration into hierarchical superstructures. Why do exploration, problem solving, imitation, and/or mutual regulation lead to this sort of integration almost automatically at the age of 6, yet seem so ineffective at the age of 4 (Case, in press, Chapter 15)?

2. The fact that so many parallel integrations take place during the same time period. Presumably, children's opportunities for exploration, problem solving, imitation, and mutual regulation vary widely from domain to domain. Yet as long as children are provided with a few minutes of such experience within the laboratory prior to testing, they appear to perform at the same level across a wide variety of domains (Case, 1982). Why is this the case?

Although other interpretations of these phenomena are no doubt possible, my own view is that the data indicate the presence of a set of very general factors that are *not* invariant in development, and that set a limit on the effectiveness of the processes that *are* invariant. One factor I believe to be particularly important is the size of a child's short-term storage space.

The Role of Short-Term Storage Space (STSS).   It is a well-established fact that the total attentional resources of the human organism are severely limited, and that they must be divided between two functions: executing current operations, and storing or retrieving the products of operations that were executed a few seconds or milliseconds earlier. In contemporary cognitive psychology, a subject's total attentional resources are often referred to with a spatial metaphor, as his *central processing space*, or *working memory*. These terms are used by analogy to a computer, where all processing must take place in some central processing unit. Since a subject's total processing space must be divided between two functions, I shall refer to the proportion of the space that is being devoted to operating as the subject's *operating space* (OS), and the proportion being devoted to short-term storage as his *short-term storage space* (STSS).

Consider now the demands that would be placed on a subject's operating space and storage space if he or she were to integrate executive structures for enumeration and size estimation. This integration could be done in a variety of ways, the most likely of which would be by *problem solving*.

If a subject were to integrate the two structures via problem solving, the first thing he would do would be to apply his current weight-estimation executive (size scanning) and to realize that it did not work in this particular case. The next thing he would do would be to store some record of the general objective (weight estimation) towards which this structure was directed, and to search for some other control structure that would allow him to reach it. What this implies is that, at the time the subject happened to apply the enumeration structure, he would experience a total working-memory demand of

$$OP_{\text{enumeration}} + S_{\text{weight estimation}},$$

where

$$OP_{\text{enumeration}}$$

refers to the operating space required for applying the enumeration structure, and

$$S_{\text{weight estimation}}$$

refers to the short-term storage space required for keeping in mind the objective he is still trying to reach (namely, that specified by the weight-estimation structure).

Consider next the load that would be placed on a subject's working memory if she were to integrate the same two structures in the course of *exploration*. In this case, the first thing the subject would do would be to apply her enumeration executive and note that one side had more weights on it than the other. The next thing she would do would be to release the balance, note which side went down, and—by applying her weight-estimation structure—realize that the side that went down must have been heavier. To realize that enumeration could be used as a *means* for weight estimation, then, she would need to be able to handle a working-memory load of

$$OP_{\text{weight estimation}} + S_{\text{enumeration}},$$

where

$$OP_{\text{weight estimation}}$$

stands for the amount of operating space required for applying the appropriate weight-estimation structure, and

$$S_{\text{enumeration}}$$

refers to the amount of short-term storage space required for storing some record of the result of the enumeration structure's application a moment earlier.

Consider next the demands that would be placed on a subject's working memory if he were to integrate the two structures by *observation* and *imitation*. In this case the subject would have to observe someone else applying an enumeration procedure, and would have to activate some internal analogue of this process as he did so. He would then have to note what happened to the balance beam, and—again by applying his weight-estimation structure—conclude that the side that went down must have been heavier. If he were to apprehend the total pattern and imitate it, then, like the subject using exploration, he would need to handle a working-memory load of

$$OP_{\text{weight estimation}} + S_{\text{enumeration}},$$

where

$$OP_{\text{weight estimation}}$$

refers to the amount of space required for activating the weight-estimation operation, and

$$S_{\text{enumeration}}$$

refers to the amount of storage space required for remembering that the enumeration structure was applied a second or two earlier.

Consider finally the demands that would be placed on a subject's working memory if she were to integrate the two structures as a result of a brief period of *mutual regulation*, such as takes place when a child asks someone else "how you do it." In this case, the subject would have to remember what goal she wanted to accomplish, while she listened to or watched a demonstration of how to do it. She would therefore have to be able to handle a demand of

$$OP_{\text{enumeration}} + S_{\text{weight estimation}},$$

where

$$OP_{\text{enumeration}}$$

refers to the space required for processing the demonstration and attempting it herself, and

$$S_{\text{weight estimation}}$$

refers to the space required for keeping track of the goal that this procedure is designed to achieve.

In summary, then, it may be said that problem solving and mutual regulation would require a working memory of

$$OP_{\text{enumeration}} + S_{\text{weight estimation}},$$

whereas exploration and imitation would require a working memory of

$$OP_{\text{weight estimation}} + S_{\text{enumeration}}.$$

In the empirical studies we have conducted in my own research group, we have demonstrated that the amount of operating space required for executing any particular dimensional operation, such as enumeration, is approximately equal to the amount of operating space required for executing any other dimensional operation, such as size or weight estimation. Similarly, we have shown that the amount of storage space required for storing the product of such an operation is approximately the same in each case (Case, in press). This leads to an interesting conclusion; namely, that the working-memory load for assembling an integrated structure of the sort required in the balance-beam task is approximately the same no matter which particular process is used. The demand in question may be represented as

$$OP_{\text{dimensional}} + S_{\text{dimensional}}.$$

Another finding that has emerged from our research group in the last few years is also relevant. This is that 4-year-olds are not capable of handling a working-memory demand of $OP_{\text{dimensional}} + S_{\text{dimensional}}$, whereas 6-year-olds are (Case, Kurland, and Goldberg, 1982). That is, 4-year-olds cannot store a pointer to one particular dimensional operation while performing a second, whereas 6-year-olds can. This datum leads to another interesting conclusion, which is that the slow growth of children's STSS may well be the factor that delays their stage transition until the age of 6. Until children have the requisite STSS, they are unlikely to assemble a hierarchically integrated dimensional control structure by any sort of spontaneous process. Conversely, once they *do* have an STSS of this magnitude, they are unlikely *not* to assemble a structure of this sort, given exposure to the appropriate opportunities for problem solving, exploration, imitation, and/or mutual regulation.

The Role of Operational Efficiency.   If the growth of children's STSS plays an important regulating role in stage transition, a question that naturally arises is what produces the growth of STSS itself. Two distinct possibilities exist. The first is that the growth is produced by a developmental change in the size or capacity of the subject's total processing space. The second possibility is that the growth is produced by a decrease in the proportion of the subject's total processing space that must be devoted to operating. These two possibilities are illustrated graphically in Figure 2-1.

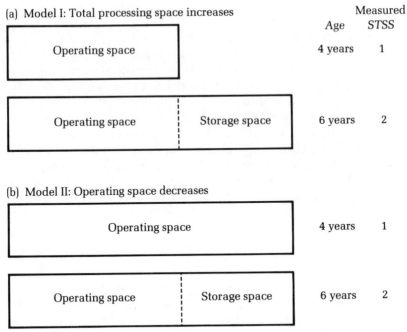

Figure 2-1
Utilization of working memory under two different
assumptions: (a) that total processing space
increases, and (b) that operating space decreases.

Historically, the model that developmental psychologists have favored has been the first one (Figure 2-1a) (Baldwin, 1894; Pascual-Leone, 1970). In the 1970s, however, researchers discovered a new type of data that called this model into question. These data showed that basic operations—operations such as visual encoding or counting—continue to undergo development for years after they have been overlearned (Chi and Klahr, 1975). Once these data were known, it seemed logical to suggest that the continued development might be accompanied by some change in operating requirements: specifically, by a decrease in the amount of operating space required for operational execution. And from there it was a short step to the hypothesis that such a change in OS might be responsible for producing the measured change in STSS (Chi, 1976; Dempster, 1977; Case, 1978).

Over the past few years, my research group has devoted a considerable amount of energy toward testing the second model (Figure 2-1b), has come to the conclusion that it is correct. The basic form of the data we have gathered is as follows. Subjects of different ages are administered two tests, one test of their STSS (using, for example, counting span) and one test of the efficiency with which they can execute the basic operations that the test of STSS entails (for counting span, counting speed would be measured). The developmental relationship between these two functions is then plotted, and shown to be linear. Next, a group of adults is taught a new operation (such as counting in a foreign language), thus temporarily reducing their operational efficiency and increasing the amount of OS they require. Finally, the STSS of the adults is determined under the new conditions and compared with that of young children who have the same degree of operational efficiency (and hence require the same amount of OS). To date we have conducted three studies of this sort, and have found essentially the same thing in each: that the STSS of young children and adults is not different for new operations (Case, Kurland, and Daneman, 1978; Case, Kurland, and Goldberg, 1982; Case, in press, Chapter 16). What these findings have led us to conclude, then, is that the total processing space of adults and children is the same, and that the measured increases in STSS with development are a function of decreases in the proportion of this space that must be devoted to executing basic operations.

The Role of Operational Practice

Once one accepts that the developmental increase in STSS is a function of a developmental increase in operational efficiency, the next question that arises is what produces the increase in operational efficiency. An obvious possibility is that this increase is a function of simple practice. Children clearly receive massive practice in basic operations—operations such as enumeration and size estimation— as they grow older. Massive practice is known to have an effect on operational efficiency (Logan, 1976), and it could also have an effect on the knowledge base that subjects have access to, thus producing the change in representational precision or "differentiation" that is observed across stage boundaries. The most parsimonious model to propose, then, is that it is operational practice that is responsible for all three developmental trends that are observed during stage transition: the increase in representational differentiation, the increase in operational efficiency, and the increase in STSS.

Unfortunately, although this may be the simplest explanation, it does not appear to be correct. We have gathered three sorts of data in my research group, all of which suggest that a more complicated model is in order. The first data show that tests of operational efficiency have almost as high a correlation with each other when they do not share any common cognitive component as when they do (Case, Kurland, and Daneman, 1979). If practice were the only factor at work, one would not expect this to be the case, since the effect of practice is known to be operation-specific. The second finding is that the efficiency of basic operations such as counting increases at the same rate, and asymptotes at the same age level, in cultures that are as different as West African villages and North American suburbs (Case, in press, Chapter 17). Since opportunities to practice counting appear to be more prevalent in the North American setting (at least as judged by West Africans who are familiar with both cultures), practice again seems unlikely to be the only factor that is at work. The third finding of relevance comes from a recent study by Kurland (1981). What Kurland did was to expose children to massive practice in counting over a period of 3 months. The subjects in his experimental group received 5,000 trials in counting, over and above whatever experience they received in their everyday life. However, in spite of this massive practice, there did not appear to be any acceleration in the development of their counting efficiency. On balance, then, it appears that while a certain minimal amount of practice is necessary to improve children's operational efficiency with age, and to produce a differentiation of their numerical representations, the ceiling that will be attained at any age will be set by other factors: factors in which either biological maturation or very general experience plays the determining role.

Unfortunately, these factors have not yet been isolated. One possibility that deserves attention, however, is the degree of myelinization of nervous tissue in the area or system of the brain that is responsible for executing the class of operations typical of each stage. For some time now, it has been known that myelinization does not proceed evenly in neurological development, but rather occurs in "waves." Different areas or systems myelinate at different rates, and have their onset and offset times at different points in development (Yakovlev and Lecours, 1967). Since there is an approximate correspondence between the myelinization that takes place in different areas of the brain at different ages, on the one hand, and the changes in the efficiency of the types of operations that these areas control, on the other, the possibility exists that the degree of myelinization may be the factor that sets the developmental ceiling on operational efficiency at any age.[4]

CONCLUSION

I began the present chapter by pointing out that the major difference between my own view of development and Piaget's is in the way in which children's intellectual structures are modeled at different stages of development. I also suggested that this difference leads to a difference in the way in which the process of stage transition is conceptualized. I would like to conclude by elaborating on this point.

In Piaget's theory, children's intellectual functioning is represented in terms of symbolic logic. This representation leads to the postulation of very general systems of logical operations, of great scope and internal cohesion. In my theory, children's intellectual functioning is represented in terms of executive control structures. This leads to the postulation of relatively specific systems of operations that are broad in general *form* but that are each assembled independently, and for purposes that are relatively specific.

The fact that both ways of modeling children's thought are structural leads to parallel assertions about children's mental processes at successive stages. In each system, for example, it is asserted that higher-order processes involve (1) the coordination of lower-order processes, (2) the differentiation of lower-order processes, and (3) the hierarchical integration of processes, or "operations on operations."

However, the fact that the two types of structure differ in their emphasis on logic and in their generality leads to different assumptions about stage transition. In Piaget's system, stage transition is seen as taking place by an internal process that is essentially logical in nature: namely, the elimination of inconsistency ("equilibration"). This development is seen as taking place in a very broad and central fashion. It is the *entire framework* to which reality is assimilated that is transformed in Piaget's system—not a particular framework for dealing with a particular class of situations.

In contrast, according to the present view stage transition takes place by a set of processes that are oriented toward achieving particular results, in particular physical and social environments. These processes include problem solving, exploration, imitation, and mutual regulation, all of which share a certain number of fundamental subprocesses, namely goal setting, novel-sequence generation, utility evaluation, executive restructuring, and consolidation. In my theory, then, the general change that takes place in the child's view of reality is not seen as being the result of a general structural change. Rather, it is seen as being the result of a number of specific structural changes that occur within a general systemic constraint.

As even the most passionate advocates of Piaget's theory would concede, the sort of general logical structure he has proposed makes it very difficult for him to explain the "specific" factor in development: the existence of low intertask correlations, for example, or experimentally induced developmental accelerations in one local problem domain. In contrast, these phenomena are quite easy to explain within the context of my theory, since children's opportunities for engaging in processes such as exploration, as well as their talents and motivations, have a strong domain-specific component.

It is important to realize, however, that in addition to having the above weaknesses, Piaget's theory also has a number of impressive strengths. As might be expected, these have to do with its ability to account for the "general" factor in development: for example, the common form that children's control structures share across domains, once the children are exposed to the appropriate opportunities for learning; or the very slow rate of progress that appears to characterize the spontaneous development of the system as a whole. It is because I believe that these general aspects of development are every bit as important to explain as the specific ones, that I have included a second class of factor in my theory of stage transition. What I have suggested is that, although particular executive structures are assembled into hierarchically integrated structures in a relatively local fashion, each specific act of assembly is constrained by a general systemic limitation: the size of a subject's short-term storage space. This space is seen as growing very gradually, in response to equally gradual increases in the efficiency of different classes of operation. And the efficiency of these operations is assumed to develop in turn as a function of some minimal amount of specific operational practice, on the one hand, and some general experience and/or maturation, on the other. A possible mechanism by which general experience and maturation might increase efficiency has also been suggested: neurological changes in myelinization.

Only time will tell if the model I have proposed is a viable one. However, if both the general and the specific aspects of stage transition are to be explained, it seems to me that only two options are available. Either one must propose a specific model of structural change acting within a general systemic constraint, as I have done, or else one must propose a *general* model of structural change, as Piaget did, and add a model of the specific factors that accelerate or retard the application of this general structure to particular social and physical situations.

NOTES

[1] For a description of children's control structures in these domains—from birth through adolescence—see Case, in press, Chapters 7–11.

[2] A question for basic research is *how* this restructuring takes place. In investigating this question, the role of affect should not be ignored. When a successful solution is reached, the result is normally a change in affective state. This change may lead to the maintenance of the successful schemes in a state of high activation for a few seconds, thus producing the equivalent of "mental rehearsal."

[3] For evidence of this spontaneous counting tendency in children, see Gelman (1978).

[4] For a elaboration of the myelinization model, see Case (in press, Chapter 17).

REFERENCES

Abramovitch, R., Carter, P., and Lando, B. Sibling interaction in the home. *Child Development*, 1979, *50*, 997–1003.

Baldwin, J. M. *The development of the child and of the race.* New York: Macmillan, 1894.

Biemiller, A. J. The effect of varying conditions of exposure to a novel object on manipulation by human infants. M.S. thesis, Cornell University, 1966.

Bruner, J. S. The course of cognitive growth. *American Psychologist*, 1964, *19*, 1–15.

Bryant, P. E. The understanding of invariance by very young children. *Canadian Journal of Psychology*, 1972, *26*, 78–96.

Case, R. Intellectual development from birth to adulthood: A neo-Piagetian interpretation. In R. Siegler (Ed.), *Children's thinking; What develops?* Hillsdale, N.J.: Erlbaum, 1978.

Case, R. The search for horizontal structure in children's development. *Genetic Epistemologist*, 1982, *11*, 6–15.

Case, R. *Intellectual development: A systematic reinterpretation.* New York: Academic Press, in press.

Case, R., Kurland, D. M., Daneman, M., and Emanuel, P. Operational efficiency and the growth of M-space. Paper presented at the biennial meeting of the Society for Research in Child Development, San Francisco, 1979.

Case, R., Kurland, D. M., and Goldberg, J. Operational efficiency and the growth of short-term memory span. *Journal of Experimental Child Psychology*, 1982, *33*, 386–404.

Chi, M. T. H. Short-term memory limitations in children: Capacity or processing deficits? *Memory and Cognition*, 1976, *4*, 559–572.

Chi, M. T. H., and Klahr, D. Span and rate of apprehension in children and adults. *Journal of Experimental Child Psychology*, 1975, *19*, 434–439.

Dempster, F. N. Short-term storage capacity and chunking: A developmental study. Ph.D. thesis, University of California, Berkeley, 1977.

Flavell, J. H. An analysis of cognitive-developmental sequences. *Genetic Psychology Monographs*, 1972, *86*, 279–350.

Gelman, R. Counting in the preschooler: An analysis of what does and does not develop. In R. S. Siegler (Ed.), *Children's thinking: What develops?* Hillsdale, N.J.: Erlbaum, 1978.

Halford, G. S. Toward a redefinition of cognitive developmental stages. In J. R. Kirby and J. B. Biggs (Eds.), *Cognition, development, and instruction.* New York: Academic Press, 1980.

Klahr, D., and Wallace, J. G. *Cognitive development: An information processing view.* Hillsdale, N.J.: Erlbaum, 1976.

Liu, P. An investigation of the relationship between qualitative and quantitative advances in the cognitive development of preschool children. Ph.D. thesis, University of Toronto, 1981.

Logan, G. D. Converging evidence for automatic perceptual processing in visual search. *Canadian Journal of Psychology*, 1976, *30*, 193–200.

Meltzoff, A. Imitation, intermodal co-ordination, and representation in early infancy. In G. Butterworth (Ed.), *Infancy and epistemology*. London: Harvester Press, 1981. New York: St. Martin's Press, 1982.

Noelting, G. Stages and mechanisms in the development of the concept of proportionality in the child and adolescent. In *Piagetian theory and the helping professions*. Los Angeles: University of Southern California, 1975.

Pascual-Leone, J. A mathematical model for the transition rule in Piaget's developmental stages. *Acta Psychologica*, 1970, *32*, 301–345.

Piaget, J. *The origins of intelligence in children.* New York: International Universities Press, 1952. (M. Cook, Trans.; original French ed., 1936.)

Piaget, J., and Fot, C. *The epistemology and psychology of functions.* Dordrecht, the Netherlands: D. Reidel Publishing Co., 1977.

Saxe, G. B. Counting and conservation: A developmental investigation of numeric symbolization and its relation to numeric conception. Ph.D. thesis, University of California, Berkeley, 1975.

Siegler, R. S. Three aspects of cognitive development. *Cognitive Psychology*, 1976, *8*(4), 481–520.

Siegler, R. S., and Robinson, M. The development of numerical understandings. In H. W. Reese and L. P. Lipsitt (Eds.), *Advances in child development and behavior*, Vol. 16. New York: Academic Press, 1981.

Stern, D. *The first relationship.* Cambridge, Mass.: Harvard University Press, 1977.

Watson, M. W., and Fischer, K. W. A developmental sequence of agent use in late infancy. *Child Development*, 1977, *48*, 828–836.

White, B. *The first three years of life.* New York: Avon Books, 1975.

Yakovlev, P., and Lecours, A. R. The myelogenetic cycles of regional maturation of the brain. In A. Minkowski (Ed.), *Regional development of the brain in early life.* Oxford: Blackwell and Mott, 1967.

Processes of Cognitive Development: Optimal Level and Skill Acquisition

Kurt W. Fischer and Sandra L. Pipp

Development, learning, and problem solving all involve systematic change in behavior over time. Despite this general similarity, the differences among the three phenomena have been a focus of controversy in developmental psychology for decades, and the dispute has tended to produce two opposing camps, at least in stereotype. One group, including most learning theorists and many proponents of the information-processing approach, portrays development as a long-term accumulation of learned behaviors or rules (for example, Klahr and Wallace, 1976; Skinner, 1969). The processes of acquisition of these behaviors are described primarily in environmental terms, involving conditioning and other specific types of experience. The other group, including Piaget, many Piagetians, and some information-processing theorists, sharply distinguishes learning from development, and argues that development is the more important and fundamental process (Piaget, 1936/1952, 1970). The processes of development are depicted as mainly organismic, involving genetic factors, the properties of the person's mind, and other types of endogenous influences.

In presenting our theory, we wish to emphasize that learning is not opposed to development and that environmental factors are not opposed to organismic ones. Learning and development should not be contrasted but should be treated as inextricably linked. Explaining them will require concepts that specify how environment and organism jointly affect fundamental psychological processes. Of course, many thinkers in the history of the developmental sciences have called for theories that treat organism and environment as interacting (for example, Piaget, 1936/1952; Sameroff, 1983), but it is not enough to state such an ideal. Theorists need to build models that include concrete specifications of both environmental and organismic influences on the same processes.

In our approach, called "skill theory," two types of processes are posited to explain development and learning: optimal level and skill acquisition. Both processes function in a manner that inter-

Preparation of this article was supported by a grant from the Carnegie Corporation of New York to the first author and a grant from the Foundation for Child Development to the second author. The statements made and views expressed are solely the responsibility of the authors. We would like to thank the following individuals for their contributions to various aspects of the article: Bennett Bertenthal, Daniel Bullock, Roberta Corrigan, Helen Hand, Susan Harter, Sheryl Kenny, Robert McCall, Marilyn Pelot, David G. Thomas, and Malcolm Watson.

twines organismic and environmental influences. *Optimal level* is the upper limit of a person's general information-processing capacity, the most complex type of skill that he or she can control. Over relatively long age spans, the individual's optimal level increases, producing changes in the kinds of skills that the person can construct. These changes can be characterized in terms of a series of hierarchically organized developmental levels. *Skill-acquisition processes* determine how the skills are actually constructed—how the person moves from a particular skill in a given context to a more complex or general skill. In skill theory, these acquisition processes are defined in terms of a set of transformation rules that specify how a particular skill can be transformed or rewritten to form a new skill.

This article will outline the nature of the two types of processes, the ways they are influenced by both organism and environment, and the manner in which they jointly produce both learning and development. More detailed treatments of skill theory are available in Fischer (1980b) and in Fischer and Corrigan (1981). Methods for studying the hypothesized processes are described in Fischer and Bullock (1981) and in Fischer, Pipp, and Bullock (in press).

Although concepts similar to optimal level and skill acquisition are used in several other approaches, skill theory changes the concepts in important ways by defining them so that organism and environment are intertwined. A skill is always controlled by a person in a specific environment or context. Both the person and the context affect the processes by which the skill occurs and develops. A skill is thus bound by the set of contexts to which it has been applied and by the capacity and history of the person controlling it.

OPTIMAL LEVEL

Optimal level is a concept that combines organism and environment to explain large-scale changes in development. Again, it specifies the upper limit on the complexity of skill that an individual can control. For a person to function at that upper limit, however, the person's performance must be induced and supported by environmental factors. If environmental influences are ignored, as is the case, for example, in Piaget's (1971) theory, then the pervasive effects of the environment become "noise" that drowns out developmental levels. Investigators who fail to consider environmental influences have difficulty documenting that levels exist at all.

In order to explain how optimal level functions, it is necessary to first outline the series of developmental levels postulated in skill theory. Then we will be able to describe how optimal level influences

Level   I   II   III   IV

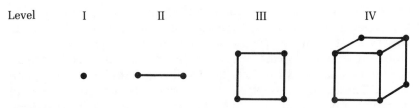

Figure 3-1
A metaphor for the cycle of four levels within each
tier of skill structures.
Reprinted from Fischer. Copyright 1980 by the
American Psychological Association.

behavior, including both how the individual's capacities change and
how environmental conditions affect the use of those capacities.

The Ten Levels of Development

Skill theory predicts a series of ten developmental levels, occurring
in three cycles or tiers. The levels and tiers are defined structurally,
in terms of behavioral sets or categories (sensorimotor actions, representations, and abstractions) and types of relations between those
sets, as shown in Table 3-1. For a given optimal level, the most complex type of skill that an individual can control has the structure
characteristic of that level. The person also retains the ability to
control skills with the structures characteristic of all previous levels.

Within each tier, there are four successive developmental levels,
each involving a new type of skill organization. Figure 3-1 provides
a geometric metaphor for the structures of the levels: from point to
line to plane to solid. At the first level, which is similar to a point,
the person can control variations in only one set: one action, one
representation, or one abstraction. At the second level, he or she can
combine several sets to produce a new structure, as points can be
combined to make a line. This structure, termed a mapping, defines
a simple relation between two or more sets. The third level, analogous to the joining of lines to make a plane, involves the integration
of several mappings to produce a system, a relation between two or
more subsets of two or more sets. Finally, the person combines several systems at the fourth level to produce a system of systems, as
planes can be joined to make a solid. This new structure is a new
building block—a new set at the first level of the next tier, as shown
in Table 3-1. That is, the fourth level of one tier is literally the first
level of the next tier, beginning the cycle over again. Thus the cycle
of levels of sensorimotor actions eventually produces representa-

tions, and the cycle of levels of representations eventually produces abstractions. [Cycles of four levels have also been posited independently by Biggs and Collis (1982) and by Case (1978); however, those cycles are defined differently.]

The development of pretend play with dolls illustrates the tier for representations. We choose this example because predictions about pretend play based on skill theory have been extensively tested in a series of experiments (Corrigan, 1983; Fischer, Hand, Watson, Van Parys, and Tucker, in press; Hand, 1981a, 1981b; Watson, 1981; Watson and Amgott-Kwan, in press; Watson and Fischer, 1977, 1980; Westerman, 1980). In the following description of the development of representations involving pretend play, we will not repeat these citations but will only cite additional relevant articles.

At about 2 years of age in middle-class children, the first level— *single representations*—emerges. A single representation is symbolized by R for Level 4 in Table 3-1. One of the many abilities that arise from single representations is the ability to treat a doll as an independent agent, as if it were acting on its own (Fischer and Jennings, 1981). In the simplest representation of this type, the doll carries out a single action, such as walking across a table or drinking from a cup. Within a level, children can use skill-acquisition processes to transform the simplest skills into more complex skills at the same level. An example of such a complex skill for representations is a behavioral role, a cluster of actions relating to a single social category, such as doctor. The child can make the doll carry out several actions appropriate for a doctor—for instance, putting on a doctor's coat, giving an inoculation, and dispensing medicine. Or the child can make another doll act like a patient by having this doll perform actions like saying "I have a tummy ache," taking medicine, and going to bed.

At the second level, *mappings*, the child can go beyond the separate representations of the previous level and form a mapping relating two or more representations, as symbolized in Table 3-1 by the structure for Level 5: R connected with T by a straight line. In pretend play, the child can coordinate two dolls in a social interaction; that is, he or she can combine *behavioral* roles to form a *social* role. The doctor and the patient no longer perform their actions independently, but interact in a stereotyped manner. The patient tells the doctor that she is sick, for instance, and then the doctor examines her throat and tells her to take some medicine to get better. He gives her the medicine, and she swallows it and says she will feel better soon. Many similar relations of social categories can be mastered with representational mappings, such as the relations of father with child and husband with wife. Social categories besides

Table 3-1
Ten Levels of Skill Structures*

Level	Name of structure	Sensorimotor† tier	Representational† tier	Abstract tier	Estimated age region of emergence
1	Single sensorimotor set	[A] or [B]			3–4 mos.
2	Sensorimotor mapping	[A — B]			7–8 mos.
3	Sensorimotor system	$[A_{G,H} \leftrightarrow B_{G,H}]$			11–13 mos.
4	System of sensorimotor systems, equivalent to a single representational set	$\begin{bmatrix} A \leftrightarrow B \\ \updownarrow \\ C \leftrightarrow D \end{bmatrix} \equiv$	[R]		20–24 mos.
5	Representational mapping		[R — T]		4–5 yrs.

6	Representational system	$[R_{I,K} \leftrightarrow T_{J,K}]$	6–7½ yrs.
7	System of representational systems, equivalent to a single abstract set	$\begin{bmatrix} R \leftrightarrow T \\ \updownarrow \\ V \leftrightarrow X \end{bmatrix} \equiv [\mathscr{C}]$	10-12 yrs.
8	Abstract mapping	$[\mathscr{C} - \mathscr{F}]$	14–16 yrs.
9	Abstract system	$[\mathscr{C}_{A,B} \leftrightarrow \mathscr{F}_{A,B}]$	18–20 yrs.
10	System of abstract systems, equivalent to a single principle	$\begin{bmatrix} \mathscr{C} \leftrightarrow \mathscr{F} \\ \updownarrow \\ \mathscr{G} \leftrightarrow \mathscr{H} \end{bmatrix}$	24–26 yrs.‡

* Boldface capital letters designate sensorimotor sets; italic capital letters designate representational sets, and script capital letters designate abstract sets. Multiple subscripts designate differentiated components of a set; whenever there is a horizontal arrow, two or more subsets exist by definition, even when they are not expressly shown. Long straight lines and arrows designate a relation between sets or systems. Brackets designate a single skill.

† Sensorimotor structures continue after Level 4, and representational structures after Level 7, but the formulas become so complex that they have been omitted. To fill in the sensorimotor structures, simply copy the pattern in the representational tier, replacing each representational set with the sensorimotor formula for Level 4. Similarly, to fill in the representational structures, copy the pattern in the abstract tier, replacing each abstract set with the representational formula for Level 7.

‡ Since little research has been done on development at this level, this age region must be considered highly tentative.

roles can also be related in a mapping, as in concrete social reciprocity: "You acted nice to me, so I'll be nice to you."

The third level of representations requires the coordination of at least two mappings to produce a *system*, a relation of two or more subsets of two or more representations, as symbolized in Table 3-1 by the structure for Level 6: $R_{J,K}$ connected with $T_{J,K}$ by a double-headed arrow. In pretend play, the child can make two dolls simultaneously carry out two intersecting concrete social roles. One doll can be both doctor and father to the other doll, who is both his patient and his daughter. For play involving the family, a man and a woman can each fill both job and parental roles at the same time, such as lawyer/father and psychologist/mother. Similarly, a man can fill both father and husband roles and a woman both mother and wife roles at the same time (Fischer and Watson, 1981; see also Harter, in press). Children's spontaneous comments at around 6 or 7 years of age often demonstrate this new understanding of intersecting roles: one 7-year old ran up to her grandmother and exclaimed, "Grandma, I get it! You're my grandmother, *and* you're Mommy's mother too!"

At the fourth and final level of the representational tier, the child coordinates two or more systems to produce a *system of systems*, which is a *single abstraction*. In Table 3-1, the two systems are designated at Level 7 by (1) R connected to T by a horizontal arrow, and (2) V connected to X by a horizontal arrow. The relation of the two systems within the higher-order system is indicated by the vertical arrow. The structure at this level forms a new building block for the next cycle—a single abstraction, symbolized by $\mathscr{E}$. In pretend play, for example, a 12-year-old girl can coordinate her system for understanding her mother's and father's parental and spouse roles (mother/wife and father/husband) with her system for understanding the parental and spouse roles of her best friend's mother and father. The result is an abstraction for the family as a system of parental and spouse roles. With this new level, the adolescent enters a new tier, in which over many years she will progress through three additional levels of abstractions (Fischer, Hand, and Russell, 1983).

Together, the sensorimotor, representational, and abstract tiers produce ten cognitive developmental levels, as shown in Table 3-1. The right-hand column of the table shows the age regions in which each level seems to first develop. These estimates are based on research with middle-class populations, and should be used cautiously.

Many cognitive developmental approaches have posited developmental levels, but the levels of skill theory differ in at least two important ways from the levels or stages of other contemporary approaches (such as Case, 1978; Huttenlocher and Burke, 1976; Pascual-Leone, 1970). First, for most other approaches, large-scale changes in development involve increases in the number of items in short-term store or working memory, whereas for skill theory they entail a fundamental change in the organization of behavior. Second, other approaches typically assume that when people have reached a certain stage or level, most of their skills exist at that level. Skill theory, on the other hand, assumes that the optimal level merely sets the upper limit on skills. Below that limit, behavior varies widely across levels. Indeed, one of the major tasks of cognitive developmental theory, we believe, is to explain variations in behavior within and across developmental levels. To investigate these variations, however, a clear empirical criterion is needed for determining how to assign behaviors to levels.

Spurts in Optimal Performance

A fundamental problem with many descriptions of stages or levels of development is that no clear criterion is stated for what type of behavioral change merits designation as a level. Children learn new behaviors and develop new capacities almost every day, yet most of these new acquisitions are not typically classified as demonstrating the emergence of a new level. To identify these pathbreaking behaviors, developmentalists need to concern themselves with what constitutes a level.

A straightforward criterion postulated in skill theory is that with the emergence of a new optimal level, the individual will show a developmental spurt—a large, rapid advance in many behaviors. That is, a person's optimal performance in a domain will improve sharply when a new cognitive developmental level is emerging. The spurt will not occur instantaneously, of course, but it will occur in a relatively short age interval. For a given developmental level, such spurts will take place across many content domains, and the spurts in the various domains will cluster in an age region for each individual. Figure 3-2 illustrates a cluster of spurts in a hypothetical person across three domains from Level 7 to Level 8 (abstract mappings), the level that is hypothesized to emerge at 14 to 16 years in middle-class adolescents.

According to this analysis, every change in level will be marked by a cluster of spurts in optimal performance at a given age region across a variety of domains. When the entire range of ten levels is considered, the following portrait emerges: Optimal performance increases with age, but the increase varies systematically, alternating between periods of rapid change (spurts) and periods of slow change.

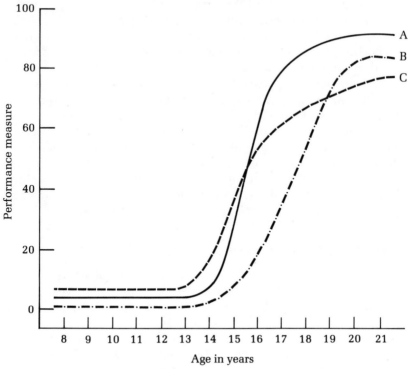

Figure 3-2
A hypothetical cluster of spurts resulting from the
emergence of a new developmental level in three
domains. Curves A, B, and C represent the
different behavioral domains. The spurts were
chosen to indicate the emergence of Level 8
(abstract mappings).

A cluster of spurts in optimal performance across a wide range of
domains indicates the emergence of a developmental level, which
is characterized by a new, qualitatively different type of skill structure. [Other factors besides optimal level can produce developmental
spurts too, as described by Fischer and Bullock (1981), but the
breadth of domains showing a spurt from such factors will always
be much narrower than for optimal level.]

As we have mentioned, neither children nor adults automatically
function at their optimal level. In every domain, individuals must
work to construct more complex skills; their optimal level merely
limits the complexity of the skills they can construct. In addition,
most spontaneous behavior seems to involve skills below the per-

son's optimal level, especially for older children and adults (Fischer, Hand, and Russell, 1983; Hand, 1981b).

There exist few studies that allow assessment of whether there are spurts in optimal performance at certain periods in development. The major reason for this deficit is that investigators seldom use methods that allow assessment of the rate of development. Fortunately, methods are available that provide such assessments, and that are easy to use in both cross-sectional and longitudinal studies. To assess for spurts, a study must include two key components: a developmental scale on which the quantity of change can be measured, and a gauge for measuring the speed of change. Several studies using such methods are described in detail in Fischer, Pipp, and Bullock (in press).

The Environmental Conditions for Detecting Levels

Having a method that can detect developmental spurts is only the first step, however. The researcher also needs to know where to look for spurts. One of the most fundamental questions for the researcher to ask is, what are the environmental conditions under which spurts are likely to occur? The task for the researcher is to test under conditions designed to elicit optimal performance. A useful strategy is to assess under a variety of conditions in order to determine how behavior varies (Davison, King, Kitchener, and Parker, 1980; Hand, 1981b).

Two of the most potent environmental influences are practice and instruction, which typically produce dramatic improvement in performance. A third important factor seems to be environmental support, the provision of cues indicating the kind of performance that is expected. Without such cues, performance frequently seems to drop below the person's capability (Hand, 1981b; Watson and Fischer, 1980; Vygotsky, 1978). A straightforward way to assess optimal level is to study performance under conditions that provide practice, instruction, and environmental support. (At times, of course, the three factors are not independent but overlap.) Under such conditions, people will perform at or near their upper limit for that domain.

In a study in progress in our laboratory, for example, we chose the domain of arithmetic because it is a standard topic of instruction in school (Kenny and Fischer, in preparation). Performance of each subject was assessed on eight specific problems under four conditions in which the degree of practice and support varied. The problems were all designed to test Level 8 abstract mappings, which involve combining two abstractions in a relation (Fischer, Hand, and

Russell, 1983). Each problem required explanation of one of four relations between similar arithmetic operations: how does addition relate to subtraction, multiplication to addition, division to subtraction, and multiplication to addition? To date, 96 subjects have been tested, four of each sex for each year ranging from 9 to 20 years of age. All subjects were middle-class white students living in Denver.

We will discuss only the two most extreme of the four conditions. Students were initially tested in the *spontaneous* condition, which is similar to most standard testing situations in cognitive and educational research: The experimenter presented each student with the eight problems without giving the student any opportunity to practice or any cues as to what constituted a good answer. This condition did little to promote optimal performance. Later in the same session, the student was shown a good answer to each problem and was reminded that he or she would be tested again in approximately two weeks.

The condition providing the most opportunity for optimal performance, the *practice-and-support* condition, occurred in the second session. Students were again shown a good answer to each problem, the answer was taken away, and they were asked to give their own answer. Thus they not only had time to practice the tasks, but they were given immediate support for an appropriate answer. The dependent measure for each condition was percentage of correct answers.

The results strongly supported the optimal-level hypothesis. In the spontaneous condition, performance showed a slow, gradual improvement from 15 to 20 years of age, but never reached as high as 50 percent correct, as shown in Figure 3-3. In the practice-and-support condition, performance spurted sharply between 15 and 16 years, from near 0 to over 80 percent correct. That is, under environmental conditions like those in most research, there was no spurt evident, but under conditions promoting optimal performance, a dramatic spurt occurred as predicted.

Indeed, the spurt occurred at the same age for virtually all subjects. This finding probably resulted from the homogeneity of the sample tested. With subjects differing more in educational and demographic characteristics, there probably would have been more variation in age. Fortunately, when there are such variations in age, spurts can still be detected by examination of the performance profiles of individual subjects: under optimal-performance conditions, most individuals will either pass most tasks or fail most tasks at the criterial developmental level.

Studies from several laboratories have shown similar spurts in diverse domains; these spurts are consistent with most of the levels

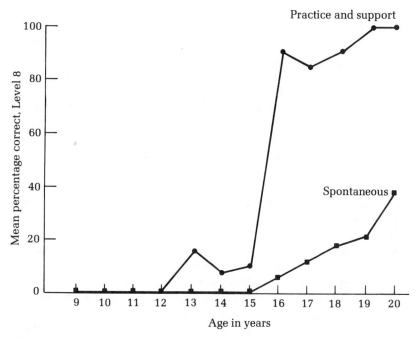

Figure 3-3
Changes with age in the percentage of Level 8
arithmetic problems solved under two conditions.
Every subject performed eight Level 8 problems in
each condition. Eight subjects, four of each sex,
were tested at each age. The same subjects
performed under both conditions.

predicted by skill theory. (See Corrigan, 1983; Emde, Gaensbauer,
and Harmon, 1976; Jaques, Gibson, and Isaac, 1978; Kenny, 1983;
McCall, 1983; O'Brien and Overton, 1982; Peters and Zaidel, 1981;
Selman, 1980, p. 184; Tabor and Kendler, 1981; and Zelazo and Leonard, 1983).

Biological Correlates of Levels

Our emphasis on the environmental conditions for detecting developmental levels has highlighted the environmental side of skill development, but the organismic side needs to be taken seriously as
well. Optimal level is a property of a specific combination of organism and environment—of a person under particular environmental
conditions. Several researchers have suggested that the emergence

of developmental levels may be accompanied by major biological changes in children, including changes in brain size and brain waves (Emde, Gaensbauer, and Harmon, 1976; Epstein, 1974, 1980; Kagan, 1982; White, 1970). Indeed, a number of developmental spurts in the biological variables seem to parallel the spurts in behavior documented in psychological research.

Although we were initially skeptical about the generality of such biological correlates of cognitive development, we nevertheless sought out data on head circumference and on brain waves, using the electroencephalogram (EEG) for the latter. These data were analyzed to determine whether spurts in those variables appeared at appropriate ages for each level. To our surprise, the biological variables did seem to spurt in the appropriate age region for every level for which we could find relevant data (Levels 1 through 9). With the EEG, for example, global measures reflecting the entire spectrum of waves typically seemed to demonstrate a spurt for each new developmental level. Figure 3-4, illustrating one such measure based on data collected by the Swedish neuroscientists Matousek and Petersen (1973; John, 1977), shows statistically significant spurts for Levels 5, 6, 7, 8, and 9, starting approximately at ages 4, 8, 12, 15, and 19, respectively. There is also a probable spurt for Level 4 at about 2 years.

Of course, these data can only be taken as suggestive at this time, since no studies have systematically examined both brain-wave and psychological changes in the same people. Existing data indicate that for at least some biological variables, patterns like that in Figure 3-4 may obtain only for groups, not for individual children. Also, we caution against thinking of the biological changes as prerequisites in any simple sense for the psychological changes.

How Optimal Level Functions

According to the optimal-level hypothesis, then, development is *both stage-like and gradual at the same time.* When individuals are functioning at their upper limit, development spurts in a relatively short period to a new level of skill. When they are not performing at their limit, change occurs gradually over a longer period. Most of the time, individuals are not performing at their optimal level, and consequently most development is gradual.

During periods when a new optimal level is emerging, developmental changes in familiar domains can occur at a rapid rate. After the optimal level has emerged, skills in those same domains will show slower, less dramatic change in complexity and generalization. The periods of slow change in optimal performance do not indicate

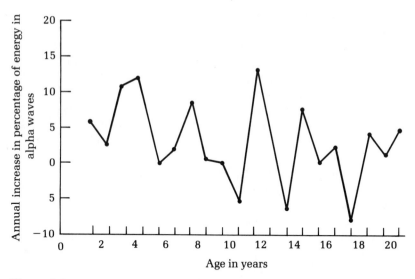

Figure 3-4
The increase in the percentage of energy in alpha
waves as a function of age. An
electroencephalogram was obtained from the
occipital-parietal area, and the percentage of
energy was calculated by dividing the amount of
energy in alpha waves by the total amount of
energy in all waves.
Data from Matousek and Petersen (1973).

developmental stasis, however. The person never lacks additional
skills to learn, because there are always new domains to master. The
emergent capacity must be extended to many diverse domains, and
it must be strengthened to the point that the individual can use it
even when there is little environmental support. This extension and
elaboration of the capacity both consolidates the person's skills and
prepares for the emergence of the next optimal level.

The way that a new optimal-level capacity is extended to diverse
domains highlights a major difference between skill theory and com-
petence/performance models such as those of Piaget (1957, 1971) and
Chomsky (1965). In the latter approaches, a general structure believed to be present in the mind can be straightforwardly applied to
new domains. For instance, Piaget's *structure d'ensemble* (structure
of the whole) for concrete operations emerges at 6 to 7 years, and it
is automatically applicable to any content. The reason that it does
not generalize to all contents immediately is that objects and events

differentially resist application of the structure. The competence is thus considered to be present, although sometimes the child cannot demonstrate it in performance (Bullock, 1981; Stone and Day, 1980).

Optimal level functions very differently. When people develop a new optimal level, they have the capacity to construct skills at the new level, but they do not actually have any competences at that level until those skills are built. An individual must always work to construct particular skills in specific domains. There are no powerful competences that are somehow prevented from eventuating in performance.

In summary, although much research remains to be done, a number of independent strands of evidence do support the optimal-level hypothesis, including the particular levels postulated in skill theory. The upper limit on the complexity of skills that a person can construct seems to develop through a series of qualitatively different levels, each of which is characterized by a cluster of spurts in optimal performance. Most of the systematic changes in behavior that constitute development, learning, and problem solving, however, are affected only modestly by this upper bound. Optimal level, after all, specifies only a limit on skills that can be mastered. To explain the many systematic changes in skills below the upper limit, another set of developmental processes must be invoked: processes of skill acquisition.

TRANSFORMATION RULES FOR ANALYZING SKILL ACQUISITION

Skill theory gambles that thought and behavior can be fruitfully described structurally, and that development, learning, and problem solving can be explained by transformations of these structures (Fischer, 1980a). The transformations can be characterized in terms of a limited set of rewrite rules that specify how given skill structures can be transformed to produce new skill structures.

The transformation rules are one of the most important mechanisms by which skill theory predicts and explains sequences in development. New skills are mastered in a succession of many small steps, each of which is specified by a transformation rule. The sequence of skill acquisition within a domain can thus be described by reference to the initial skill structure and the series of transformation rules used. Development, learning, and problem solving all involve these same basic transformations.

Five different transformation rules have been specified, and we suspect that more will be discovered. There are four rules for predicting steps within a developmental level: substitution, focusing, compounding, and differentiation. The fifth rule, intercoordination, deals with movement to a new level—with how skills at one level are combined to produce a new skill at the next level. All five rules have been formally defined as algebraic rewrite rules for skill structures, and principles for ordering the results of the transformations have also been explicated (Fischer, 1980b).

A Developmental Sequence Illustrating the Transformations

To illustrate the transformation rules, we will analyze a developmental sequence involving all five rules. The sequence begins with three Level 5 skills for social rules. These skills are rewritten by the five different transformations, which are ordered according to skill-theory principles to produce the sequence shown in Table 3-2. This sequence has been tested and confirmed in several studies (Watson, 1981; Watson and Fischer, 1980).

The initial Level 5 mappings deal with the social roles of doctor/patient, nurse/patient, and father/child, as shown for step 1 in Table 3-2. Recall that a social role always involves a relation between a primary role, such as a doctor, and a complementary role, such as patient. To enact the doctor/patient role, for example, a girl pretends that a doctor doll examines a patient doll, who interacts appropriately. For the nurse/patient role, she pretends that a nurse doll examines a patient doll, who again interacts appropriately. For the father/child role, she makes a man doll treat a child doll as his daughter, who also interacts appropriately.

The simplest of the within-level transformation rules is *substitution*, a type of generalization in which a skill is mastered through one task and then transferred to a second, similar task. An individual may show such transfer when all but one of the components in the second skill structure are the same as those in the first structure, and when the single different component can be generalized to the second task. The Level 5 skill for doctor/patient shows an instance of such transfer when the type of patient is changed, as shown in step 2 of Table 3-2. The child first learns to make a doctor interact with a girl patient and then transfers that skill to the interactions of a doctor with a woman patient.

Some of the within-level transformations involve the combination of two previously existing independent skills, such as two of the social roles in step 1. In one type of combination, called *focusing*, a person uses two related skills in succession, shifting from one to the other within a single task or situation (Gottlieb, Taylor, and Ruderman, 1977; Hand, 1981a; Harter, in press; Watson, 1981). In step

Table 2
Examples of the Transformation Rules in the Domain of Social Roles

step	Type of transformation	Cognitive level	Role-playing skill	Example of behavior	Formula for transformation	Skill structure
1	Initial skills	5: Representational mappings	Social role of doctor or	The child pretends that a doctor doll examines a patient doll, who responds appropriately.		$[R_D — S_P]$
			Social role of nurse or	The child pretends that a nurse doll examines a patient doll, who responds appropriately.		$[T_N — S_P]$
			Social role of father	The child pretends that a father doll takes care of a child doll, who responds appropriately.		$[R_F — S_C]$
2	Substitution		Doctor role with woman patient	The child pretends that a doctor doll examines a woman doll, who responds appropriately.	$Sub[R_D — S_P] =$	$[R_D — T_P]$
3	Focusing		Shifting between doctor role and nurse role	The child pretends that a doctor doll examines a patient doll, who responds appropriately; and	$Foc[(R_D — S_P),(T_N — S_P)] =$	$[(R_D — S_P) > (T_N — S_P)]$

4	Compounding		then she switches to having the nurse doll examine a patient doll, who responds appropriately.		
		Social role of doctor with complementary roles of nurse and patient	The child pretends that a doctor doll examines a patient doll and is aided by a nurse doll. Both patient and nurse respond appropriately.	$[R_D - S_P] + [T_N - S_P] = [R_D - T_N - S_P]$	
5	Intercoordination	6: Representational systems	Intersection of doctor and father roles and their complements	The child pretends that a doctor doll examines a patient doll and simultaneously acts as a father to the patient, who is his son or daughter. The patient doll acts appropriately as both patient and offspring.	$[R_D - S_P] \cdot [R_F - S_C] = [R_{D,F} \leftrightarrow S_{P,C}]$

Note. In the formulas, the italicized capital letters stand for the child's representation of a particular doll as an independent agent: R for a man doll, S for a child doll, and T for a woman doll. The subscripts designate the role or roles that the child represents for each doll, as follows: C = child; D = doctor; F = father; N = nurse; P = patient. See Fischer (1980) for elaboration of the notation. The sequence has been tested and confirmed in several studies (Watson 1981; Watson & Fischer 1980).

3 of Table 3-2, the two skills are doctor/patient and nurse/patient. The child first has the doctor doll examine the patient doll, who interacts appropriately. Then the child simply shifts her focus from the doctor to the nurse: the nurse doll examines the patient doll, who again interacts appropriately. There is no integration between the two types of social roles: they are simply strung together.

Like all transformations, focusing arises from the collaboration of person and environment. The person possesses two or more related skills for a given situation but can apply only one of the skills at a time. Nevertheless, the situation tends to elicit both skills. The result is that the person effectively links the two skills together by focusing on first one skill and then the other.

The two Level 5 skills can be integrated by another type of within-level transformation, *compounding*. Two skills at a given level are combined to form a more complex skill that unifies the components at that level. In our play example, the child may combine the two role skills, doctor/patient and nurse/patient, to form a new compounded structure, doctor/nurse/patient, as shown in step 4 in Table 3-2. The child exhibits this new structure by making the doctor doll and the nurse doll jointly examine the patient doll, who responds appropriately to both of them. Note how this skill is different from the one based on focusing. In compounding, the three actors are made to carry out an integrated interaction; in focusing, the two initial skills remain separate and are linked only temporally.

The fourth transformation, *differentiation*, refers to the process by which one skill is separated into distinct components. This process seems always to accompany application of one of the other transformation rules, and consequently is not shown as a separate step in Table 3-2 (although it can be used by itself to predict developmental steps). Following Werner (1948), skill theory postulates that combination and differentiation occur together. In development, relatively global skills become more differentiated through combination, which Werner usually called integration.

For example, the compounded skill of doctor/patient/nurse in step 4 of Table 3-2 contains more highly differentiated components than the two uncompounded skills, doctor/patient and nurse/patient. In the uncompounded skills, a doctor can interact with a patient, or a nurse can interact with a patient. So long as these skills remain separate, many appropriate doctor, nurse, and patient behaviors will not be differentiated, even if the child also possesses a third uncompounded skill for the doctor/nurse role. The behavior of the doctor, for instance, will not include ways of (1) having the doctor interact with the patient to the exclusion of the nurse, (2) having the doctor interact with the nurse to the exclusion of the patient, or (3) having the doctor interact with the nurse and the patient simultaneously. In the compounded structure these behaviors can be differentiated, and as a result, all three roles will become both clearer and richer.

The last transformation, *intercoordination*, is the one rule that describes how skills can be combined to move behavior to a higher level. In conjunction with optimal level, it specifies how a person's skills at one level are transformed to the next level. At the beginning of the process, the child has two well-formed skills at a given level. The two skills function separately from each other until some object or event in the world induces the child to relate the two skills. If at this point the child is capable of the next developmental level, he or she will unravel the relationship between the two skills, gradually intercoordinating them. This unraveling will include a series of microdevelopmental steps involving the other transformations, and it will culminate in the intercoordination.

For example, two Level 5 social roles can be intercoordinated into a Level 6 understanding of the intersection between social roles. In one Level 5 skill, a child pretends that a doctor doll examines a patient doll who interacts appropriately. In another Level 5 skill, the child pretends that a father doll interacts with a daughter doll who responds appropriately. By intercoordinating these two social roles, the child constructs a Level 6 role intersection in which a doctor who is also a father interacts appropriately with a patient who is also a daughter. As a result of the intercoordination, the child can control the relations between the several social roles and so can understand that two people interacting can fulfill two complementary roles at the same time. Once this simple Level 6 role intersection has been mastered, more complex intersections can be built by means of the other transformations, such as the addition by compounding of a nurse who is also the patient's mother.

The five transformation rules specify different ways of rewriting skills. Within a domain, the rules can be used to analyze and predict sequences of skill acquisition, including both steps that must be ordered in a sequence and steps that cannot be consistently ordered with respect to one another. It is no trivial matter to predict developmental sequences (Bertenthal, 1981; Fischer and Bullock, 1981; Flavell, 1972; Siegler, 1981), and the transformation rules seem to provide a useful framework for making such predictions.

Many Paths from a Few Transformations

Cognitive developmentalists, especially Piagetians, commonly assume that there is one, and only one, path for development in any domain (for example, see Piaget, 1970). That is, all children are believed to pass through the same steps or stages of development. Skill theory postulates the contrary, that when specific skills are considered, different people follow different developmental paths (Fischer and Corrigan, 1981; see also Bullock, 1981; Flavell, 1982; Kuhn and Phelps, in press). That is, the steps that people move through in mastering a domain vary enormously in detail from one person to the next.

Variations in the environment alone will produce such differences, because every person's specific experiences are different from every other person's. For example, the types of dolls available to a preschool child will influence the types of social roles the child will construct when playing with those dolls. The child who plays with a baby doll and a mommy doll is likely at an early age to construct a skill for acting out a mother–child relationship, whereas the child who plays with two baby dolls or with a doctor doll and a nurse doll will construct different role skills. Likewise, various 9-year-olds will master the skills of addition through different paths, depending on their experiences with numbers and arithmetic tasks (Lawler, 1981).

Similarly, variations in the person alone will produce differences in developmental paths. People seem to differ greatly in the facility with which they can master certain kinds of materials, as illustrated by the wide variations in verbal, spatial, and mathematical abilities (Horn, 1976; Sternberg, 1980). When individual variations in motivation, activity level, and other such factors are also considered, it would seem that based on these variations alone, individuals will demonstrate important differences in developmental paths.

Since skills always involve influences from both the person and the environment, the degree of variation in developmental sequences will inevitably be large. It will be difficult to find two children who spontaneously develop through exactly the same steps in any domain.

There are, of course, important equivalences of skills across individuals, especially when those skills are analyzed globally. Various 9-year-olds, for example, have skills for addition that typically produce the same answers to simple addition problems. Likewise, in pretend play, preschoolers living in similar environments show many equivalences in the general types of developmental paths they demonstrate, as illustrated by the sequence outlined in Table 3-2. In fact, the developmental levels postulated in skill theory describe one highly global type of equivalence. When sequences are described in more detail, however, every child will show a different developmental path.

Although developmental paths may vary widely, the transformation rules underlying them do not vary, according to skill theory. The many paths can all be characterized by the same small set of transformation rules. It is the skills that individuals start with and the ways in which they use the transformation rules that differ, and that cause developmental paths to vary. The postulate that all skill acquisitions at all ages involve the same limited group of transformations is similar to the position taken by many information-processing theorists: that the same fundamental acquisition processes occur in development, learning, and problem solving at all ages (see Goodman, 1980; Klahr and Wallace, 1976; MacWhinney, 1978; Sternberg, 1980).

How Optimal Level Limits Transformations

The transformation rules specify how skills can be changed, and thereby predict which sequences of skill acquisition can occur. However, application of the rules is limited by the person's optimal level. The type of transformation that can be applied to existing skills is restricted by the highest level of which the individual is capable.

The most basic form of this restriction involves the transformation rule for moving to a higher level, intercoordination. With two skills that are already at the person's optimal level, intercoordination cannot occur, because the person is not capable of building a skill beyond his or her upper limit. In the social-role example, a $4\frac{1}{2}$-year-old girl who has several Level 5 skills for social roles can make those skills more complex via the other transformations; but if Level 5 is her optimal level, she cannot intercoordinate two of the skills to form a Level 6 role intersection.

Another form of limitation is hypothesized to occur when a new optimal level is first emerging: the person cannot yet apply the within-level transformations to the simple skills just built at the new level. For substitution and focusing, the period of this limitation may be brief; but for compounding, it is probably longer. Consider a 6-year-old girl who has just begun to be capable of Level 6 and has constructed a simple role intersection such as the relation of doctor/father to patient/daughter. She will not immediately be able to extend that intersection by compounding—by adding, say, nurse/mother. For all within-level transformations, the duration of this limit is brief relative to the age interval between levels. By the time the girl becomes $6\frac{1}{2}$ or 7 years old, she will be able to compound her skill to include three role intersections.

For each optimal level, then, there is a development of the ability to apply the within-level transformation rules. As the level initially emerges, the person cannot apply the transformations. This limitation gradually recedes, first for the simpler rules and finally for compounding. At that point, the only restriction is on moving to a higher level. This upper bound remains until the next optimal level begins to emerge.

OTHER IMPLICATIONS OF OPTIMAL LEVEL AND THE TRANSFORMATION RULES

We have argued that optimal level and the transformation rules specify two types of processes that explain changes in the organization of behavior in cognitive development, learning, and problem solving. Because of the fundamental nature of the two processes, they should manifest themselves in diverse arenas, including two of the most investigated phenomena in modern cognitive research: individual differences in intelligence, and limitations on memory.

Individual Differences in Intelligence

According to skill theory, levels and transformation rules are relatively independent in normal development. A plausible hypothesis about individual differences in intelligence can be derived from this analysis: Variations in intelligence involve two separate factors—optimal level and skill acquisition. At a given age, people do not vary widely in optimal level; most individuals develop each optimal level at about the same age. On the other hand, skill-acquisition processes demonstrate large individual differences (Flavell, 1982). In children, performance on standard intelligence tests varies as a function of both factors, but skill-acquisition processes account for much more of what psychologists traditionally assess on such tests.

By this hypothesis, variations in the age of emergence of each optimal level are relatively small within a normal population and show little correlation with intelligence-test performance after the level has emerged. People who grow up in normal environments develop each new level in the same age period, unless they have some kind of organic impairment producing mental retardation. For instance, Level 6 representational systems begin to develop at 6 to $7\frac{1}{2}$ years of age, and Level 7 single abstractions at 10 to 12 years, as described in Table 3-1. Optimal levels, according to this hypothesis, show a developmental pattern that is strongly canalized—characteristic of most members of the human species in a wide range of environments (McCall, 1981; Wohlwill, 1973).

The hypothesis that optimal level is strongly canalized seems to be most clearly supported for infant development. Different populations of normal infants show not only the same succession of four levels of development but also remarkable similarities in the age of emergence of each level. If spurts in developmental change are used to index emergence of a level, the ages for the levels seem to be 3 to 4 months, 7 to 8 months, 11 to 13 months, and 20 to 24 months— the ages for Levels 1 to 4, as shown in Table 3-1 (Corrigan, 1983; Fischer, 1982; Kagan, 1982; McCall, 1983; Zelazo and Leonard, 1983).

For later levels, there have been fewer analyses of the ages of emergence. Nevertheless, a number of studies do seem to converge on similar ages for each level (for example, Biggs and Collis, 1982; Epstein, 1974, 1978; Fischer, Hand, and Russell, 1983; Jaques, Gibson, and Isaac, 1978; Kenny, 1983; Kitchener, 1983; Peters and Zaidel, 1981; Tabor and Kendler, 1981). During childhood, levels seem to develop at approximately 4, 7, and 11 years; in adolescence and adulthood, they appear to emerge at 15, 19, and perhaps 25 years (see Table 3-1).

Unlike optimal levels, processes of skill acquisition differ enormously across individuals, producing great variation in the breadth and flexibility of skills. In general, high intelligence means that the individual can build more complex, flexible, and generalized skills at each optimal level, employing the transformation rules more easily and frequently. These abilities also vary widely across domains, with individuals showing varying degrees of facility at using the skill-acquisition processes in, for example, spatial versus verbal tasks (Horn, 1976).

The large individual differences in acquisition processes mean that under most testing conditions, people of the same age will show apparently wide variability in their optimal levels. However, when they are tested under environmental conditions that produce optimal performance, the discrepancies in optimal levels will mostly disappear. The reason is that people who have broader and more flexible skills will demonstrate their optimal level more easily under the usual testing conditions. That is, the same optimal level will be evident to a greater or lesser extent in different people, depending upon how broadly and flexibly each person can use that capacity in the specific domains tested.

One interesting test of this analysis involves very intelligent children. If the two-process model is correct, exceptionally bright children will initially develop each optimal level at the same age as children of average intelligence. Once the new level has emerged, however, bright children will quickly construct a wide range of skills at that level, whereas other children will take a much longer time to extend their new capacity to a wide range of skills.

Support for this hypothesis comes from several studies of children with IQ scores above 150. Webb (1974), for example, tested very bright children between 6 and 11 years of age on several of Piaget's concrete-operational and formal-operational tasks. The children under 10 years of age performed splendidly on the concrete-operational tasks, giving unusually rich responses, but they failed the formal-operational tasks. Only the children between 10 and 11 years began to pass the formal-operational tasks. This is the same age at which children of normal intelligence produce their first formal-operational skills (Fischer, Hand, and Russell, 1983; Martarano, 1977).

Two other studies have reported a similar lack of precocity in the emergence of new developmental levels in very bright children (Brown, 1973; Lovell and Shields, 1967). Further tests of the hypothesis are obviously called for, but care will have to be taken to ensure that the tasks provide clear tests of each level. Many behaviors are intrinsically ambiguous, in that they can be performed with skills at two or more different developmental levels (Fischer, Pipp, and Bullock, in press; Hand, 1981b; Roberts, 1981).

The pattern of development for retarded, handicapped, and mentally ill children is also of interest. One hypothesis is that some categories of children have virtually the same optimal level as normal children, but because of deficits in their skill-acquisition processes or their performance capabilities, they are typically unable to demonstrate their level. Lancy and Goldstein (1982), for example, suggest that autistic children show such a pattern.

Some types of mentally retarded children, on the other hand, probably evidence a delay in the development of optimal level. Seibert, Hogan, and Mundy (in press) found that in a group of retarded children, the chronological ages for the first three developmental levels seemed to be greatly delayed. Remarkably, however, the mental ages at which the children demonstrated those levels were virtually identical to the chronological ages for normal infants. (Mental ages were based on the Bayley infant intelligence test.)

Traditionally, Piagetian and psychometric approaches have been seen as opposed to each other. Piaget (1970) emphasizes the commonalities across people in the development of intelligence, whereas psychometricians focus on individual differences in intelligence (Horn, 1976; Sternberg, 1980). The two-process analysis suggests that these two approaches may, in fact, be compatible, with each approach emphasizing one of the two processes of intelligence.

Two Types of Memory Limitations

The concepts of optimal level and skill acquisition also promise to illuminate the nature of limitations on human memory. Many theories of cognitive development based on the information-processing approach posit that one of the fundamental bases of large-scale developmental changes is improvement in short-term or working memory. But the nature of the developmental limitations on such memory processes has proven to be a puzzle. Researchers have had difficulty in determining both the character of the development of working memory itself and the role of memory in cognitive development more generally.

Theories that posit substantial memory changes in childhood generally assume two conflicting forms. In one form, children's memory capacity actually increases with development, with the size of the short-term store growing from one item to two to three, and so forth (Huttenlocher and Burke, 1976; Pascual-Leone, 1970). In the second type of theory, memory resources remain constant, but there are developmental changes in the efficiency with which the resources can be allocated, with the result that there is a seeming increase in capacity (Case, Kurland, and Goldberg, 1982; Chi, 1978; Dempster, 1978). Thus, both approaches acknowledge that there are developmental changes in children's working memory and that those changes involve increases in the number of items that can be sustained in memory (Case, 1978). What is in dispute is the mechanisms underlying those increases.

We would like to suggest that the nature of changes in short-term or working memory can be clarified by a model that differentiates changes in the structures that can be sustained in working memory from changes in the number of items that can be sustained. That is, limitations on working memory take two different forms, based on the two processes postulated in this Chapter—optimal level and skill acquisition. For optimal level, the limit is on the type of skill structure the person can construct and control. For within-level acquisition processes, on the other hand, the limit is on the number of components that can be combined in a single skill. Although both processes affect how the resources of working memory can be allocated, the nature of the effects differs.

A rise in optimal level increases the efficiency of processing, but the growing efficiency comes not from an increase in the number of items that can be held in working memory but from a change in the type of structure that can be controlled. The emergence of a new optimal level provides the capacity to reorganize skills in a more efficient way. A shift in an individual's optimal level, then, increases memory resources because the new structural level leads to more efficient processing.

In contrast, within-level acquisitions place greater demands on processing. Because optimal level limits the reorganization of a skill, the within-level transformation rules are used to create more complex (and sometimes more baroque) skill structures at a given level. These more complex skill structures require more memory resources than do the simpler structures of that level.

Consider the developmental sequence of transformations outlined in Table 3-2. Most of the sequence involves within-level transformations. In step 4, for instance, the child moves from a simple Level 5 social role, such as the interaction of doctor and patient, to a compounded Level 5 role combining doctor, nurse, and patient. At Level 5 the child can construct many similar compounded skills, such as the combination of a doctor, a girl patient, and the patient's father. A simple social role involves two components (doctor and patient). A compounded role involves three components (doctor, patient, and father). If compounding is repeated, skills that are even more complex can be built, as when interaction occurs among four agents—say, a doctor, a patient, the patient's father, and the patient's sister. As each new component is added by compounding, the child must control a larger number of items, and consequently there is an increase in the demands on working memory.

When the child becomes capable of constructing Level 6 skills, the four-component compounded Level 5 skill can be reorganized to form a Level 6 system. In such a system, two representations that each contain two related subsets are coordinated to form a role intersection, as shown in Table 3-2. For example, at Level 6, two people can interact in such a way that each occupies two intersecting roles: the adult male can be both doctor and father, and the girl can be both patient and daughter. According to our analysis, this Level 6 skill will require smaller working-memory demands than the four-component compounded Level 5 skill, even though the number of role categories within each skill is exactly the same.

The relation between optimal-level shifts and the within-level transformations is thus as follows: A shift to a new optimal level produces the capacity for a larger functional working memory, because structures at the new level are more efficient. The reorganizations resulting from the new level reduce processing demands and thereby make possible the synthesis of more complex structures at the new level via the within-level transformations.

The characterization of memory changes in terms of number of items does not hold for level changes, but it does seem to hold for any one type of within-level transformation. In those special cases, the increase in memory load can be characterized in terms of the number of components held in working memory. For our example involving compounding of social roles, the number of components increased from two to three to four.

Across the types of transformations, however, number of components may not be a useful metric, since the qualitative differences between transformations seem to imply different effects on working-memory capacity. The transformations can be viewed as distinct ways to juggle the demands of the task within the constraints posed by optimal level. Practice with a task can increase the ability to juggle components within a level, although it cannot produce a reorganization beyond the person's optimal level (Fischer and Bullock, 1981; Hirst, Spelke, Reaves, Caharack, and Neisser, 1980). Faced with the constraints of optimal level, a person may attempt to solve a task by adding on components, shifting from one component to another, or substituting one component for another. Each of these types of transformations has a different effect on working-memory capacity.

The transformation of compounding may be the most costly in terms of working memory, because compounded skills involve the integration of all components in a single skill. To activate a compounded skill, the individual must combine all the components and relations between components. In our doctor example, the compounded skill for doctor/nurse/patient required the simultaneous coordination of all three categories and their relations. Limits on memory capacity within a level should therefore be especially apparent in compounded skills.

A larger number of components can be controlled with the transformation of focusing, where two or more skills are linked together in sequence. Because of the sequential structure of focusing, the several skills do not necessarily occupy processing space at the same time. Focusing can be produced by a cue in the environment, which leads the person to shift focus from one skill to another. In that case, the person controls each of the two skills separately, with the environment providing the link between them. Thus virtually no new short-term-memory demands arise from a shift of focus, because the environment—not the person—acts as the link. If the person does acquire control of a shift of focus, however, some additional memory load is added, since he or she must supply an associative tag leading from the first skill to the second.

The transformation rule of substitution also places a small demand on memory, because it involves the simple transfer of an established skill to a new (but similar) situation. The only new processing required is that one component of the substituted skill be applied to a new object or event. If multiple components are substituted, then each one adds an additional demand on working memory. Once the substituted skill has been practiced, however, these processing demands disappear.

For the transformation rule of differentiation, the memory demand depends on the type of combination involved, since differentiation always occurs in conjunction with one of the other rules.

In summary, the within-level transformations produce greater demands on working memory, and given any one type of transformation the increase can be treated as a change in the number of items in memory. Reorganization of skills at a new optimal level, on the other hand, leads to a decrease in memory load—that is, to an increase in effective working memory. Memory changes between levels arise from the new structure of skills at each successive level, not from a simple increase in the number of items in memory.

CONCLUSION

Two different types of processes are involved in developmental transitions and in many other systematic changes in the organization of behavior. Optimal level is the upper limit on the complexity of skills that the person can construct, and it develops through a series of hierarchically organized levels that seem to be closely tied to age. Skill-acquisition processes are the rules by which a skill can be transformed into something more complex or advanced. Together, these two types of processes account for both large and small changes in cognitive development. They also suggest several hypotheses, including the following:

1. Stage-like change to a new optimal level is most evident when a person is tested under environmental conditions that produce optimal performance. Under the testing conditions typically used in psychological research, optimal performance is not assessed, and consequently developmental change is slow and gradual. When environmental conditions are taken into account, it becomes evident that stage-like and gradual change can both occur in the same person.

2. Individual differences in intelligence reflect two relatively independent factors corresponding to the two types of processes. Although normal individuals all develop from one optimal level to the next at about the same age, most individual variations in intelligence arise from differences in the facility with which people can use the transformation rules to build skills both at and below optimal level.

3. Limitations in short-term or working memory are of two independent types: (1) those imposed by the skill structures charac-

teristic of each optimal level, and (2) those imposed by the person's capacity for using the within-level transformations to coordinate multiple components in skills at or below optimal level.

4. Systematic changes in the organization of behavior in domains that are conventionally described in terms of learning and problem solving involve the same skill-acquisition processes that produce development.

Our hope is that the distinction between two developmental processes in skill theory will prove useful in the ways suggested by these hypotheses. Then skill theory could not only explain changes in the organization of behavior in cognitive development, but it could also suggest ways to move psychology toward an integration of some of its separate parts. Learning, memory, problem solving, intelligence testing, and cognitive development would all seem to have a great deal in common. We believe that one of psychology's next tasks is to explain those commonalities.

REFERENCES

Bertenthal, B. I. The significance of developmental sequences for investigating the what and how of development. In K. W. Fischer (Ed.), *Cognitive development*. San Francisco: Jossey-Bass New Directions for Child Development, No. 12, 1981.

Biggs, J., and Collis, K. *A system for evaluating learning outcomes: The SOLO taxonomy*. New York: Academic Press, 1982.

Brown, A. L. Conservation of number and continuous quantity in normal, bright, and retarded children. *Child Development, 44*, 376–379.

Bullock, D. On the current and potential scope of generative theories of cognitive development. In K. W. Fischer (Ed.), *Cognitive development*. San Francisco: Jossey-Bass New Directions for Child Development, No. 12, 1981.

Case, R. Intellectual development from birth to adulthood: A neo-Piagetian interpretation. In R. Siegler (Ed.), *Children's thinking: What develops?* Hillsdale, N.J.: Erlbaum, 1978.

Case, R., Kurland, D. M., and Goldberg, J. Operational efficiency and the growth of short-term memory span. *Journal of Experimental Child Psychology, 1982, 33*, 386–404.

Chi, M. T. H. Knowledge structures and memory development. In R. S. Siegler (Ed.), *Children's thinking: What develops?* Hillsdale, N.J.: Erlbaum, 1978.

Chomsky, N. *Aspects of the theory of syntax*. Cambridge, Mass. M.I.T. Press, 1965.

Corrigan, R. The development of representational skills. In K. W. Fischer (Ed.), *Levels and transitions in children's development*. San Francisco: Jossey-Bass New Directions for Child Development, No. 21, 1983.

Davison, M. L., King, P. M., Kitchener, K. S., and Parker, C. A. The stage concept in cognitive and social development. *Developmental Psychology*, 1980, *16*, 121–131.

Dempster, F. N. Sources of memory span differences. *Psychological Bulletin*, 1981, *89*, 63–100.

Emde, R., Gaensbauer, T., and Harmon, R. Emotional expression in infancy: A biobehavioral study. *Psychological Issues*, 1976, *10*, No. 37. New York: International Universities Press.

Epstein, H. T. Phrenoblysis: Special brain and mind growth periods. *Developmental Psychobiology*, 1974, *7*, 207–224.

Epstein, H. T. EEG developmental stages. *Developmental Psychobiology*, 1980, *13*, 629–631.

Fischer, K. W. Learning as the development of organized behavior. *Journal of Structural Learning*, 1980, *3*, 253–267.

Fischer, K. W. A theory of cognitive development: The control and construction of hierarchies of skills. *Psychological Review*, 1980, *87*, 477–531.

Fischer, K. W. Human cognitive development in the first four years. *Behavioral and Brain Sciences*, 1982, *5*, 282–283.

Fischer, K. W., and Bullock, D. Patterns of data: Sequence, synchrony, and constraint in cognitive development. In K. W. Fischer (Ed.), *Cognitive development*. San Francisco: Jossey-Bass New Directions for Child Development, No. 12, 1981.

Fischer, K. W., and Corrigan, R. A skill approach to language development. In R. E. Stark (Ed.), *Language behavior in infancy and early childhood*. Amsterdam: Elsevier/North-Holland, 1981.

Fischer, K. W., Hand, H. H., and Russell, S. The development of abstractions in adolescence and adulthood. In M. Commons, F. Richards, and C. Armon (Eds.), *Beyond formal operations*. New York: Praeger, 1983.

Fischer, K. W., Hand, H. H., Watson, M. W., Van Parys, M., and Tucker, J. L. Putting the child into socialization: The development of social roles and categories in preschool children. In L. Katz (Ed.), *Current topics in early childhood education*, Vol. 5. Norwood, N.J.: Ablex, in press.

Fischer, K. W., and Jennings, S. The emergence of representation in search: Understanding the hider as an independent agent. *Developmental Review*, 1981, *1*, 18–30.

Fischer, K. W., Pipp, S. L., and Bullock, D. Detecting developmental discontinuities: Method and measurement. In R. Harmon and R. N. Emde (Eds.), *Continuities and discontinuities in development*. New York: Plenum Press, in press.

Fischer, K. W., and Watson, M. W. Explaining the Oedipus conflict. In K. W. Fischer (Ed.), *Cognitive development*. San Francisco: Jossey-Bass New Directions For Child Development, No. 12, 1981.

Flavell, J. H. An analysis of cognitive-developmental sequences. *Genetic Psychology Monographs*, 1972, *86*, 279–350.

Flavell, J. H. On cognitive development. *Child Development*, 1982, *53*, 1–10.

Goodman, G. S. Picture memory: How the action schema affects retention. *Cognitive Psychology*, 1980, *12*, 473–495.

Gottlieb, D. E., Taylor, S. E., and Ruderman, A. Cognitive bases of children's moral judgments. *Developmental Psychology*, 1977, *13*, 547–556.

Hand, H. H. The development of concepts of social interaction: Children's understanding of nice and mean. Ph.D. thesis, University of Denver, 1981. *Dissertation Abstracts International*, in press.

Hand, H. H. The relation between developmental level and spontaneous behavior: The importance of sampling contexts. In K. W. Fischer (Ed.), *Cognitive development*. San Francisco: Jossey-Bass New Directions for Child Development, No. 12, 1981b.

Harter, S. Children's understanding of multiple emotions: A cognitive-developmental approach. In *Proceedings of the Jean Piaget Society: 1979*. Hillsdale, N.J.: Erlbaum, in press.

Hirst, W., Spelke, E. S., Reaves, C. C., Caharack, G., and Neisser, U. Dividing attention without alternation or automaticity. *Journal of Experimental Psychology: General*, 1980, *109*, 98–117.

Horn, J. L. Human abilities: A review of research and theory in the early 1970s. *Annual Review of Psychology*, 1976, *27*, 437–486.

Huttenlocher, J., and Burke, D. Why does memory span increase with age? *Cognitive Psychology*, 1976, *8*, 1–31.

Jaques, E., with Gibson, R. O., and Isaac, D. J. *Levels of abstraction in logic and human action*. London: Heinemann, 1978.

John, E. R. *Functional neuroscience*, vol. 2: *Neurometrics*, Hillsdale, N.J.: Erlbaum, 1977.

Kagan, J. *Psychological research on the human infant: An evaluative summary*. New York: W. T. Grant Foundation, 1982.

Kenny, S. R. Developmental discontinuities in childhood and adolescence. In K. W. Fischer (Ed.), *Levels and transitions in children's development*. San Francisco: Jossey-Bass New Directions for Child Development, No. 21, 1983.

Kitchener, K. S. Human development and the college campus: Sequences and tasks. In G. Hanson (Ed.), *Assessing student development*. San Francisco: Jossey-Bass New Directions for Student Services, 1983.

Klahr, D., and Wallace, J. G. *Cognitive development: An information processing view*. Hillsdale, N.J.: Erlbaum, 1976.

Kuhn, D., and Phelps, E. The development of problem-solving strategies. In H. W. Reese and L. P. Lipsitt (Eds.), *Advances in child development and behavior*, Vol. 17. New York: Academic Press, in press.

Lancy, D. F., and Goldstein, G. I. The use of nonverbal Piagetian tasks to assess the cognitive development of autistic children. *Child Development*, 1982, *53*, 1233–1241.

Lawler, R. W. The progressive construction of mind (one child's learning addition). *Cognitive Science*, 1981, *5*, 1–30.

Lovell, K., and Shields, J. B. Some aspects of a study of the gifted child. *British Journal of Educational Psychology*, 1967, *37*, 201–208.

McCall, R. B. Nature-nurture and the two realms of development: A proposed integration with respect to mental development. *Child Development*, 1981, *52*, 1–12.

McCall, R. B. Exploring developmental transitions in mental performance. In K. W. Fischer (Ed.), *Levels and transitions in children's development*. San Francisco: Jossey-Bass New Directions for Child Development, No. 21, 1983.

MacWhinney, B. The acquisition of morphophonology. *Monographs of the Society for Research in Child Development*, 1978, *43*(1–2, Serial no. 174).

Martarano, S. C. A developmental analysis of performance on Piaget's formal operations tasks. *Developmental Psychology*, 1977, *13*, 666–672.

Matousek, M., and Peterson, I. Frequency analysis of the EEG in normal children and adolescents. In P. Kellaway and I. Peterson (Eds.), *Automation of clinical electroencephalography*. New York: Raven Press, 1973.

O'Brien, D. P., and Overton, W. F. Conditional reasoning and the competence-performance issue: A developmental analysis of a training task. *Journal of Experimental Child Psychology*, 1982, *34*, 274–290.

Pascual-Leone, J. A mathematical model for the transition rule in Piaget's developmental stages. *Acta Psychologica*, 1970, *32*, 301–345.

Peters, A. M., and Zaidel, E. The acquisition of homonymy. *Cognition*, 1981, *8*, 187–207.

Piaget, J. *The origins of intelligence in children*. New York: International Universities Press, 1952. (M. Cook, Trans.; original French ed., 1936).

Piaget, J. Logique et équilibre dans les comportements du sujet. *Études d'Épistémologie Génétique*, 1957, *2*, 27–118.

Piaget, J. Piaget's theory. In P. H. Mussen (Ed.), *Carmichael's manual of child psychology*. New York: Wiley, 1970.

Piaget, J. The theory of stages in cognitive development. In D. R. Green, M. P. Ford, and G. B. Flamer (Eds.), *Measurement and Piaget*. New York: McGraw-Hill, 1971.

Roberts, R. J., Jr. Errors and the assessment of cognitive development. In K. W. Fischer (Ed.), *Cognitive development*. San Francisco: Jossey-Bass New Directions for Child Development, No. 12, 1981.

Sameroff, A. Contexts of development: The systems and their evolution. In W. Kessen (Ed.), *Handbook of Child Psychology*, Vol. 1. New York: Wiley, 1983.

Seibert, J. M., Hogan, A. E., and Mundy, P. C. Structures and stages in early cognitive development. *Intelligence*, in press.

Selman, R. L. *The growth of interpersonal understanding: Developmental and clinical analyses.* New York: Academic Press, 1980.

Siegler, R. S. Developmental sequences within and between concepts. *Monographs of the Society for Research in Child Development*, 1981, 46(2, Serial no. 189).

Skinner, B. F. *Contingencies of reinforcement: A theoretical analysis.* New York: Appleton-Century-Crofts, 1969.

Sternberg, R. J. Sketch of a componential subtheory of human intelligence. *Behavioral and Brain Sciences*, 1980, *3*, 573–584.

Stone, C. A., and Day, M. C. Competence and performance models and the characterization of formal operational skills. *Human Development*, 1980, *23*, 323–353.

Tabor, L. E., and Kendler, T. S. Testing for developmental continuity or discontinuity: Class inclusion and reversal shifts. *Developmental Review*, 1981, *1*, 330–343.

Vygotsky, L. *Mind in society.* Cambridge, Mass.: Harvard University Press, 1978.

Watson, M. W. The development of social roles: A sequence of social-cognitive development. In K. W. Fischer (Ed.), *Cognitive development*. San Francisco: Jossey-Bass New Directions for Child Development, No. 12, 1981.

Watson, M. W., and Amgott-Kwan, T. Transitions in children's understanding of parental roles. *Child Development*, in press.

Watson, M. W., and Fischer, K. W. A developmental sequence of agent use in late infancy. *Child Development*, 1977, *48*, 828–836.

Watson, M. W., and Fischer, K. W. Development of social roles in elicited and spontaneous behavior during the preschool years. *Developmental Psychology*, 1980, *16*, 483–494.

Webb, R. A. Concrete and formal operations in very bright 6- to 11-year-olds. *Human Development*, 1974, *17*, 292–300.

Werner, H. *Comparative psychology of mental development.* New York: Science Editions, 1948.

Westerman, M. A. Differences in the organization of mother-child interaction in compliance problem and healthy dyads. Ph.D. thesis, University of Southern California, 1979. *Dissertation Abstracts International*, 1980, *40*(10), 5031B.

White, S. H. Some general outlines of the matrix of developmental changes between five and seven years. *Bulletin of the Orton Society*, 1970, *20*, 41–57.

Wohlwill, J. F. *The study of behavioral development.* New York: Academic Press, 1973.

Zelazo, P. R., and Leonard, E. The dawn of active thought. In K. W. Fischer (Ed.), *Levels and transitions in children's development.* San Francisco: Jossey-Bass New Directions for Child Development, No. 21, 1983.

4

Mechanisms of Cognitive Development and the Structure of Knowledge

Frank C. Keil

I t has become a cliché to say that research in cognitive development has usually provided only "snapshots" of cognitive competencies at various points in development, and that it has told us very little about how the child progresses from snapshot to snapshot. At a 1959 conference of the Social Science Research Council on children's thought, several participants (among them, Kessen, 1962; Simon, 1962) pointed out this snapshot problem. Simon, for example, stated that "we know very little about the kind of dynamic system with which we are dealing in the development of the child" (p. 150), and called for a bipartite theory that would describe competence at a particular stage and "a learning program governing transitions from stage to stage" (p. 155). The Newell and Simon (1963) General Problem Solver was suggested as such a learning program.

Twenty years later, there is a new emphasis on studying the mechanisms of transition in development. Researchers are trying to restore some dignity to the study of learning itself. Brown (1981) asks why learning has become such a neglected issue, and proposes that more attention be given to longitudinal studies, training studies, and detailed analyses of expert/novice differences in local domains. Similarly, Rumelhart and Norman (1978) argue that "the study of learning has been slighted" (p. 37) and suggest three general modes of learning as the basis for further investigations.

This new emphasis on the dynamics of developmental change, however, does not necessarily mean that we should shift all our attention to the study of learning as a process. Even if one's goal is to uncover the causal mechanisms responsible for change, in many cases the answers may lie in a better understanding of the structures of mental representations. In this essay, I will present a view of learning that emphasizes local structural descriptions over computational routines or general learning procedures. The view also places an emphasis on *a priori* constraints on knowledge, and on content-bound versus content-free knowledge. Although there has undoubtedly been progress over the last twenty years in specifying general learning procedures, those specifications may give us only a very

Preparation of this paper and some of the research described herein was funded by National Science Foundation grants BNS-78-06200 and BNS-81-02655. Many thanks to Jim Cutting, Kristi Lockhart-Keil, Lianne Ritter, and especially Dick Neisser for helpful comments on drafts of this manuscript. I am also grateful to Cindy Hutton for assistance in preparation of the paper.

incomplete understanding of transition mechanisms, by having overemphasized the roles of such procedures and underemphasized the importance of the knowledge structures themselves.

To a certain extent, the point of this essay is obvious: that the nature of one's current representations and the *a priori* constraints on those representations influence how new material is learned. A somewhat stronger and less obvious claim is that the actual dynamics of change—the causal developmental factors, the precipitating states, and the like—depend primarily on the structure of what is known and on how that knowledge is to be used in the world. Even longitudinal studies may be most informative by providing snapshots at much closer intervals rather than by focusing on learning itself. Training studies may be most useful for testing whether the presence of some structure leads to a type of transition; they are much less likely to be successful as simulations of the process of natural learning, except when the knowledge involved is of a kind that is normally learned in training-type settings. (Such knowledge may include much of the curricula of formal schooling, however).

In this essay, I will focus on types of cognitive change that seem to represent qualitative shifts or discontinuities, on the assumption that it is in such cases that transition mechanisms are least well understood. Cases in which there is a more or less continuous accretion to a homogeneous knowledge base require less attention to structural descriptions and may reflect general learning procedures more directly.

SOME EXAMPLES OF STRUCTURE-DEPENDENT TRANSITION MECHANISMS

To illustrate how structural descriptions of local knowledge are often crucial to understanding mechanisms of transition, I will consider four examples of apparently discontinuous changes in cognitive development: the appearance of new higher-order relations, the resolution of internal inconsistencies or contradictions, the influence of boundary conditions, and the characteristic-to-defining shift.

The Appearance of New Higher-Order Relations

In some cases, dramatic and relatively rapid changes in knowledge can occur because knowledge structures become differentiated or articulated to such a degree that they suddenly make new relations apparent.

One example of this mechanism can be seen in the development of metaphor. Metaphorical ability does not, as some researchers formerly assumed (for example, see Asche and Nerlove, 1960), develop either as a general monolithic skill or as a gradual accretion on a case-by-case (metaphor-by-metaphor) basis. The ability to comprehend metaphors is more a consequence of the structure of the relevant knowledge needed to create metaphors. This dependence on knowledge structure can be seen by examining those word meanings that cluster together in various conceptual domains known as "semantic fields." If a group of words forms a closely related set of meanings (for instance, the cooking terms boil, bake, fry; or the eating terms chew, gobble, munch, nibble), then they form a semantic field (cf. Lehrer, 1978).

Semantic fields develop as coherent units. When two fields become sufficiently differentiated that a common set of relations between them can be perceived, a whole class of metaphors caused by the juxtaposition of the two fields becomes comprehensible. Since a child is able to juxtapose some semantic fields to perceive metaphorical relations much earlier than other fields, the development cannot be described as the emergence of a general metaphorical skill. Thus, young children are usually able to perceive metaphorical relations between animal terms and automobiles ("the car is thirsty"), but no relations between human eating terms and ways of reading a book ("he gobbled up the book"). Moreover, since whole groups of metaphors emerge at the same time in a manner predicted by semantic-field structure, any gradual-accretion theory that does not make detailed reference to structure also is inadequate (Keil, submitted ms.).

These examples do not mean that our ability to juxtapose semantic fields may not also have to be acquired; but they diminish the probable complexity and importance of such an ability. If even preschoolers can reliably juxtapose some fields and thereby apprehend metaphors, then developmental change seems less a consequence of this ability per se and more a consequence of the richness of knowledge of the associated fields. It may be that the ability itself constantly increases its power and extendability as well. Sternberg and Downing (1982), for example, have argued that higher-order relations cannot be mapped in a sophisticated manner until adolescence, perhaps as a consequence of formal operations, where higher-order relations are defined as analogies between analogies. Assuming that a sizable number of complex metaphors are metaphors between metaphors, this account would suggest that general improvement in metaphorical ability occurs when children become able to process these more complex relations.

It would be a mistake, however, to infer from such a study that most of metaphor development is a consequence of general shifts in processing ability. The semantic-field effect, which appears to be the primary factor in younger children, cannot be accounted for by such a view. Moreover, highly intelligent adults will also fail to comprehend metaphors if one of the domains is unfamiliar to them (consider computer metaphors about cognition), though presumably their general metaphorical abilities are fully developed. Finally, it might be possible to uncover extremely simple higher-order analogies that children much younger than adolescents can interpret, or to show that if the domain chosen is one in which young subjects have a great deal of expertise and knowledge, they can understand "sophisticated" analogies. Since Sternberg and Downing did not focus on this issue, we can't be sure. If such skills were to be demonstrated, however, they would suggest that the ability to apprehend higher-order relations is more dependent on a particular knowledge structure than has previously been thought.

The semantic-field explanation of metaphor development suggests that, more generally, transitions in cognitive development occur when knowledge in certain domains becomes sufficiently differentiated that it suddenly reveals new relations to other domains through analogies, similarities, and so on. Whereas it might be possible to explain the continuous differentiation of knowledge in any one domain largely in terms of a content-free general learning procedure (for example, one in which a new node gets added to the network structure after a given number of concepts or rules instantiate that node), such an account seems ill suited to explain transitions resulting from the interaction of two domains. With such interactions consideration of the structures of the domains themselves seems to be essential. Presumably, wherever a cognitive ability depends on the interaction of two conceptual domains, a transition effect might be seen. In addition to metaphorical analogies, other such abilities might include appreciation of humor, causal thinking, and knowledge of social conventions, among others.

Resolution of Internal Inconsistencies or Contradictions

Sometimes change is necessitated by the discovery that two aspects of knowledge have developed to the point where they are incompatible and create contradictions or opposing solutions to the same problem. Bower (1979) has proposed such dilemmas in an infant's development of procedures for perceiving objects, and has argued that when the contradictions between procedures becomes manifest, they create an impetus for the infant to form a more complex rule.

For example, Bower (1974) stated that a typical 3-month-old has conflicting rules pertaining to objects: one set of rules is applicable to stationary objects ("to find an object, look in its usual place"), and another set is applicable to moving objects ("to find an object, look along its pattern of movement"). Consequently, when stationary objects move or when moving objects stop, the infant is faced with the conflicting rules and makes errors in performance. The two contradictory rules must become resolved through combination into a new rule: "to find an object that has been seen to move, follow the pattern of movement; to find a moving object that no longer moves, look for it stationary" (Bower, 1974, p. 218).

The notion of contradiction becoming an impetus for a new developmental change has figured prominently in a number of cognitive developmental theories (for example, Piaget's 1970); the important point here is the emphasis on structural descriptions. The child acquiring syntax might develop movement rules for negation and Wh questions that are otherwise adequate, but that when combined to yield negative questions are incompatible. The same notion can be applied to rules concerning conservation problems (Piaget, 1970).

Of course, the Piagetian account has a strong underlying process assumption. When a contradiction between two rules becomes salient, it causes a disequilibrium. This starts the process of equilibration, wherein cognitive structures are modified (via the process of accommodation) so as to reduce conflict and move the cognitive system closer to a state of equilibrium. But these processes are present throughout development, and thus cannot in themselves explain specific instances of developmental change. They only become active or get "triggered" when knowledge structures differentiate to a point at which a contradiction becomes apparent. And that pattern of resolution depends primarily on the structures of the conflicting bodies of knowledge—not upon the very general and continuously present process of equilibration.

Contradictions arise most frequently when two separate components of a system develop independently and then become combined. The combination apparently makes the contradiction salient. It would seem that for a resolution to occur, the contradiction must be made evident to the child rather than remaining implicit. When the contradiction results in obvious performance errors on relevant tasks, it is immediately revealed.

Internal contradictions, then, create instabilities that cause a drive for a new form of representation. Inconsistencies and contradictions may be contrasted with another type of structural incompatibility that occurs when developing knowledge structures threaten or temporarily violate boundary conditions.

The Influence of Boundary Conditions

A different sort of transition occurs when boundary conditions laid down by *a priori* constraints on knowledge could be potentially violated, or are temporarily violated by the development of a knowledge system. Thus, a child might be acquiring a certain type of knowledge at a relatively constant rate, when suddenly some aspect of that structure threatens violation of a universal constraint on cognition. (By "universal," I mean that it holds across all individuals, cultures, and so on—not necessarily across all cognitive domains.) A rapid change might then be seen as the child seeks to modify the structures so as to avoid that incompatability.

One example comes from my own work on ontological knowledge (Keil, 1979; Keil, 1983). I have argued that children's knowledge of certain basic semantic and conceptual distinctions can be modeled as tree structures that usually obey a hierarchical constraint known as the M-constraint. The M-constraint, which states that these structures are pure hierarchies as opposed to partial lattices, is proposed to be a universal structuring tendency for ontological knowledge.

The tree structures representing young children's ontological knowledge are grossly truncated versions of the average adult hierarchical tree (that is, the children's version has two or three branches instead of 15). These tree structures indicate which classes of predicates can be sensibly combined with which classes of terms. As the branches differentiate, the child may add new predicates and terms to the tree, or may move old ones in a regular manner until a predicate or term is positioned so that it violates the M-constraint. When such a violation occurs, one often sees discontinuities in development, as children restructure their trees to avoid continuing to violate the constraint.

For example, young children often judge that all physical-object predicates can be sensibly applied to events and abstract objects (for instance, "the idea is green" might be considered a meaningful concept). This results in a collapsed tree structure that honors the M-constraint. If the child, however, discovers that a particular abstract object or event cannot take a particular physical-object predicate, that discovery in itself could cause a violation of the constraint. Very few children are found in such states; they appear to leave them by rejecting almost immediately thereafter the application of all physical-object predicates to the offending term, and relocating it in the hierarchical tree in such a way that the violation no longer exists.

(Sommers [1970] has argued that similar restructurings may have happened in the minds of adults throughout the history of science, as a result of new scientific discoveries that temporarily violated the constraint.) The reason only a few children are found in these transitional states (that is, violating the constraints) is apparently that a violation creates an instability that must be resolved.

Such situations, in which a constantly developing structure temporarily exceeds a cognitive constraint, cause a marked qualitative and discontinuous change in structure. The violation provides a strong impetus to restructure the knowledge so as to honor that constraint, all the while preserving previously attained knowledge.

An analogous case of a threatened violation of a universal constraint causing a restructuring has been suggested by Bever and Langedoen (1971) in an analysis of the historical development of relative-clause structure. When one change in the language—that is, a loss of certain noun-phrase inflections—resulted in a violation of a constraint or subordinate clauses, a second change—an optimal relative pronoun becoming obligatory—occurred shortly thereafter to correct the violation.

The arguments about the resolution of inconsistencies also carry implicit process assumptions, but again, the suggestion is that these processes are relatively simple in nature and are unlikely to offer any insights as to how particular transitions occur. Thus, the only process assumption for such resolutions need be that when a strong inconsistency becomes salient, there is an increased pressure to seek out alternative representation structures. How such structures are sought out might again be simple in terms of a process characterization. Faced with an inconsistency, the child might use a general inductive procedure, guided by the boundary conditions, to generate a new, more compatible set of rules.

Changes caused by temporary or threatened violations of boundary conditions are different in several ways from those caused by inconsistencies and contradictions. For one thing, the form of a given inconsistency is vastly more difficult to predict, as it may depend on a particular relation between idiosyncratic rules created by the child. On the other hand, in the constraints case, a more fundamental and universal violation is observed and then rectified. Secondly, the inconsistency may be present for some time before the child has reason to recognize it, and this may occur only as two components are combined. Again, it must become salient for it to be resolved. Violations of universal constraints appear to be noticed as soon as they occur, and may only be precipitated by the gradual differentiation of one set of rules. In many cases, the knowledge structure may never exceed the boundaries set down by a most restrictive constraint. In other cases, however, the constraint is more like a bias, and a brief violation might be tolerated as a transition state.

The Characteristic-to-Defining Shift

It has been noticed for some time and in a variety of tasks that children progress from exemplar-based representations to more rule-based representations (for example, see Vygotsky, 1962). This progression is often indicated by a dramatic shift in emphasis in the child's thinking, away from characteristic features of a concept and toward defining features. For instance, young children may consider age, appearance, and behavioral disposition to be fundamental to the meaning of "uncle" and may ignore the kinship definition, whereas older children will focus on the kinship definition even in the face of highly uncharacteristic features.

Traditionally, this shift was thought to occur at a specific point in development and to represent a general change in cognitive ability (Vygotsky, 1962). Recent work (Keil and Batterman, in press), however, shows that the shift occurs at different times for different concepts, suggesting that it is determined primarily by the structures of the concepts themselves rather than by a general transition from instance-bound knowledge to more rule-governed knowledge. The structural factors that precipitate this shift are not well understood. The nature of the shift is especially puzzling, given that in some cases, the abandonment of an exemplar-based representation causes a temporary backslide in developmental performance. (For example, in semantic development, children sometimes progress from an exemplar-based representation by means of which they are correct much of the time, to a faulty analytic definition that causes them to make more mistakes [Carey, 1978; Keil and Carroll, 1980].)

The important point for this discussion is that the nature of the change from one form of knowledge to another does not represent a global change in the manner of representation, or the advent of a new learning strategy. Instead, it appears to reflect the particular properties of the structures of specific concepts. Understanding and predicting the characteristic-to-defining shift for any concept depends more on a precise description of the nature of that concept than on any general transition mechanisms.

In more recent work, Lianne Ritter and I have explored more explicitly the influence of local conceptual domains on the characteristic-to-defining shift. Children were given several terms from various semantic fields, such as cooking (boil, bake, fry), moral acts (lie, steal, cheat), and kinship (uncle, aunt, cousin). The shift was shown to occur at widely differing ages for the different conceptual domains, but at roughly the same time for the terms within each domain. Clearly, then, a primary determinant of when the shift occurs is the degree of knowledge the child has of a particular domain.

Summary of the Four Examples

None of the four types of transitions I have described is easily explainable by appeals to general learning procedures or processes of transition. Beyond the general description of the phenomenon, further insight is dependent on detailed characterizations of the structure of the knowledge involved. One cannot speak of learning mechanisms or transition mechanisms in isolation, independent of the content of the knowledge they operate on. This point of view follows from the assumption that the complexity and richness of human cognition lie much more in prestored knowledge structures than in general-purpose computational routines or procedures.

Of course, even the most general process-oriented learning accounts recognize the need for knowledge structure, but the tendency is to assume that the structure varies little across different domains, and thus that the process of learning is affected only slightly or not at all by the properties of structures in each of the domains. These sorts of content-independent mechanisms, then, attempt to explain most of developmental change without reference to knowledge structures. The general laws and patterns of cognitive development are assumed to be the same across all conceptual domains.

The critical role of structure in particular domains is not restricted to just these four types of transitions. Chi (1978), for example, has in a series of studies raised doubts about the traditional accounts of memory development that refer primarily to changing procedures and strategies. She has shown that many of the supposedly general changes in memory-processing ability are mostly dependent on the degree of expertise children have in the conceptual domain being tested. Her account does not focus on transitions *per se*, but the emphasis on specific knowledge structures instead of general processes is clear. It is now necessary to address this structure/process dichotomy more directly.

THE STRUCTURE/PROCESS DILEMMA

In addition to favoring content dependency, the preceding examples of transition mechanisms emphasized the role of already present representations rather than ongoing heuristics and strategies. Is this distinction valid or bogus?

In adult cognition, the structure-versus-process distinction has been controversial, and many believe that there are some fundamental indeterminacies that cannot be resolved (cf. Anderson, 1978). The troublesome examples, such as computer programs, are well known. These have a structure and an organization, but they also represent procedures that can be used to handle knowledge (Newell, 1972). Moreover, almost any functioning system that is described as mostly structure and a little process can, with enough ingenuity, be redescribed as mostly process and a little structure. (For example, contrast the model of semantic memory in Glass and Holyoak [1975] with that in Smith, Shoben, and Rips [1974].)

Despite these ambiguities, there is a widespread belief that structure and process can be distinguished, and the claim made here is that structure plays a more important role than process in explanations of many instances of cognitive change. Unlike computers, humans may not be capable of general procedures consisting of many stages of processing with elaborate loops, serial chains, and the like. Our ability to succeed in complex tasks may lie more in elaborate representations than in complex computational routines.

It is surprising how little unambiguous evidence has been found in support of complex processing routines that are not directly derived from a specific knowledge base. From syntax to pattern perception, few models with multiple intermediate stages have held up. For example, the early syntactic-processing models that relied on serial application of real-time transformations failed because no evidence could be found for such processing stages (cf. Fodor, Bever, and Garrett, 1974). These early models have been superseded by theories with simpler processing stages and with correspondingly more complex prestored structures and structural constraints. Bresnan (1978), for example, has greatly simplified transformations by building a much more complicated set of structural relations into the lexicon. Similarly, Chomsky and Lasnik (1977) have profoundly reduced the complexity of transformations by increasing the roles of structuring constraints, filters, and the like.

Our best knowledge of how adults solve complex tasks for which "structure-heavy" and "process-heavy" solutions are both possible suggests a preference for structure. Consider the chess expert's reliance on prestored structures and patterns, as compared to the chess computer's elaborate computational routines. Chase and Simon's (1973) elegant work on expert and novice chess players has illustrated that the primary difference between the two is not so much in general procedures (depth of search and so forth) as in the amount and chunking of prestored knowledge. The expert may store routines as well as static arrays, but the crucial contrast is between prestorage and on-line computation. Although a range of possible models with different structure/process trade-offs can always be constructed, most natural cognitive systems may have a tendency to trade off multiple stages of processing and elaborate computational routines for prestored knowledge.

As mentioned above, Newell and Simon (1962) have proposed the General Problem Solver as a learning program that provides a mechanism of transition in cognitive development. It is interesting that even with all of its subsequent developments, the crux of the model is an extremely simple set of procedures interacting with increasingly complex structures. A content-free description of the General Problem Solver is reduced to little more than the sequence, "notice problem; establish goal; try to attain goal; if unsuccessful, try different goal path."[1] This is not to say that a great many investigators haven't found this simple means–end heuristic and the more general notion of production systems useful in models of problem solving and learning; but such a general sequence helps us very little in understanding specific transitions in cognitive development. Moreover, the process is so powerful that it cannot be used to make predictions, since it can model virtually any pattern of data.

Much of the insight into the problem solving and learning in the Newell and Simon program is in their description of the knowledge structures that are brought to a problem, and of how the problem itself is encoded or represented. Simon (1981), for example, has speculated that "solving a problem simply means representing it so as to make the solution transparent." Elsewhere, Simon and Hayes (1976) and Hayes and Simon (1977) have shown how formally identical problems can differ in difficulty by a factor of 2, "because different problem instructions cause subjects to adopt different problem representations even when the problems are isomorphic" (Hayes and Simon, 1977, p. 21). Obviously, we can't have models of cognitive change without explicit or implicit process models, but the most successful models so far have been so simple and general that they have provided little insight into how transitions occur in specific domains.

Humans are capable of engaging in complex chains of processing, but when they do, the processing is embedded within, and done in reference to, a specific knowledge structure. The process, then, is guided by and is derivative of the structure of the knowledge, rather than being an independent set of "boxes" with patterns of information flow. Even in two of the most apparently clear cases of pure processing—the calculation of arithmetical solutions and digit span—it is striking how much these processes depend on knowledge structures of the relevant domains. Consider, for example, Professor

A. C. Aitken, described by Hunter (1968) as "probably the most expert mental calculator of whom detailed records exist" (p. 341). Whereas Aitken certainly engaged in lengthy chains of computation when calculating fractions to 40 or more decimal places, what is perhaps most impressive about his performance is the extraordinary amount he knew about numbers and their properties. Hunter felt that these were among the most basic features of Aitken's ability. Aitken differed less from novices in having some large, all-purpose computational capacity than in having an extremely rich memory structure with which to guide calculations and organize them.

Similarly, Ericsson, Chase, and Faloon (1980) demonstrated that one subject's ability to increase his digit span from 7 digits to over 70 was largely a consequence of his developing a rich retrieval structure organized hierarchically around meaningful clusters of numbers. The content dependency of this system is vividly illustrated by the same subject's failure to show virtually any improvement in his ability to recall strings of letters. Performance on this lengthy serial task was, therefore, a consequence of his having a content-specific hierarchical structure to guide recall.

If the assumption about the limitations of general processing capacity is true, then it warrants an emphasis on structure rather than on process in the analysis of mechanisms of transition. Though one might be interested in the dynamics of development, clarification of these dynamics might still depend mainly on the specification of the representations that are in the domain and the range of the learning function. Even a gradual accretion of knowledge through induction can proceed only under the guidance of domain-specific constraints that limit the hypothesis space (Keil, 1981).

There may indeed be general learning procedures that are very simple and limited in application. Their limitations can be seen in the poor performance of subjects attempting to learn information that has no intrinsic or easily imposable structure. Many of our most effective strategies serve to encode the learned information into some sort of relational structure that greatly simplifies the task. But once that structure is introduced, it takes on a life of its own and fundamentally influences the nature of learning itself.

DOMAIN SPECIFICITY

I have argued for a view of learning and transition whereby a limited set of general learning procedures take complex domain-specific knowledge structures as inputs and give others as outputs. This interpretation places a special emphasis on structure and prestored knowledge. An additional distinction is needed to fully specify this view: it involves the extent of domain specificity.

Without sets of constraints that demarcate certain natural domains of cognition with their own unique distinguishing properties, theorists of transition mechanisms have two choices. They can argue either that knowledge structures of all types have the same formal properties and are learned in the same way, or that virtually every learning situation dictates its own unique patterns of learning and its own forms of representation. Both views, however, seem to lack explanatory power and become *ad hoc* in application.

The first view is likely to be associated with a very powerful general learning procedure or set of procedures. But to the extent that knowledge structures in different domains do exhibit unique distinguishing properties, the patterns of transition in each domain will not be explainable by general learning procedures, and will instead require different accounts tailored to each domain but without general principles motivating them.

Alternatively, the danger in excessively microscopic, task-specific views of learning is that we may learn less and less about principles of cognitive functioning and more and more about the task and the environment. We learn very little about the intrinsic properties of human intellectual systems if every description of every learning situation is different. Moreover, to the extent that these learning situations involve types of knowledge that we have no specific natural predispositions to structure, the knowledge and strategies will immediately reflect the structure of the task and the environment. This is not to deny the value of such approaches when the goal is to improve learning performance on some task, but they may tell us little about general principles of learning. I doubt that there are as many mechanisms of transition or types of strategies as there are learning situations. If there are, what we learn from the study of one task will tell us little about the next task we study.

The notion of constrained faculties views humans less as all-purpose learning machines and more as biological organisms that have, through the course of evolution, developed specialized "mental organs" that are used to deal with different aspects of their physical and mental worlds (cf. Fodor, 1972). Each organ imposes its own set of constraints on the types of knowledge structures it uses, such that we have different domains of cognition with different formal properties. There are not, however, as many organs as there are tasks and situations, and thus the total number of cognitive domains with different formal properties may be relatively small. There may also be domain-general principles of learning that we fall back on to learn artificial or unfamiliar information, or when we are required to learn under bizzare task demands. Unfortunately, under the premise of controlling for irrelevant information, psychologists since Ebbinghaus have tended to look only for content-free, domain-general principles of learning, with the consequences that the principles that are uncovered may be only marginally relevant to the sorts of natural knowledge we most often acquire.

In stressing this point, Neisser (1978) has been highly skeptical of the value of general theories of memory and learning. He argues that the patterns and properties of memory and learning (and forgetting) may be fundamentally different for different types of memory tasks, situations, and content domains. Neisser believes that it is futile to speculate about general learning procedures until we have understood learning and remembering in an adequate range of realistic situations. What these procedures eventually turn out to have in common may be quite unlike our present conceptions of mechanisms of learning. Here I wish to suggest that such procedures may indeed exist (candidates include analogy perception and induction), but that they are so simple and general that they cannot give us insights into mechanisms of transition, except where the mechanisms are for those special types of knowledge that defy any sort of structural organization.

CONCLUSIONS

The view of constrained cognitive faculties presented here suggests a research strategy that examines how principles of structural change interact with different domains of cognition. For some kinds of knowledge (such as language) humans seem to have evolved natural predispositions to structure and acquire them, while for others, (such as chess) we haven't any specific predispositions. How are the transition mechanisms likely to differ in the two cases? One might suspect at least two differences. In the case of types of knowledge for which we have strong predispositions, one might expect to see strong structural relations immediately in effect, and a relatively minor role for any general learning procedure. In a domain for which we have no a priori constraints, the initial stages of learning may rely heavily on general principles of learning until structural relations are uncovered. The structural relations that are subsequently discovered will gradually make the learner rely less on general learning principles and more on the structure of the task and the environment.

Novices' performances might be more explainable in terms of general learning procedures, whereas experts might require more structural accounts: compare novice and expert chess players, for example. Obviously, internal and external structural constraints are involved in both cases, but the relative importance may be different. In chess learning, there will be few transitions caused by violations of universal boundary conditions, and perhaps there will be correspondingly more transitions caused by internal contradictions and inconsistencies.

The danger of a view with homogeneous representations generated by powerful all-purpose learning procedures is that it fails to account in any principled manner for the sorts of transitions we commonly observe. By focusing more on content-dependent structures, it is possible to gain further insight into such transitions. But one has gone too far if all structure is seen as a direct reflection of the task at hand. Mechanisms of transition then become consequences solely of the structure of the environment and the task, and the only general principles of learning will be generalizations about the environment. I favor a compromise view: that humans have a relatively small number of specialized cognitive faculties as well as some more general learning procedures and forms of representations.

Human beings, especially children, are not impressive as all-purpose computational machines. In comparison to even the most modest microcomputer they fare dismally, being able to keep only a few variables in "working memory" at any time, and having the capacity to perform a relatively small number of successive operations on them. What computations we do make are dependent upon our having rich knowledge of the task domain and of how we fit into it. If one examines some of the most magnificent intellectual skills humans exhibit, from long-distance navigation without charts or instruments (Gladwin, 1970), to chess mastery, to number calculation, in each case true master performers do not usually have a larger "working memory" or general computational capacity; rather, they know a great deal more than most people know about the domain involved. Computational skills, when they do exist, are parasitic off specific knowledge structures.

Children have magnificent intellectual skills as well, even if their talents may appear more mundane at first blush. But again, children's great ability to learn may not be a consequence of a great inductive computer as much as it is a consequence of a marvelous intermeshing between certain structural predispositions in local cognitive domains and the structure of what is learned. For this reason, general laws of problem solving or induction may not be useful in explaining specific changes, especially the more discontinuous or qualitative ones. It may be relatively simple to posit a process mechanism that keeps adding one more node to a decision tree or knowledge network, but such an account falters when the structure undergoes dramatic change, for then one must look much more at the structure itself. Transitions can be best understood by adopting what Flavell (1982) has called "the heterogeneous view" of cognitive development, in which domain-specific structures (and their derivative processes) are favored over global learning procedures and forms of representation.

In sum, models of cognitive development can differ widely in the extent to which they are "structure-heavy" versus "process-heavy," and in the extent to which they rely on prestorage versus computation. Although some computers may learn best in a process-heavy computational fashion, humans for the most part do not, especially in natural conceptual domains and in those cases where clear transitions occur. Put differently, one way to study cognitive development is to look for general principles of learning and problem solving, and to make from these subsidiary inferences about the structure of the knowledge acquired. I am arguing for the opposite: an approach in which the investigator explores the structure of the knowledge acquired and of the information to be learned in the specific domains, and from *these* makes inferences about how transitions in cognitive development occur.

NOTE

[1] I thank Dick Neisser for originally making this argument about the General Problem Solver.

REFERENCES

Anderson, J. R. Arguments concerning representations for mental imagery. *Psychological Review*, 1978, 85(4), 249–277.

Asche, S. E., and Nerlove, H. The development of double function terms in children: An exploratory investigation. In B. Kaplan and S. Wapner (Eds.), *Perspectives in psychological theory: Essays in honor of Heinz Werner*. New York: International Universities Press, 1960.

Bever, T. G., and Langedoen, D. T. A dynamic model of evolution of language. *Linguistic Inquiry*, 1971, 2, 433–463.

Bower, T. G. R. *Development in infancy*. San Francisco: W. H. Freeman and Company, 1974.

Bower, T. G. R. *Human development*. San Francisco: W. H. Freeman and Company, 1979.

Bresnan, J. A realistic transformational grammar. In M. Halle, J. Bresnan, and G. A. Miller (Eds.), *Linguistic theory and psychological reality*. Cambridge, Mass.: M.I.T. Press, 1978.

Brown, A. L. Learning and development: The problems of compatibility, access and induction. *Human Development*, 1981, *25*, 89–115.

Carey, S. The child as a word learner. In M. Halle, J. Bresnan, and G. Miller (Eds.), *Linguistic theory and psychological reality*. Cambridge, Mass.: M.I.T. Press, 1978.

Chase, W. G., and Simon, H. A. The mind's eye in chess. In W. G. Chase (Ed.), *Visual information processing*. New York: Academic Press, 1973.

Chi, M. T. H. Knowledge structures and memory development. In R. S. Siegler (Ed.), *Children's thinking: What develops?* Hillsdale, N.J.: Erlbaum, 1978.

Chomsky, N., and Lasnik, H. Filters and controls. *Linguistic Inquiry*, 1977, *8*(3), 425–504.

Ericsson, K. A., Chase, W. G., and Faloon, S. Acquisition of a memory skill. *Science*, 1980, *208*, 1181–1182.

Flavell, J. H. On cognitive development. *Child Development*, 1982, *53*, 1–10.

Fodor, J. Some reflections on L. S. Vygotsky's *Thought and language*. *Cognition*, 1972, *1*, 83–95.

Fodor, J. A., Bever, T. G., and Garrett, M. F. *The psychology of language*. New York: McGraw-Hill, 1974.

Gladwin, T. *East is a big bird*. Cambridge, Mass.: Harvard University Press, 1970.

Glass, A., and Holyoak, K. J. Alternative conceptions of semantic theory. *Cognition*, 1975, *3*(4), 313–339.

Hayes, J. R. and Simon, H. A. Psychological differences among problem isomorphs. In N. J. Castellan, D. B. Pisoni, and G. R. Potts (Eds.), *Cognitive Theory*, (vol. 2). New York: Halstead, 1977.

Hunter, I. M. L. Mental calculation. In P. C. Wason and P. N. Johnson-Laird (Eds.), *Thinking and reasoning: Selected readings*. Hamondsworth, England: Penguin Books, 1968.

Keil, F. C. *Semantic and conceptual development: An ontological perspective*. Cambridge, Mass.: Harvard University Press, 1979.

Keil, F. C. Constraints on knowledge and cognitive development. *Psychological Review*, 1981, *88*(3), 197–227.

Keil, F. C. On the emergence of semantic and conceptual distinctions. *Journal of Experimental Psychology: General*, 1983, *112*(3), 357–385.

Keil, F. C. Semantic fields and the acquisition of metaphor. Manuscript submitted for publication.

Keil, F. C., and Batterman, N. A characteristic-to-defining shift in the development of word meaning. *Journal of Verbal Learning and Verbal Behavior*, in press.

Keil, F. C., and Carroll, J. J. The child's conception of "tall": Implications for an alternative view of semantic development. *Papers and Reports on Child Language Development*, 1980, *19*, 21–28.

Kessen, W. "Stage" and "structure" in the study of children. *Monographs of the Society for Research in Child Development*, 1962, *27*(3), 65–86.

Lehrer, A. Structure of the lexicon and transfer of meaning. *Lingua*, 1978, *45*, 95–123.

Neisser, U. Memory: What are the important questions? In M. M. Gruneberg, P. M. Morris, and R. N. Sykes (Eds.), *Practical aspects of memory*. London: Academic Press, 1978.

Newell, A. A note on process/structure distinctions in developmental psychology. In S. Farnham-Diggory (Ed.), *Information processing in children*. New York: Academic Press, 1972.

Newell, A. and Simon, H. A. GPS, a program that simulates human thought. In E. A. Feigenbaum and J. Feldman (Eds.), *Computers and Thought*. New York: McGraw-Hill, 1963.

Piaget, J. Piaget's theory. In P. H. Mussen (Ed.), *Carmichael's manual of child psychology*, 3rd ed., vol. 1. New York: Wiley, 1970.

Rumelhart, D. E., and Norman, D. A. Accretion, tuning, and restructuring: Three modes of learning. In J. W. Cotton and R. L. Klatzky (Eds.), *Semantic factors in cognition*. Hillsdale, N.J.: Erlbaum, 1978.

Simon, H. A. An information processing theory of intellectual development. *Monographs of the Society for Research in Child Development*, 1962, *27*(3), 150–162.

Simon, H. A. *The sciences of the artificial*, 2nd ed. Cambridge, Mass.: M.I.T. Press, 1981.

Simon, H. A., and Hayes, J. R. The understanding process: Problem isomorphs. *Cognitive Psychology*, 1976, *8*, 165–190.

Simon, H. A., and Newell, A. Computer simulation of human thinking and problem solving. *Monographs of the Society for Research in Child Development*, 1962, *27*(3), 137–149.

Smith, E. E., Shoben, E. J., and Rips, L. J. Structure and process in semantic memory: A featural model for semantic decisions. *Psychological Review*, 1974, *81*, 214–241.

Sommers, F. The calculus of terms. *Mind*, 1970, *79*, 1–39.

Sternberg, R. J., and Downing, C. J. The development of higher-order reasoning in adolescence. *Child Development*, 1982, *53*(1), 209–221.

Vygotsky, L. S. *Thought and Language* (E. Haufmann and G. Vakar, Trans.). Cambridge, Mass: M.I.T. Press, 1962. (Original work published 1934)

5 Transition Processes In Quantitative Development

David Klahr

[M]ore than 50 years have passed since Piaget first began to demonstrate that children's behavior is governed by their knowledge, rather than their lack thereof. By asking how children's knowledge generates the robust regularities in their behavior, Piaget established the theoretical and empirical precedent for the current focus on the development of knowledge. Even a casual perusal of today's developmental journals yields an unambiguous impression about the primary goals of cognitive developmental research:

1. To discover what children know. That is, to describe knowledge *states*.

2. To explain how they come to know it. That is, to describe the processes governing *transition* between states.

The two topics have received unequal attention, with the major portion of the published work addressing the former at the expense of the latter.

Perhaps that is why the editor of this book asked the contributors to "present their views on how children transit from one state to another in the course of their development." This is the fundamental question faced by cognitive developmentalists, and a fully satisfactory answer is not yet available. However, in recent years, there have been increases in our understanding of cognitive development in particular knowledge domains. These advances derive from discoveries of (1) new procedures for assessing and representing young children's knowledge states, and (2) new methods of formulating theories of transition and change.

KNOWLEDGE STATES AND TRANSITION PROCESSES

I believe that one fruitful way to approach the developmental issue "in the large" is to start with a reasonably complete account of the development of a particular, but fundamental, knowledge domain.

This chapter was supported in part by a grant from the National Science Foundation, and in part by the Spencer Foundation. The ideas presented here evolved over many years of continuing collaboration with Iain Wallace. Helpful comments on an earlier draft came from Brain MacWhinney, Robert Neches, Michael Scheier, Robert Siegler, and Robert Sternberg. Requests for reprints should be addressed to David Klahr, Department of Psychology, Carnegie-Mellon University, Pittsburgh, Pa. 15213.

In this chapter, the general themes of states and transition are imbedded in a substantive context: knowledge about quantity. Although the specific knowledge states I describe all refer to what is loosely termed "quantitative development," I will argue for the generality of the proposed transition processes.

Knowledge States

The emphasis on children's knowledge states has led to advances in the related areas of *knowledge representation* and *knowledge assessment*. By the former, I mean descriptive formalisms for characterizing the structures and processes in which children's knowledge is embedded. Knowledge representation has become a central issue in developmental psychology, warranting chapters devoted exclusively to the topic in at least two recent developmental publications (Klahr and Siegler, 1978; Mandler, 1982). The diversity of the new approaches to representation is exemplified by various descriptions of children's knowledge in terms of rules (Haith, 1980; Siegler, 1976), scripts (Nelson, 1978), skill hierarchies (Fischer, 1980), semantic nets (Gentner, 1975), grammars (Stein and Glenn, 1977), and production systems (Young and O'Shea, 1981).

These representational inventions have been accompanied by corresponding improvements in methodologies for knowledge *assessment*. Examples can be found in such diverse areas as infant quantification (Gelman, 1972a; Strauss and Curtis, 1981), scientific principles (Siegler, 1976), analogical reasoning (Sternberg, 1977), memory development (Brown, 1978; Case, 1983; Chi, 1976), and problem solving (Klahr and Robinson, 1981; Spitz and Borys, 1984), to mention but a few.

In this chapter, I will exploit both of these advances. I will draw on studies using new types of assessment of quantitative knowledge in infants and young children, and I will use the newly emergent formulation of *self-modifying production systems* to describe the developmental process that yields increasingly sophisticated quantitative knowledge. In the next few paragraphs, I will give a very brief description of what a production system is, and indicate how it can be used to describe a particular knowledge *state*. Then, I will present a state description of a "mature" form of conservation of number. This state description will subsequently be elaborated by focusing on its fundamental components: the quantifiers. That discussion will be followed by a developmental account—without detailed mechanisms. Next, I will describe some of the rudiments of self-modifying production systems; and finally, I will indicate their relevance to the question of transition.

Production-System State Descriptions.   Unambiguous theories of knowledge states are a prerequisite for theories of transition, because a transition theory can be no better than a theory of what it is that is undergoing transition. During the last decade, several investigators have formulated state descriptions for knowledge domains in terms of *production systems*. The domains include seriation (Baylor and Gascon, 1974; Young, 1976), class inclusion (Klahr and Wallace, 1972), conservation and quantification (Klahr and Wallace, 1976), and balance-scale prediction (Klahr and Siegler, 1978).

A production system consists of a set of rules—called productions—written in the form of condition/action pairs; the conditions are symbolic expressions for elements of knowledge that might be present at some instant. A production system operates via a recognize/act cycle. During the recognition portion of the cycle, all the condition sides of all the productions are compared with the current contents of the immediate knowledge state. This immediate knowledge can be interpreted as primary or short-term memory (Waugh and Norman, 1965), as "M-space" (Pascual-Leone, 1970), as short-term-plus-intermediate-term memory (Bower, 1975; Hunt, 1971), or, more generally, as the currently activated portion of long-term memory.

Thus, the conditions are tests on the momentary "state of awareness' of the system. A sequence of condition elements is interpreted as a test for the simultaneous existence of that particular conjunction of individual knowledge elements. If, for a given production, all the condition elements happen to be true at some instant, we say that the production is "satisfied." If only one production is satisfied, then it "fires": the actions associated with it are taken. These actions can modify the knowledge state by adding, deleting, or changing existing elements in it, or they can correspond to interactions—either perceptual or motor—with the environment. If more than one production has its conditions satisfied, then the satisfied productions are placed into the conflict set; a conflict-resolution principle is applied; and one production fires. The act portion of the cycle executes the actions that are associated with the fired production. Then the next cycle commences. Although the human information-processing system contains an enormous number of productions, only a limited subset of long term memory is active at any one moment, and hence only a handful of productions are potentially satisfied at any instant.

Figure 5-1 shows a simple production system. P1 says that if you have a circle and a plus, replace them with a triangle. P2 says replace a triangle with a circle; P3 says that if you have two circles, replace them with a square and a plus.

Data Base

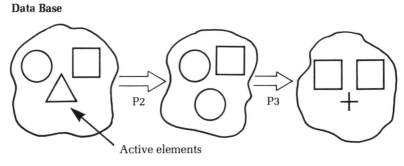

Active elements

Productions

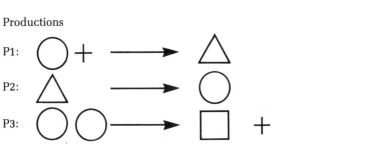

Figure 5-1
A simple production system with some active
elements

If this production system were to operate on the active elements shown here—comprising a circle, a triangle, and a square—it would behave as follows. On the recognition portion of the first cycle, only P2 would have all of its conditions matched. It would fire, consuming its input and adding a circle to the knowledge state. On the next cycle, neither P1 nor P2 would be able to find a complete match, but P3 would be satisfied. It would fire, effectively replacing the two circles with a square and a plus. At this point, none of the productions would be satisfied and the system would halt.

Although one can demonstrate the logical equivalence between production systems and any of several alternative formalisms, production systems have some important practical and theoretical advantages for modeling states and transitions. The context sensitivity of production systems enables them to represent the sequential, goal-directed aspect of human cognition while maintaining the potential for interruptability. The modularity of production systems makes them particularly well suited for modeling developmental changes, because individual rules can be added, deleted, or modified without extensive consideration of the other productions.

Production systems were originally used by developmental psychologists to model children's knowledge at fixed points in time: these systems were *state descriptions*. With respect to the short time span of the performance in question (for example, a seriation task), such models were *dynamic*: they transformed one transitory knowledge state into another. However, with respect to the longer time scale of cognitive development, the earliest models were *static*: they had no capacity to change.[1] Although there might be a sequence of models representing increasingly mature knowledge states [as in the Baylor and Gascon (1974) seriation models], the early production systems had no self-modification capability.[2]

Transition

The characterization of children's behavior as "rule-governed" (cf. Haith, 1980; Siegler, 1976) is implicit in all of the knowledge mentioned earlier, and is explicitly manifested in production systems. If knowledge can be described in terms of rules, then it follows that development and learning can be conceived of in terms of rule formation, acquisition, modification, and transformation. Since such processes are themselves a form of knowledge, we can talk of *rules for learning and development*, and assume that these rules are represented in the same general form as the things that are to be learned.

Soon after the appearance of production-system models for knowledge states, psychologists began to formulate *self-modifying* production systems. The rules for modifying the production systems were stated as productions to modify other productions. These "second-generation" production systems *do* have the capacity for self-modification: they are models of transition that transform a state description from one level of performance to the next (Langley, 1980; Waterman, 1975).

Later in this chapter I will describe several important features of these models, because I believe that the self-modification mechanisms utilized in such programs provide the building blocks for an information-processing theory of developmental transitions. Prior to that, I will provide an account of the development of knowledge about quantity. The account will assume that self-modification mechanisms are available, and that they can be specified with sufficient precision to be cast as computer-simulation models. Finally, in the last section of the chapter, I will attempt to demonstrate that these mechanisms are consistent with some general characteristics of cognitive development.

Theoretical Criteria

The distinction between state theories and transition theories might imply that there is a neat temporal order to theory construction. First you describe the two states of interest; then you look at the differences between them; and finally you formulate the transition model. Of course, it is not that simple. Usually, the state descriptions that one proposes are influenced by the transition mechanism that one expects to invoke. These descriptions, in turn, affect the empirical procedures that are used to generate evidence for the existence of the processes and structures that constitute the state in question.

This seems to be the case with respect to theories of quantitative development. Claims about the temporal order or earliest manifestation of different quantitative skills are derived from a particular view of the developmental processes. Indeed, much of the empirical work described in this chapter has been chosen to support the developmental account to be presented below. One never sees transitions, only by-products of transitions; so the empirical snapshots provide a major source of support for theories of transition.

In some cases, it is difficult to choose between competing state descriptions. Even after applying such evaluative criteria as empirical fit, plausibility, parsimony, elegance, and so on, we may be left with a standoff between competing theories. It is at this point that an additional criterion, one unique to developmental psychology, can be used to evaluate theories. I call this criterion *developmental tractability*. It evaluates the extent to which the competing theories, which propose two different pairs of state descriptions for earlier and later competence, can be integrated with a transitional theory: one that can actually transform the early state into the later one. Regardless of the predictive power or elegance of a theory for a given state of knowledge, if there is no plausible mechanism that might have produced that state from some previous one, then, from the viewpoint of the developmental psychologist, such a theory is seriously deficient.

CONSERVATION OF NUMBER: A STATE DESCRIPTION

In this section, I present a state description of the basic processes involved in "mature" conservation.[3] This is the target at which a developmental account of conservation acquisition must aim. The description descends to successively more specific levels of embedding: from general rules for forming relationships among quantities (in this section), to the processes that generate quantitative information in the first place (under the next major heading). The detail

Processing steps for EC

1. $Q_i(X) \longrightarrow x_i \quad Q_i(Y) \longrightarrow y_i$
2. $(x_i = y_i) \longrightarrow (X \overset{Q}{=} Y)$
3. $T_p(Y) \longrightarrow (Y')$
4. $(X \overset{Q}{=} Y)[T_p(Y) \longrightarrow Y'] \longrightarrow (X \overset{Q}{=} Y')$

Figure 5-2
Processing steps for equivalence conservation.

is necessary because the transition processes to be proposed can be understood only in terms of the kinds of quantitative information available to them.

The classic version of the number-conservation task starts with the presentation of two distinct collections of equal amounts of discrete items (for example, two rows of beads). First the child is encouraged to establish their quantitative equality, usually by quantifying each collection independently and then noting the equivalence of the two quantifications. Then the child observes as one of the collections undergoes a transformation that changes some of its perceptual features while mantaining its numerical quantity. Finally, the child is asked to judge the relative quantity of the two collections after the transformation.

To be classified as "having conservation," the child must be able to assert the continuing quantitative equality of the two collections without resorting to a requantification and comparison after the transformation; that is, the child's response must be based not on another direct observation, but rather on the realization of the "logical necessity" for initially equal amounts to remain equal under "mere" perceptual transformations.[4] A symbolic representation of an equivalence-conservation (EC) situation is shown in Figure 5-2. Each step illustrates—in an abstract form—an essential processing phase in the standard EC task.

Construction of an Internal Quantitative Representation

The first step indicates that some *quantifier* produces an internal representation of the quantities in each of the external collections X and Y. The quantifiers are shown in their most general form as Q_i, and their encodings as x_i. In any particular situation, one of three basic types of quantifiers may be used. The three quantifiers (to be described in more detail in the next major Section) are subitizing (Q_s), counting (Q_c), and estimation (Q_e).[5] These quantifiers may produce very different internal representations of the same quantity, so information about which quantifier did the encoding is maintained in the formal notation. Thus, when collection X is quantified by Q_c, the resultant internal symbol is indicated by x_c.

The distinction among the internal representations of quantity (or, more briefly, among *quantitive symbols*) is not merely a notational refinement. Rudimentary representations for two or three items quantified via Q_s may have no initial correspondence to the internal symbol generated by Q_c operating on the same collections. For example, an internal representation of a triangle is quite unrelated to an internal representation for the word "three." Although adults have all the required processes to detect the abstract numerical equivalence between the work representation and the triangular representation, the *initial* encodings remain, nevertheless, distinct. We can think of Q_s as producing something equivalent to the triangle representation, and Q_c as producing something equivalent to "three." It is thus clear why we want to distinguish the two possible encodings of a display of three things as x_s and x_c: they are likely to be distinct in the young child. Indeed, one of the things to be accounted for is the development of a fully generalized internal representation for number—for the "threeness of three."

Inferring External Equivalence from Internal Equality

The second processing step shown in Figure 5-2 is an inference rule that says that "if two internal quantitative symbols are equal, then their external referents are quantitatively equivalent with respect to the dimension in question." This distinction between knowledge about internal symbols and knowledge about external collections, is, like the distinction just made among quantitative symbols, a necessary part of a state description for what is ultimately to be a *developmental* theory. In adults, the inference that "three reds equal three blues implies that there are as many reds as blues" seems trivial. But it is a piece of knowledge about quantity that is not available to young children, even though they may be able to count small sets accurately. Piaget was probably the first to make the surprising discovery that young children may correctly count two equal collections, but fail to assert their quantitative equivalence:

> Fur . . . counts both sets, discovers that they have the same
> cardinal number, but refuses to accept that they are equivalent: "No,
> there are more pennies. There's one past the end." Similarly Aud
> counts eight pennies, says that he will be able to buy eight flowers,
> makes the exchange, and then cannot see that the sets are equivalent:

"There are more, because they're spread out." These cases clearly
show that perception of spatial properties carries more weight than
even verbal numeration (Piaget 1941/1952, p. 59)

In the somewhat more difficult situation of initial inequivalence,
Schaeffer, Eggleston, and Scott (1974) found that young children who
could correctly count four items in one set and then five in another
still did not know which set had more items. In other words, children
may have the ability to produce and order quantitative symbols well
before they have the rule shown in step 2 of Figure 5-2. They may
know that "5 comes after 4" (relational information about internal
quantitative symbols), but still not know that the collection of five
things is "more" than the collection of four things (external quantitative relation).

Encoding the Type of Transformation

The third step in Figure 5-2 represents an internal record that a
particular type of transformation was applied to one of the collections. T_p stands for a quantity-preserving transformation.[6] The other
two types of transformational classes are quantity-increasing (T_+)
and quantity-decreasing (T_-). Note that the appropriate classification of a physical act depends not only on the act itself, but also on
the dimension being quantified. For example, spreading is T_p with
respect to number, but T_+ with respect to length and T_- with respect
to density. One of the goals of a theory of conservation acquisition
is to account for the formation of such transformational classes.

Applying "the" Conservation Rule

The fourth step in Figure 5-2 represents the form of knowledge that
gives conservation its "logical necessity." It is a production that says,
in effect, "if you know that two collections were initially equal, and
that one of them underwent a quantity-preserving transformation,
then you know that the transformed collection is still equal to the
untransformed one." The fundamental question in the study of conservation is: where did this rule come from?

In fact, the basic question is too simple, for there is much more
to be known about conservation of relationships between two quantities. There are a total of nine logically distinct conservation situations involving initial inequalities as well as equalities, and quantity-changing transformations as well as quantity-preserving ones.
As shown in Figure 5-3, only seven of these can result in unambiguous outcomes. For example, in the "classic" conservation situation,

Initial relations

Types of transformation		X = Y	X > Y	X < Y
	$T_p(Y) \longrightarrow Y'$	$X = Y'$ ①	$X > Y'$ ②	$X < Y'$ ③
	$T_+(Y) \longrightarrow Y'$	$X < Y'$ ④	? ⑧	$X < Y'$ ⑦
	$T_-(Y) \longrightarrow Y'$	$X > Y'$ ⑤	$X > Y'$ ⑥	? ⑨

Figure 5-3
The full set of possible types of conservation and
nonconservation situations.

shown as Type 1, the initial relation is one of equality, the transformation is T_p, and the final relation is also equality. However, in
Type 8, the initially lesser quantitiy y has something added to it
(T_+), and the final relation between the two quantities can only be
established by a final requantification.

This elaboration of types of conservation situations is important,
for much of the contradictory evidence about the emergence of conservation results from a lack of attention to the particular type of
conservation that is being assessed. For example, Silverman and
Briga (1981) questioned Gelman's (1972b) conclusion that very
young children can conserve. They evaluated the possibility that 3-
year-olds solve small-number conservation problems by requanti-
fying the final sets, rather than by using any conservation rule. Although all of their manipulations involved Type 2 and Type 3 situations, Silverman and Briga expanded their final conclusion to the
broad (and ambiguous) category of "small-number conservation,"
asserting that their results disconfirmed Gelman's claim.

But the two studies are not comparable. In Gelman's "magic"
study, the "number invariance rule" that children evidenced was
that *in the absence of a transformation, number should not change.*
(I will extend this argument in a later section: "Elaboration of Transformational Classes.") Although superficially Gelman's study appears to have involved an inequivalence-conservation situation (that
is, a Type 2 or 3, with a surreptitious Type 8 or 9), from the children's
point of view it was really a pair of identity-conservation trials: the
two-item array was expected to remain a two-item array, and the
three-item array a three.

It is conceivable that young children could acquire a small-number identity-conservation (IC) rule analogous to the Type 1 EC rule

shown in Figure 5-3 long before they acquire the Type 2 and Type 3 rules. As for the other types, there is not much systematic empirical work, except for Siegler's (1981) discovery that the rules based on quantity-changing transformations (for example, Types 4 and 5)[7] develop prior to the analogous rules based on quantity preservation (Type 1).

QUANTIFIERS: SUBITIZING AND COUNTING

In this section I will describe some properties of both subitizing and counting in terms of their *state descriptions* at three levels: at adulthood, at about age 6, and during infancy. It is necessary to look more closely at the quantifiers before turning to a developmental account, for our theory is based on the assumption that subitizing operates in a rudimentary form very early in development.

It might be useful to summarize the structure of the presentation thus far, and to indicate where this section fits into the overall picture. Recall that in the section entitled "Theoretical Criteria," I explained that one way to assess a developmental theory was to determine the extent to which it could account for the sequence of states that were observed. With respect to quantification, then, it is important to establish just what children can do at different ages. Therefore, this section deals with some basic empirical findings and relates them to the important features of a theory of the development of quantitative skills. The section will complete the discussion of state descriptions, and will prepare us for a description of the developmental processes.

Subitizing

The phenomenology of subitizing is well known. When asked to quantify collections of fewer than four objects, adults respond very rapidly, with little conscious effort and high accuracy. The answers seem to be immediately and directly available, with no intermediate calculations. The subitizing experience is easily distinguished from the counting experience, which requires conscious attention to maintaining the correspondence between items counted and the count words, partitioning of the array into counted and uncounted items, and so on.

Subitizing in Adults.   When subjects quantify random dot patterns, their reaction times (RTs) and error rates reveal a clear discontinuity at $n = 3$ or 4, as shown in Figure 5-4 (Chi and Klahr, 1975). For

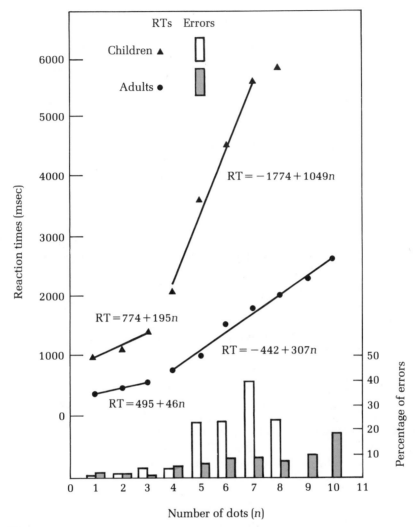

Figure 5-4
Reaction times (RTs) and error rates for children
and adults in quantifying random dot patterns.
From Chi and Klahr (1975, Figure 1).

adults, from $n = 1$ to $n = 3$ the *slope* of RT versus n is about 50
msec: RT increases about 50 msec with each additional item to be
quantified. The slope changes to about 300 msec per item for n from
4 to 10 items. Error rates jumped from nearly zero for $n < 4$ to from
8 to 10 percent for $4 < n < 10$.[8] These results support the subjective
distinction between $\mathbf{Q_s}$ and $\mathbf{Q_c}$, but they do not support the "im-

mediate-apprehension" view of Q_s, for it does take more time to operate on larger collections. To the extent that "pure" perceptual processes are typically characterized as highly parallel, Q_s cannot be a simple, purely perceptual process: some sequential processing must be occurring.

Furthermore, the view of Q_s as some kind of pattern recognizer cannot be reconciled with the results of studies in which subjects had to quantify complex block configurations (Chase, 1978). Using stimuli similar to the Shepard–Metzler block configurations, but varying the quantity from 1 to 10 blocks, Chase found RT patterns— for individual subjects—very similar to those in Figure 5-3. For most subjects, the upper limit of Q_s was $n = 3$, and for a few it was $n = 4$. Whereas it seems plausible that one, two, and three *dots* could be recognized as a familiar pattern, it is unlikely that people would have pattern recognizers for line drawings of small block configurations. More recently, Van Oeffelen and Vos (1982) found that people can subitize *groups* of dots as well as individual dots. They used displays of from 13 to 23 dots that could be grouped into from one to eight clusters. The displays were shown for brief periods, and the subjects had to report how many clusters of dots they saw. When the number of clusters was within the subitizing range, subjects were very accurate, but their performance deteriorated sharply when there were more than four clusters.

Thus, Q_s appears to be partially controlled by higher-order cognitive processes that determine the *target* of the quantification effort (for example, dots, cubes, dot clusters), and by some inherent limitation whereby the visual field can be rapidly segmented into only three or four perceptual chunks. Q_s is likely to be a side effect of a more general hierarchically organized perceptual process (cf. Palmer, 1977).

Subitizing in Preschoolers and Infants: Recent Evidence.   Kindergarten children given the dot-quantification task produced the RT results shown by the upper curves in Figure 5-4. Also, their subjective reports for the Q_s range were similar to those of adults. We have concluded from these results that by the age of 6 years, children have both Q_c and Q_s available to them, although both processes are substantially slower than their fully mature versions.

At the time we were formulating our theory of the development of quantifiers (Klahr and Wallace, 1973), there was little evidence about the nature of infant quantification ability. The argument over whether Q_s was developmentally prior to Q_c was based in part on the developmental-tractability criterion, and in part on whether or not preschoolers used Q_c or Q_s in situations where either would suffice (Gelman and Gallistel, 1978; Gelman and Tucker, 1975; Schaeffer, Eggleston, and Scott, 1974).

In the past few years it has been found that infants can make discriminations among small numerosities. By utilizing appropriate variations in stimulus materials, investigators have found that these discriminations are based not on brightness, total contour, extent, density, or surface area, but on number *per se* (Starkey and Cooper, 1980; Starkey, Spelke, and Gelman, 1980; Strauss and Curtis, 1981, 1984). Typically, infants are habituated to a particular numerosity (for example, $n = 2$). Then they are presented with post-habituation arrays of either the same numerosity or one very close to it ($n = 2$ or 3). If they dishabituate to the novel numerosity but not to the familiar one, they have demonstrated the ability to discriminate between the two quantities. Collectively, these studies demonstrate that infants as young as 4 months can discriminate 2–3 and 3–4, but not 4–5.

We now know that 4-month-old infants can perform rudimentary number discriminations long before they can have acquired the complex, socially transmitted mechanisms required by Q_c. Can we then conclude that these infants possess a precursor of Q_s? Strauss and Curtis (1981) suggest a cautious interpretation. Although their results "demonstrate that some numerosities can be discriminated by infants even though they possess no knowledge of counting," they warn that these findings "do not necessarily imply that the infant has a cognitive awareness of number and can 'represent' numerosity" (p. 1151). In order to evaulate this position, it is necessary to consider just what might be involved in the representation of numerosity.

A quantifier encodes an external stimulus into an internal quantitative symbol. The extent to which the quantifier is truly numerical depends on the extent to which it produces an internal symbol that has numerical properties—in particular, the properties of ordinality and cardinality. A full discussion of the properties of the quantitative symbols produced by the precursors of Q_c and Q_s would take us too far afield from the main theme of this chapter, which is the development of conservation rules that utilize Q_c and Q_s. All we need to assume about the infant representations of quantity is that they include at least cardinal informaticn. This seems reasonable, because the habituation to a particular numerosity, when many other perceptual dimensions are varying, could only result from repeated encoding of the cardinality of the set size.

Cardinality without ordinality is only half of the story, however, and Strauss and Curtis' caution is probably prudent, for nothing from the infant labs has yet demonstrated that early quantification produces ordinal information. Several investigators, including Bullock and Gelman (1977), Estes (1976), Siegel (1971, 1977), and Silverman and Briga (1981), have demonstrated that by age 3, children can make judgments about relative numerosity. There is some disagreement about whether the relative judgments are based on number or on some correlated dimension, such as length or density (McLaughlin, 1981), but the weight of evidence appears to favor the position that preschoolers can utilize the ordinal property of number. The interesting question now concerns the extent to which *infants* can extract such information, and investigations are under way to answer this question.[9] Although we have argued elsewhere for a rudimentary quantitative representation that contains both cardinal and ordinal information,[10] for the purposes of this chapter we need to assume only that infants have a Q_s that produces reliable encodings of small cardinalities.

Counting

The complexity of counting has been convincingly demonstrated by Gelman and Gallistel's (1978) analysis of the five "counting principles" that children must understand before Q_c can produce reliable encodings of quantity. The elaboration of the principles into a computational model that can actually *do* counting is an even more impressive statement of the underlying complexity of Q_c (Greeno, Riley, and Gelman, 1981). It seems quite implausible that much of this would be available to a 4-month-old infant. Indeed, investigations of even a single component of Q_c—the ability to recite the list of number names—have revealed a protracted developmental course, typically not completed until well into the preschool years (Siegler and Robinson, 1981). It is difficult to see how Q_c could initially provide the reliable encodings necessary for the child to detect any quantitative invariants.

Nevertheless, Starkey, Spelke, and Gelman (1980) have derived from their infant studies the possibility that "infants possess a primitive form of nonverbal counting" that "may underlie (some) subitizing phenomena," and that "could share some component processes with verbal counting" (p. 9). What might this "nonverbal counting" be in infants? It certainly could not include the technology embodied in the counting principles, but it might include processes for attention deployment and symbol generation. Because such processes are common to both counting and subitizing, the infant capacity might be viewed as a precursor to either or both of the adult quantifiers. However, the similarity to Q_s derives from the finding that the upper limit of the infant discrimination seems to be three

Specific consistent sequences

(a) $\mathbf{Q}_s$(cookies) ... ${}_o3_s$ ... pick them up in hand ... look $\mathbf{Q}_s$(cookies in hand) ... ${}_n3_s$ ... ${}_o3_s$ ... ${}_n3_s$

| Quantify a small collection via $\mathbf{Q}_s$ | Observe a transformation | Quantify the resultant collection | Compare ${}_o3_s = {}_n3_s$ |

(b) $\mathbf{Q}_s$(dolls) ... ${}_o2_s$ ... push together ... $\mathbf{Q}_s$(dolls) ... ${}_n2_s$ ... ${}_o2_s = {}_n2_s$

Figure 5-5
Examples of specific consistent sequences of time-line entries (a) ${}_o3_s$: old quantitative symbol for $\underline{3}$ objects produced by subitizing. ${}_n3_s$: new quantitative symbol for $\underline{3}$ objects produced by subitizing. (b) ${}_o2_s$ and ${}_n2_s$: old and new quantitative symbols for two objects produced by subitizing.

or four objects. This coincides with the break on the curves for both children's and adults' quantification times.[11]

DEVELOPMENT OF CONSERVATION OF NUMBER

Assuming, then, that initially only $\mathbf{Q}_s$ provides reliable encodings of small numerosities, how are the conservation rules ultimately acquired? In order to answer this question, it is necessary to describe some of the general properties of the developing information-processing system.

The Time Line

One of the fundamental capacities posited by the theory is the ability to store and analyze an encoded record of ongoing processing. This *time line* is analogous to a trace of the run of a computer program; only it is stored internally, where it is accessible to the system's basic processes for self-modification.[12] The time line and its associated analyzers can be viewed as an attempt to further specify Piaget's appealing but mysterious notion of "reflective abstraction" (Piaget, 1971); it provides a means for the system to ruminate about the efficacy of its own processing episodes. Rather than directly examining its own knowledge structures, the system regards the *results* of its actions; that is, the symbolic trace of its behavior.

Two hypothetical sequences of time-line entries relevant to quantity are shown in Figure 5-5. Entries are made in the time line at the conclusion of processing episodes. These include, in this case, simple goal-directed sensorimotor episodes, such as picking up some objects, and quantification, via Q_s, of small collections. At the early point in development represented by the sequences in Figure 5-5, the infant stores in the time line a sequence of very specific encodings of these events (as well as others, indicated by the ellipses). First, using Q_s, the infant might quantify a collection of cookies (Figure 5-5a), producing as a result a subitizing quantitative symbol for three cookies. Then he or she might encode the transformation of "picking up," followed by another execution of Q_s. Finally, the infant might notice the relation between the "old" 3 ($_o3_s$) and the "new" 3 ($_n3_s$) for cookies, and store that, too, in the time line.

This set of encodings—a symbolic record of quantification, transformation, requantification, and comparison of contiguous quantitative symbols—is called a *specific consistent sequence*. It is *specific* to the objects (in this example, cookies), to the number and quantifier (that is, to the particular quantitative symbol produced by Q_s), and to the transformation (picking up). It is *consistent* because both Q_s (with respect to three items) and picking up (also with respect to three items) are relatively reliable and error-free. One can imagine this particular specific sequence being entered many, many times in the time line; indeed, sufficiently often that even with uncontrolled variations in the irrelevant intervening time-line entries, the consistent pattern is detectable: the signal begins to emerge from the noise.

Other specific consistent sequences are also stored in the time line: an example of one involving different objects (dolls), a different number (2), and a different transformation (pushing together) is shown in Figure 5-5b.[13] As indicated earlier, the entries in the time line are available for inspection by the system's procedures for regularity detection. These processes look for recurrences in the stream of specific consistent sequences, and from them attempt to form *common consistent sequences*. An example of how such a common consistent sequence might be formed is diagrammed in Figure 5-6.

Generalization over Time-Line Sequences

The basic process involved is generalization. One of the three features of the specific consistent sequences from one set of experiences is compared with another, and the feature that varies is generalized while the others remain invariant. For example, Figure 5-6a shows a case in which a specific numerosity representation from Q_s and a specific transformation are discovered to be invariant with respect to the particular objects involved. The generalization produces new information in the time line: the Q_s symbol for two things, followed by spreading and requantification, followed by the discovery that

(a) **Generalization over objects**

$$\left.\begin{array}{l}\text{two dolls}\\\text{two cookies}\\\text{two fingers}\end{array}\right\} \ \ldots \ \text{spread apart} \ \ldots \ \left\{\begin{array}{l}\text{two dolls}\\\text{two cookies}\\\text{two fingers}\end{array}\right.$$

$$_0 2_s \ \ldots \ \text{spreading} \ \ldots \ {}_n 2_s \ \ldots \ {}_0 2_s = {}_n 2_s$$

(b) **Generalization over quantitative symbols (numbers)**

$$\left.\begin{array}{l}_0 2_s\\_0 1_s\\_0 3_s\end{array}\right\} \ \ldots \ \text{spreading} \ \ldots \ \left\{\begin{array}{l}_n 2_s\\_n 1_s\\_n 3_s\end{array}\right.$$

$$\text{any} \ {}_0 X_s \ \ldots \ \text{spreading} \ \ldots \ {}_n X_s \ \ldots \ {}_0 X_s = {}_n X_s$$

(c) **Generalization over transformations**

$$_0 X_s \ \ldots \ \left\{\begin{array}{l}\text{spreading}\\\text{rotating}\\\text{compressing}\end{array}\right\} \ \ldots \ {}_n X_s \ \ldots \ {}_0 X_s = {}_n X_s$$

(d) The three types of generalization produce **common consistent sequences**:

$$_0 X_s \ \ldots \ T_p(X) \ \rightarrow \ X' \ \ldots \ X_s \ \ldots \ X_s = X_s$$

$$_0 X_s \ \ldots \ T_{+/-}(X) \ \rightarrow \ X' \ \ldots \ X_s \ \ldots \ X_s \neq X_s$$

Figure 5-6

Examples of generalization over time-line entires
for (a) objects, (b) quantitative symbols, and (c)
transformations, to produce (d) common consistent
sequences.

the second symbol is the same as the first. The time line now contains
a record of activity at a slightly higher level of abstraction than before,
although it is still quite limited in generality.

The next generalization shown occurs over the quantitative symbol. The minimally generalized sequences shown in Figure 5-6b are
examined by the same regularity detectors that produced them. In
this instance, the generalization process detects the variation in number and the constancy in transformation. In subsequent processing
episodes, the system inserts information into the time line at this
new level of generality: *any* Q_s symbol, followed by spreading and
requantification, followed by the discovery that the first and second
Q_s symbols are the same.

The partially generalized sequences shown in Figure 5-6b are
then further generalized, this time over the particular transformation
that is involved. If the early symbols from Q_s contain only cardinal
information, then at first the only transformational generalizations
will be to T_p or $T_{+/-}$ as a class. That is, the only reliable regularities

Redundancy elimination

Observe, predict, verify . . .   ultimately eliminate verification
Given an IC transformation within the Q_s range, produce a "rule"
or "production":

If you know   then you also know
$(_o\mathbf{x}_s)\,[T_p(X) \;\longrightarrow\; X'] \;\longrightarrow\; {}_o x_s = {}_n x_s$

Figure 5-7
Summary of rule formation via redundancy
elimination for identity conservation.

will be those that include, as part of the requantification and comparison process, information that the transformation produced either
the same or a different quantitative symbol.[14] With sufficiently many
of these sequences, the generalization mechanisms will produce the
common consistent sequences shown in Figure 5-6d: highly generalized encodings of quantification and transformation regularities
(still limited to Q_s, however, since only Q_s has been producing the
reliable encodings of the environment). Two forms of common consistent sequences are illustrated in Figure 5-6d. The first corresponds
to quantity-preserving transformations, and the second to quantity-
changing transformations.

Rule Formation via Redundancy Elimination

Common consistent sequences of the types shown in Figure 5-6d
contain some redundant information. The initial Q_s is followed by
the observed T_p (or $T_{+/-}$), which is always followed by another Q_s,
which in turn is followed by a determination that the two quantitative symbols are the same (or are different). The developing system
has a general principle of avoiding unnecessary processing—of redundancy elimination—and this principle is manifested in this case
by processes that form a rule from the sequence. After repeated oc-
currences of observations that, with respect to x_s, and say, T_p, the
old and the new quantities are the same, the redundancy-elimination
processes form a rule about T_p. The process is sketched in Figure 5-
7.

The new rule is limited to the range of n for which Q_s has been
providing reliable encodings. There is solid evidence that the first
conservations occur within the subitizing range (Cowan, 1979; Siegler, 1981).[15] Although there is nothing in the logic of the time-line
processing that favors Q_s over Q_c, the added complexity of Q_c renders
it an unlikely source of the requisite quantitative regularity. It has

been shown repeatedly that preschoolers can reliably count quantities well beyond their conservation range (Gelman, 1972a). If counting provided the initial basis for the formation of conservation rules, it would be hard to explain why there remains a lag of several years between reliable counting of some level of n and conservation of n things.

Suppose, instead, that the earliest conservations are specific to the internal representations produced by Q_s, as we have argued. Then the lag can be explained as a consequence of either or both of two processes. If all conservations evolve from the initial subitizing-based rules, then the lag would be due to the additional effort required for the time-line processing to detect the co-occurrence of both counting and subitizing symbols for the same quantification episode. If counting at first generates its own independent set of conservation rules, then the simple fact that counting starts later could explain the temporal discrepancy. In either case, there appears to be a period of several years when young children are using subitizing-based rules for conserving small numbers while simultaneously using counting to quantify larger collections.

Individual Variation in Conservation Acquisition

The processes that analyze the time line are postulated to be available to all infants, but the course of quantitative development is highly dependent on the particular experience of the individual. Most obvious is the expected variation in the specific items (balls, dolls, fingers, and so on) and transformations (spreading, rotating, compressing, and so on) that form the initial time-line entries. Another variation lies in the sequence of generalizations. The object, number, transformation sequence used in Figure 5-6 is not the only possible permutation of the three classes of generalizations. Depending on environmental experience, any generalization sequence might occur.

The most interesting potential variations are differences in the level of generalization at which rules may be formed. Figure 5-8 shows two orthogonal "dimensions" of change that can be effected by time-line processing: *data generalization* and *rule formation*. As illustrated in the example, the redundancy-elimination processes might produce a rule that was only partly generalized, say with respect to only 4 items and spreading, or perhaps with respect to a particular object. That is, a child might know that compressing conserves two or three pieces of candy, well before the child has the more general rule shown in Figure 5-7. These two dimensions are similar to those proposed by Newman, Riel, and Martin (1982) in their discussion of the cultural specificity of cognitive acquistions.

$_o3_s$ $\ldots$ spreading $\ldots$ $_n3_s$ $\ldots$ $_o3_s = {}_n3_s$

$_o3_i$ $_n3_i$ $_o3_i \quad {}_n3_i$

Rule formation

$_o4_s$ $\ldots$ spreading $\ldots$ $_n4_s$ $\ldots$ $_o4_s = {}_n4_s$ $\Longrightarrow$ $_o4_s$ and spreading $\longrightarrow$ $_o4_s = {}_n4_s$

$_o4_i$ $_n4_i$ $_o4_i \quad {}_n4_i$

$\Downarrow$ **Data generalization**

x_s $\ldots$ spreading $\ldots$ x_s^1 $\ldots$ $x_s = x_s^1$

$_ox_i$ $_nx_i$ $_ox_i \quad {}_nx_i$

Figure 5-8
Divergent paths of data generalization and rule
formation. $_o3_i$: old quantitative symbol for
collection of 3 items, produced by either $\mathbf{Q_s}$, $\mathbf{Q_c}$ or
$\mathbf{Q_e}$,

Newman et al. note that Piaget's (1972) proposal that formal-operational reasoning is domain-specific—even in adults—is paradox-
ical, given the purportedly abstract nature of the psychological structures that support formal operations. Their resolution is to

> recognize that there are two orthogonal dimensions along which
> knowledge can be characterized. A vertical dimension, "concrete to
> abstract," refers to the nature of the knowledge itself, that is, the
> level of abstraction at which some phenomenon is understood. The
> horizontal dimension, "specific to general," refers to the range of
> contexts to which the knowledge in question applies.

It seems that Newman et al.'s "concrete to abstract" is similar to our
rule-formation dimension, whereas "specific to general" corresponds to data generalization.

Expected diversity in developmental paths is not unique to the
theory being proposed here. Fischer (1980), focusing on the structural rather than the procedural properties of cognitive development,
makes a similar point. He argues that with respect to an individual's
attainments in a particular domain (such as number concepts), "unevenness must be the rule in development" (p. 513); and that with
respect to individual differences,

> for virtually every skill at every one of the levels, different
> individuals can take different developmental paths within a skill
> domain, and usually the end products of the different paths will be
> skills that are equivalent for most purposes. . . . [but] the different
> paths within a domain are often significant. (p. 514)

The process of "early" (or partially generalized) rule formation helps to explain the lack of coherence in children's "numerical understandings" (Siegler and Robinson, 1981):

> Preschoolers could have used their knowledge of counting to compare numerical magnitudes but they did not seem to. They could have used their knowledge of comparing to add numbers . . . but again they did not seem to . . . [E]arly mathematical skills may develop in relative isolation from one another. (p. 70)

Elaboration of Transformational Classes

This is not to say that no empirical predictions can be made about the appearance of conservation-related behaviors. With respect to the transformational classes, the first regularities detected would be those in which no transformation at all was encoded in the time line between two successive quantifications of the same collection. That is, the system would first come to expect that discrete quantity is constant in the absence of any transformation.[16]

It is precisely this form of "quantity permanence" that was assessed by Gelman's well-known "magic" studies (Gelman, 1972b). When 2-year-old children do not see a transformation, they expect small discontinuous quantity to remain invariant. When confronted with an array that has undergone a surreptitious numerical transformation, they show surprise.[17] Note that expecting quantitative invariance in the absence of an observed transformation is a simpler piece of knowledge than expecting it in the face of a specific kind of transformation (of a T_p, for example).[18] This first level in the elaboration of transformation classes is depicted in Figure 5-9a. If no transformation has been detected, then the expectation is that repeated quantification of the same collection should yield the same subitizing symbol. If any transformation has been observed, then there is uncertainty about what to expect. In an experiment involving pairs of sequential transformations of continuous quantity, Halford (1975) found that 4-year-old children expected almost any pair of transformations to produce a change in the original quantity.

The next level, shown in Figure 5-9b, involves the elaboration of transformations into either $T_{+/-}$ or non-$T_{+/-}$. Although I have been referring to the transformations that neither increase nor decrease quantity as "quantity-preserving" transformations (that is, as T_p), they are more appropriately characterized as a residual category: their meaning derives from what they don't do rather than from what they do. The tests in Figure 5-9b first determine whether or not any transformation has occurred. If not, the expectation is one of quantitative invariance. If there has been a transformation, a further test

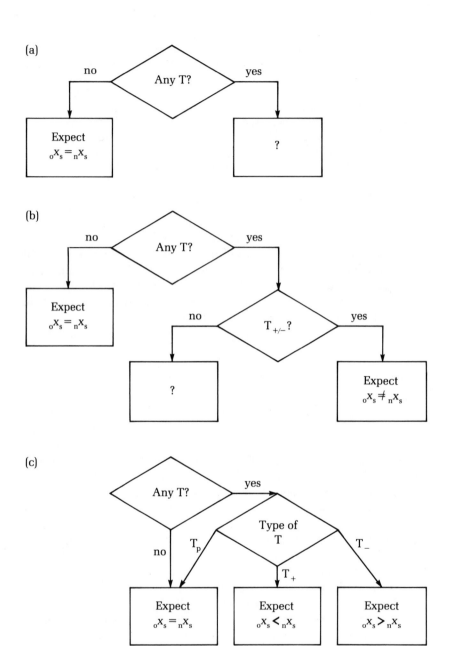

Figure 5-9
Elaboration of transformational classes.

is made to determine whether or not it is $T_{+/-}$. If it is, then a quantitative change is expected; if it is not, then no prediction is made.

Finally, in the full elaboration of transformations shown in Figure 5-9c, the specific transformation, if there is one, is directly linked with its corresponding quantitative relation. Evidence that this is a fairly late acquisition is provided by Siegler's (1981) study of the emergence of conservation rules.[19]

According to the theory presented here, "having conservation" is a consequence of acquiring the transformational knowledge illustrated in Figures 5-3 and 5-9. It does not depend on knowledge about inversion or compensation, although such knowledge may well be acquired concurrently with the acquisition of the conservation rules. This position is consistent with the results of Silverman and Rose's (1982) review of dozens of empirical studies of the relationship between compensation and conservation:

> Developmental studies support the conclusion that the ability to conserve can be attained without the ability to compensate. Further, conservation training literature points to the same conclusion. (p. 80)

MECHANISMS FOR SELF-MODIFICATION

In previous sections, I presented a state description of conservation, followed by an account of how time-line analysis leads to the new knowledge structures that support conservation. In this section, I will describe some of the mechanisms that are being used in various self-modifying production systems, and then discuss their relevance to the processes that govern the acquisition of conservation. The systems will be described at a nontechnical level, since space constraints preclude a detailed treatment of the required mechanisms.

Conflict Resolution

Before describing self-modification techniques, I should say a little more about the *conflict-resolution rules* mentioned earlier. Recall that when more than one production's conditions are satisfied, the production-system interpreter has to decide which one to "fire." Conflicts arise frequently in systems of even modest complexity, and the conflict-resolution rules are very important, especially in systems that are continually creating their own new productions. Although there are several distinct conflict-resolution rules that have been used in various production-system implementations (Anderson, Kline, and Beasley, 1980; Forgy, 1979; Langley, 1984; Newell, 1973),

I will discuss only the two that are most important for self-modifying systems.

Specificity.   The specificity rule selects the more specific of two otherwise equivalent productions from the conflict set. That is, if one production has conditions A and B satisfied while the other has conditions A, B, and C satisfied, then the specificity rule will choose the latter over the former.

Strength.   Productions can have a *strength* associated with them. This strength is established when they are first created, and it is modified by the system in appropriate circumstances. The conflict-resolution rule that utilizes production strength will prefer the stronger of two productions in the conflict set. The stronger production is usually the one that has led to the most desirable functioning in the past. A newly created production is typically relatively weak, and a well-established one is typically strong. If the system is about to create a new production and it discovers that the same production already exists, then it will simply strengthen the existing one (Langley, 1984). Thus, initially weak productions that may be winnowed out by the strength conflict-resolution rule will, if they are repeatedly recreated, eventually become strong enough to be selected by that same process.

Discrimination

Discrimination is achieved by taking an existing production and adding more tests to its condition side. For example, if we had a production for a concept-learning task that represented the current hypothesis as

if RED and LARGE, then say YES,

and we discovered that the production was overly general, then we might want to change it to be more specific. By creating a new production having the two initial conditions plus an additional one, we might get

if RED and LARGE and TRIANGLE, then say YES.

The creation of discriminating productions usually occurs in the context of environmental feedback, and the system need only have access to the local context that caused the overly general response. Thus, it is not very difficult to decide which productions might be the most fruitful candidates for modification. Actually, the existing productions are not modified. Instead, a new production is created, and the old and new version coexist. They may follow a period during which the faulty rule still dominates the correct one. Such cases would correspond to situations in which training and experience appear to have no effect on behavior, even though the underlying correct production is getting stronger with each episode. Eventually, the conflict-resolution rules and strengthening procedures described above will ensure that the appropriate production will control behavior.

Langley (1984) proposes a system that depends entirely on discrimination as a learning and developmental mechanism. His system always starts with the most general rules possible, and then slowly builds up more and more discriminating versions of them. Langley has used this procedure to construct self-modifying production systems for concept learning, problem solving, language acquisition, and concrete operations on the balance scale.

Generalization

There are two ways to make a production more general. The first is to simply reverse the procedure for discrimination; that is, to create a new production with fewer condition elements than the one that already exists. The second way is to replace specific condition elements with variables that can be matched to any members of a class. In an algebra-learning self-modifying production system, Neves (1978) takes productions that initially refer to specific integers and creates new productions that refer just to numbers. For example, a production that starts, "if there is a 4 on the left side of the equation . . . " might get replaced with one that starts, "if there is a number . . . "

The discrimination and generalization processes can compensate for each other's excesses. Anderson and Kline (1979) describe a system that uses discrimination to recover from situations in which an overly general version of a production has been created. In the context of a concept-learning task, their system compares the situation existing when a rule is correctly applied with the situation that occurs when the same rule is incorrectly applied. Based on the differences between these two situations, the system then constructs a less general (more discriminated) version of the overly general rule.[20]

Composition

Composition is based on the idea that whenever a set of productions repeatedly fires in the same sequence, it may be possible to *combine* the set into a single production. The new production would be composed from the conditions and actions of the original set, and it would enable the system to achieve what had previously taken several recognize/act cycles in a single cycle. For example, if the system repeatedly executes the two productions

P1: if A and B, then C

and

P2: if C, then D and E,

then they could be combined into the single production

P3: if A and B, then D and E.

The next time that conditions A and B occur, the system will get to states D and E without going through the intermediate state C; it will thus get there in one step rather than two.

Composition was used by Lewis (1978) to account for two effects of practice observed with adults: speed-up and the Einstellung effect (Luchins, 1942). Its importance in a developmental context derives from the fact that, unlike discrimination and generalization, it does not depend directly on environmental feedback. The form of composition described above is based on the detection of repeated production sequences and is therefore *indirectly* dependent on what the system is encountering in the environment, but not in the sense of direct feedback about the correctness of a piece of processing. Furthermore, it is possible to do composition via a purely "syntactic" analysis cf the form of the production set, without any procedural-trace information.[21]

Domains of Application

Production systems that utilize these self-modification processes have been constructed to acquire knowledge in several different contexts, including: learning to solve algebra problems (Neves, 1978); learning to solve a puzzle by repeatedly doing it (Anzai and Simon, 1979); developing efficient procedures for arithmetic (Neches, 1984) and for concept learning, schema abstraction, and language acquisition (Anderson, Kline, and Beasley, 1980; Langley, 1980); and discovering descriptive laws (Langely, 1977). Langley, Neches, Neves, and Anzai (1981) give an integrative review of this work, and offer a general characterization of the different self-modifying mechanisms that have been used.

Neches' work is especially relevant. He has constructed a system called HPM (for "heuristic procedure modification") that elaborates the basic idea of composition. HPM has a set of potentially useful ways of transforming strategies to make them more efficient. These heuristics include things such as building units, deleting unnecessary steps, saving partial results (so that they need not be recomputed), and reordering sequential steps. The heuristics operate by observing the procedural trace and determining whether or not their application is appropriate. The most extensive application of HPM has been in the context of learning to add. HPM starts with a strategy that is equivalent to children's first-acquired addition process: counting out the augend, counting out the addend, and then counting out the entire set. By applying several of its heuristics, HPM eventually modifies this strategy to the more efficient "min model." It starts the count at the larger of the two arguments, and then "counts on" the additional amount determined by the minimum argument. The most important feature of this model is that *both strategies are correct*, so the system does not change because of feedback from the environment that some error has occurred. Rather, its internal heuristics, always seeking ways to make the system more efficient, detect the inefficiencies and redundancies automatically and act on them.

Self-Modification Mechanisms and Conservation Acquisition

The time-line analysis described previously led to three major effects: the increasing generality of time-line entries, the formation of productions embodying the full set of conservation rules, and the elaboration of tests for transformational classes. How do the self-modifying procedures just presented generate the necessary effects for conservation acquisition?

Generalization over time-line sequences is accomplished by processes similar to those described earlier. Overly general rules are corrected by discrimination processes. The entries in the time line represent productions at increasingly higher levels of abstraction and generality, as the regularity-detection mechanisms examine not only the tokens for each production system's execution, but also the productions that constitute the node referred to by the token in the time line. These mechanisms then construct higher-order nodes corresponding to the common elements in the combined systems.[22] These processes are closer in flavor to Neches' HPM than to any of the other systems I have described.

Rule formation via redundancy elimination is based on procedures very similar to the composition processes explained above. It is a process that functions without any explicit external direction. The elaboration of transformational classes is accomplished via discrimination (and generalization) processes that do depend on some sort of feedback about the adequacy of the current classification of observed transformations.

I have briefly outlined some systems that can modify their productions through processes such as generalization, discrimination, composition of related conditions, and chaining of action sequences. These mechanisms provide some of the basic building blocks for a self-modifying production system that, starting with no substantive knowledge about quantity beyond the rudimentary Q_s, ultimately "acquires" conservation.

In order to construct a production system that could acquire sufficient knowledge to "have" conservation, it has been necessary to formulate increasingly powerful production-system architectures. In particular, implementation of mechanisms to generate and analyze time-line entries has added considerable complexity to the simple production-system interpreter described at the outset of this paper. It is clear that production-system approaches to developmental theory represent a strategic bet that such complexity is the necessary price of combining specificity with developmental tractability. To the best of my knowledge, there are no other equally specific proposals for how self-modification might come about.

SELF-MODIFYING SYSTEMS: LEARNING OR DEVELOPMENT?

Having proposed self-modifying production systems as viable formalisms for a theory of cognitive development, I will conclude by addressing the difficult distinction between learning and development. One frequently stated evaluation of such systems is that they may account for learning, but they certainly do not capture the "essence" of development (cf. Beilin, 1981; Neisser, 1976). But what could be the basis of such an evaluation? If we look at the many dichotomies that have been used to distinguish learning from development, the self-modifying systems appear to be more appropriately placed in the development category than in the learning category.

• *Spontaneous versus imposed.* Much of development appears to occur "on its own," without any external agent instructing, inducing, or urging the change. So, too, for some of the self-modifying systems. Time-line processing occurs continuously, and results in changes whenever the system detects the appropriate circumstances. it has the flavor of the experience-contingent spontaneity that purportedly distinguishes development from learning.

• *Qualitative versus quantitative.* This distinction has occupied philosophers and developmentalists for many years, and I can only suggest one modest clarification. Look at a program that has undergone self-modification, and ask whether the change is quantitative or qualitative. For example, in the Anzai and Simon (1979) work, it seems to me that the change from depth-first search to a recursive strategy could only be characterized as qualitative, and hence more of a developmental change than a learning one. Similarly, in Neches' (1981) model of heuristic procedure modification, the system transforms an inefficient strategy for addition (counting out the augend, counting out the addend, and then counting out the total set) into an efficient one (starting with the maximum of the two arguments and then "counting on" the other argument). It is difficult to characterize this as simply a change in which more of some pre-existing feature is added to the system: "qualitative change" seems the appropriate designation.

• *Structural reorganization versus local change.* Developmental theories, particularly those with a strong emphasis on stages (cf. Fischer, 1980), usually demand structural reorganization as a requirement for development, while viewing local changes as the province of learning. Clearly, some of the basic mechanisms in self-modifying production systems operate on a relatively local basis. Indeed, one of the great advantages of production systems is that they do not require vast systemic knowledge of the consequences of local changes. But when we begin to look carefully at changes in information-processing systems, the distinction between "local" and "structural" changes becomes blurred. Changing a few conditions in an existing production (a local change) may radically alter the firing sequence of it and all its previous successors, producing very different patterns of activation in working memory and in the time line. This in turn would result in different patterns of regularities being detected in the time line, and, ultimately, in a different set of generalizations and rules. Thus, from local changes come global effects, and from incremental modifications come structural reorganizations.[23]

• *Reflective abstraction versus practice with knowledge of results.* The systems described in this chapter constitute a very different class of models from earlier models of paired-associate learning (Feigenbaum, 1963) or concept learning (Gregg and Simon, 1967). Such models were clearly intended to account for learning in situations with externally supplied feedback about the correctness of the current state of the system. The self-modifying production systems do not necessarily get this sort of explicit feedback from the environment. Instead, many of the processes that seek pattern and regularity in the time line are completely self-contained, in the sense that they examine the trace of the system's own encodings in the absence of any clear indications of a "right" or "wrong" response. As noted earlier, the time-line processes can be viewed as a mechanization of Piaget's "reflective abstraction."

These dichotomies are not independent, nor do they exhaust the possible contrasts between learning and development. This listing should suffice, however, to show that at the level at which such contrasts are stated, there is little basis for the claim that information-processing models in general, or self-modifying production systems in particular, are inherently inadequate to capture the essence of cognitive development. This chapter is an argument for just the opposite point of view. Information-processing theories of the sort described here provide us with a powerful new language with which to write the answer to the opening question: "How do children transit from one state to another in the course of their development?"

NOTES

[1] The distinction between what is static and what is dynamic depends on the "grain" of the time interval being considered. An excellent discussion of the structure/process dichotomy and its implications for developmental psychology can be found in Newell (1973).

[2] This early state of the art led to a lot of erroneous assertions about the inherent limitations of information-processing models. For a positive and constructive response to those criticisms, see Kail and Bisanz (1983).

[3] The view of conservation acquisition presented here summarizes and extends my earlier work with J. G. Wallace (Klahr and Wallace, 1973, 1976).

[4] There are two classes of conservation tasks. In *equivalence conservation* (EC), there are two equal collections at the outset, and one of them is transformed. In *identity conservation* (IC), there is only collection, and the comparison is made between its initial and its final values (Elkind, 1967).

[5] Previously, we called these "quantification operators." Gelman has used both "estimators" (Gelman, 1972b) and "numerosity abstractors" (Gelman and Gallistel, 1978) for the same processes. Thus, the literature contains the somewhat confusing reference to subitizing and counting as two kinds of estimators. In this chapter the term "quantifier" includes the terms subitizing, counting, and estimation.

[6] Previously (Klahr and Wallace, 1976), we called this a "perceptual" transformation.

[7] More appropriately called "nonconservation rules."

[8] Although the details of these particular results—such as the exact location of the break and the linearity of the lower curve—have been subject to some strident critism (Allport, 1975), the basic conclusion is sound: subitizing and counting are different processes.

[9] See Cooper (1984) and Strauss and Curtis (1984) for the most recent work on this question:

[10] See the discussion of relative-magnitude determination in Klahr and Wallace, 1976, pp. 74–76.

[11] Our view that primitive forms of subitizing are closely tied to the specific quantitative context will be challenged if preliminary results by Starkey and Spelke (1981) turn out to be reliable. The found that for $n = 2$ or 3, infants can do cross-modal matching between simultaneous visual and sequential auditory patterns. This would argue for a highly abstract representation of small quantities.

[12] The time-line notion is more fully described in Klahr and Wallace 1976. There are formidable problems in implementing it in general form, but it has been applied in the context of arithmetic-strategy transformations (Neches, 1981), and it has been partially implemented for the conservation-acquisition domain described in this chapter (Wallace, 1979; Wallace, Klahr, and Bluff, 1984). An important feature of self-modifying production systems is their ability to represent and examine their own "procedural traces" (Langley, Neches, Neves, and Anzai, 1981), or, in our terms, to generate and analyze a time line.

[13] In order to simplify the discussion, only the identity-conservation sequences will be described at this point. The basic mechanisms for the acquisition of equivalence-conservation rules are the same as those to be described here.

[14] As the semantics of the transformations become encoded in the time line, the Q_s symbols can acquire the appropriate orderings as a function of the effects of transformations upon their comparison operation. A full discussion of this issue would take us too far afield at this point. All we need to assume is that the system can discriminate quantity-preserving transformations from others, be they addition or subtraction.

[15] Cowan has also concluded that the rules for identity conservation are acquired prior to those for equivalence conservation.

[16] Acredolo (1981) offers an interesting version of this position, in what he calls an "identity theory" of conservation acquisition.

[17] No such expectations would be formed with respect to *continuous* quantity (for example, length or density), because the en-

codings generated by rudimentary forms of Q_e are not sufficiently reliable at this point for any regularities to be detected. This is one reason why the children in the "magic" studies were not surprised by surreptitious changes in length or density. Another reason why the children were surprised by unexpected changes in number but not in length or density is that in the training phase of these studies, the children clearly established number as the discriminating feature between "winners" and "losers." Once the basis of the discrimination was removed, the children were surprised.

[18] The expectation of quantity permanence is implicit in infant habituation studies also. The increased attention to quantitative change (but not to changes in length, density, and so on) suggests that infants have similar expectations about discrete quantity not changing in the absence of some observed transformation.

[19] Siegler has proposed a similar sequence of conservation models. His are necessarily more complex because they include tests for the size of the collection and because they are descriptions of the equivalence-conservation paradigm, rather than the identity-conservation situation discussed here.

[20] See Langley (1983) for a discussion of the history of generalization and discrimination programs.

[21] Composition poses some very difficult and still unresolved problems that get to the core of the status of production systems as psychological theories. An elegant treatment of some fundamental issues can be found in Lewis (1984).

[22] See Wallace, Klahr, and Bluff (1984) for a detailed description of thse processes.

[23] There is no paradox here: poets have long been sensitive to the profound effects of local decisions:

Two roads diverged in a wood, and I—
I took the one less traveled by,
And that has made all the difference.

Robert Frost

REFERENCES

Acredolo, C. Acquisition of conservation: A clarification of Piagetian terminology, some recent findings, and an alternative formulation. *Human Development*, 1981, 24, 120–137.

Allport, D. A. The state of cognitive psychology. *Quarterly Journal of Experimental Psychology*, 1975, 27, 141–152.

Anderson, J. R., and Kline, P. J. A learning system and its psychological implications. In *Proceedings of the Sixth International Joint Conference on Artificial Intelligence*, Tokyo, Japan, 1979.

Anderson, J. R., Kline, P. J., and Beasley, C. M., Jr. Complex learning processes. In R. E. Snow, P.-A. Federico, and W. E. Montague (Eds.), *Aptitude, learning, and instruction: Cognitive process analyses*, Vol. II. Hillsdale, N.J.: Erlbaum, 1980.

Anzai, Y., and Simon, H. A. The theory of learning by doing. *Psychological Review*, 1979, *86*, 124–140.

Baylor, G. W., and Gascon, J. An information processing theory of aspects of the development of weight seriation in children. *Cognitive Psychology*, 1974, *6*, 1–40.

Beilin, H. Piaget and the new functionalism. Address given at the Eleventh Symposium of the Piaget Society, Philadelphia, 1981.

Bower, G. H. Cognitive psychology: An introduction. In W. K. Estes (Ed.), *Handbook of learning and cognitive processes*, Vol. I. Hillsdale, N.J.: Erlbaum, 1975.

Brown, A. L. Knowing when, where, and how to remember: A problem of metacognition. In R. Glaser (Ed.), *Advances in instructional psychology*, Vol. 1. Hillsdale, N.J.: Erlbaum, 1978.

Bullock, M., and Gelman, R. Numerical reasoning in young children: The ordering principle. *Child Development*, 1977, *48*, 427–434.

Case, R. *Intellectual development: A systematic reinterpretation*. New York: Academic Press, 1983.

Chase, W. G. Elementary information processes. In W. K. Estes (Ed.), *Handbook of learning and cognitive processes*, Vol. 5. Hillsdale, N.J.: Erlbaum, 1978.

Chi, M. T. H. Short-term memory limitations in children: Capacity or processing deficits? *Memory and cognition*, 1976, *4*, 559–572.

Chi, M. T. H., and Klahr, D. Span and rate of apprehension in children and adults. *Journal of Experimental Child Psychology*, 1975, *19*, 434–439.

Cooper, R. G. Early number development: discovering number space with addition and subtraction. In C. Sophian (Ed.) *The origins of cognitive skills*. Hillsdale, New Jersey, Erlbaum, 1984.

Cowan, R. A reappraisal of the relation between performances of quantitative identity and quantitative equivalence conservation tasks. *Journal of Experimental Child Psychology*, 1979, *28*, 68–80.

Elkind, D. Piaget's conservation problems. *Child Development*, 1967, *38*, 15–27.

Estes, K. W. Nonverbal discrimination of more and fewer elements by children. *Journal of Experimental Child Psychology*, 1976, *21*, 393–405.

Feigenbaum, E. A. The simulation of verbal learning behavior. In E. A. Feigenbaum and J. Feldman (Eds.), *Computers and thought*. New York: McGraw-Hill, 1963.

Fischer, K. W. A theory of cognitive development: The control and construction of hierarchies of skills. *Psychological Review*, 1980, *87*, 477–531.

Forgy, C. L. *The OPS74 reference manual* (Tech. rep.). Department of Computer Science, Carnegie-Mellon University, 1979.

Gelman, R. The nature and development of early number concepts. In H. W. Reese (Ed.), *Advances in child development*, Vol. 7. New York: Academic Press, 1972a.

Gelman, R. Logical capacity of very young children: Number invariance rules. *Child Development*, 1972b, *43*, 75–90.

Gelman, R., and Gallistel, C. R. *The child's understanding of number.* Cambridge, Mass.: Harvard University Press, 1978.

Gelman, R., and Tucker, M. F. Further investigations of the young child's conception of number. *Child Development*, 1975, *46*, 167–175.

Gentner, D. Evidence for the psychological reality of semantic components: The verbs of possession. In D. A. Norman and D. E. Rumelhart (Eds.), *Explorations in cognition.* San Francisco: W. H. Freeman and Company, 1975.

Greeno, J. G., Riley, M. S., and Gelman, R. Conceptual competence in children's counting. *Cognitive Psychology.* In press.

Gregg, L. W., and Simon, H. A. Process models and stochastic theories of simple concept formation. *Journal of Mathematical Psychology*, 1967, *4*, 246–276.

Haith, M. M. *Rules that babies look by.* Hillsdale, N.J.: Erlbaum, 1980.

Halford, G. S. Children's ability to interpret transformations of a qunatity, I: An operational system for judging combinations of transformations. *Canadian Journal of Psychology*, 1975, *29*, 124–141.

Hunt, E. What kind of computer is man? *Cognitive Psychology*, 1971, *2*, 57–98.

Kail, R., and Bisanz, J. Information processing and cognitive development. In H. W. Reese (Ed.), *Advances in child development and behavior*, Vol. 17. New York: Academic Press, 1983.

Klahr, D., and Robinson, M. Formal assessment of problem solving and planning processes in preschool children. *Cognitive Psychology*, 1981, *13*, 113–148.

Klahr, D., and Siegler, R. S. The representation of children's knowledge. In H. W. Reese and L. P. Lipsitt (Eds.), *Advances in child development*, Vol. 12. New York: Academic Press, 1978.

Klahr, D., and Wallace, J. G. Class inclusion processes. In S. Farnham-Diggory (Ed.), *Information processing in children.* New York: Academic Press, 1972.

Klahr, D., and Wallace, J. G. The role of quantification operators in the development of conservation of quantity. *Cognitive Psychology*, 1973, *4*, 301–327.

Klahr, D., and Wallace, J. G. *Cognitive development: An information processing view.* Hillsdale, N.J.: Erlbaum, 1976.

Langley, P. W. BACON: A production system that discovers natural laws. In *Proceedings of the Fifth International Joint Conference on Artificial Intelligence,* Cambridge, Mass.: MIT Press, 1977.

Langley, P. Finding common paths as a learning mechanism. Unpublished manuscript, Carnegie-Mellon University, 1980.

Langley, P. A general theory of discrimination learning. In D. Klahr, P. Langley, and R. Neches (Eds.), *Production system: models of learning and development.* Cambridge, Mass.: MIT Press/Bradford Books, 1984.

Langley, P., Neches, R., Neves, D. M., and Anzai, Y. A domain-independent framework for procedure learning. *Policy Analysis and Information Systems,* 1981, 4(2), 163–197.

Lewis, C. H. *Production system models of practice effects.* Ph.D. thesis, University of Michigan, 1978.

Lewis, C. Composition of productions. In D. Klahr, P. Langley, and R. Neches (Eds.), *Production system models of learning and development.* Cambridge, Mass.: MIT Press/Bradford Books, 1984.

Luchins, A. S. Mechanization in problem solving—The effects of "Einstellung." *Psychological Monographs,* 1942, 54(248),

McLaughlin, J. A. Development of children's ability to judge relative numerosity. *Journal of Experimental Child Psychology,* 1981, 31, 103–114.

Mandler, J. M. Representation. In P. Mussen (Ed.), *Manual of child psychology,* Vol. 2. New York: Wiley, 1982.

Neches, R. *Learning through incremental refinement of procedures* in D. Klahr, P. Langley, and R. Neches (Ed.) *Production system models of learning and development.* Cambridge, Mass.: MIT Press/Bradford Books, 1984.

Neisser, U. General, academic and artificial intelligence. In L. B. Resnick (Ed.), *The nature of intelligence.* Hillsdale, N.J.: Erlbaum, 1976.

Nelson, K. How children represent knowledge of their world in and out of language: A preliminary report. In R. S. Siegler (Ed.), *Children's thinking: What develops?* Hillsdale, N.J.: Erlbaum, 1978.

Neves, D. A computer program that learns algebraic procedures by examining examples and working problems in a textbook. In *Proceedings of the Second National Conference of the Canadian Society of Computational Studies of Intelligence,* Toronto, Canada, 1978.

Newell, A. Production systems: Models of control structures. In W. G. Chase (Ed.), *Visual information processing.* New York: Academic Press, 1973.

Newman, D., Riel, M., and Martin, L. M. W. Cultural practices and Piagetian theory: The impact of a cross-cultural research program. In D. Kuhn and J. A. Meacham (Eds.), *On the development of developmental psychology.* Basel, Switzerland: Karger, 1982.

Palmer, S. Hierarchical structure in perceptual representation. *Cognitive Psychology*, 1977, 9, 441–474.

Pascual-Leone, J. A mathematical model for the transition rule in Piaget's developmental stages. *Acta Psychologica*, 1970, 32, 301–345.

Piaget, J. *The child's conception of number.* New York: Humanities Press, 1952. (C. Gattegno and F. M. Hodgson, Trans.; original French edition, 1941.)

Piaget, J. Intellectual evolution from adolescence to adulthood. *Human Development*, 1972, 15, 1–12.

Piaget, T. *Biology and knowledge.* Trans. B. Walsh. Chicago: University of Chicago Press, 1971.

Schaeffer, B., Eggleston, V. H., and Scott, J. L. Number development in young children. *Cognitive Psychology*, 1974, 6, 357–379.

Siegel, L. S. The sequence of development of certain number concepts in pre-school children. *Developmental Psychology*, 1971, 5, 357–361.

Siegel, L. S. The cognitive basis of the comprehension and production of relational terminology. *Journal of Experimental Child Psychology*, 1977, 24, 40–52.

Siegler, R. S. Three aspects of cognitive development. *Cognitive Psychology*, 1976, 8(4), 481–520.

Siegler, R. S. Developmental sequences within and between concepts. *Monographs of the Society for Research in Child Development*, 1981, 46(2, Serial no. 189).

Siegler, R. S., and Robinson, M. The development of numerical understandings. In H. W. Reese and L. P. Lipsitt (Eds.), *Advances in child development and behavior*, Vol. 16. New York: Academic Press, 1981.

Silverman, I. W., and Briga, J. By what process do young children solve small number conservation problems? *Journal of Experimental Child Psychology*, 1981, 32, 115–126.

Silverman, I. W., and Rose, A. P. Compensation and conservation. *Psychological Bulletin*, 1982, 91(1), 80–101.

Spitz, H. H., and Borys, S. V. Depth of search: How far can the retarded search through an internally represented problem space? In R. Sperber, C. McCauley, and P. Brooks (Eds.), *Learning and cognition in the mental retarded.* Baltimore, University Park Press, 1984.

Starkey, P., and Cooper, R. G., Jr. Numerosity perception in human infants. *Science*, 1980, 210, 1033.

Starkey, P., and Spelke, E. Infants can enumerate objects and events. Paper presented at the 22nd Annual Meeting of the Psychonomic Society, Philadelphia, November, 1981.

Starkey, P., Spelke, E., and Gelman, R. Number competence in infants: Sensitivity to numeric invariance and numeric change. Paper presented at the International Conference on Infant Studies, New Haven, Conn., 1980.

Stein, N. L., and Glenn, C. G. An analysis of story comprehension in elementary school children. In R. Freedle (Ed.), *Multidisciplinary approaches to discourse comprehension.* Norwood, N.J.: Ablex, 1977.

Sternberg, R. J. *Intelligence, information processing, and analogical reasoning: The componential analysis of human abilities.* Hillsdale, N.J.: Erlbaum, 1977.

Strauss, M. S., and Curtis, L. E. Infant perception of numerosity. *Child Development,* 1981, *52,* 1146–1152.

Strauss, M. S. and Curtis, L. E. *Development of numerical concepts in infancy.* In C. Sophian (Ed.) *The origins of cognitive skills.* Hillsdale, N.J. Erlbaum, 1984.

Van Oeffelen, M. P., and Vos, P. G. Configuration effects on the enumeration of dots: Counting by groups. *Memory and Cognition,* 1982, *10,* 396–404.

Wallace, J. G. Towards a sufficient theory of transition of cognitive development. In *Proceedings of the Fifth Bienniel Congress of the International Society for the Study of Behavioral Development,* University of Lund, Sweden, 1979.

Wallace, J. G., Klahr, D., and Bluff, K. A self-modifying production system for conservation acquisition. In D. Klahr, P. Langley, and R. Neches (Eds.), *Production system models of learning and development.* Cambridge, Mass.: MIT Press/Bradford Books, 1984.

Waterman, D. Adaptive production systems. In *Proceedings of the Fourth International Joint Conference on Artificial Intelligence.* Cambridge, Mass.: Artifical Intelligence Laboratory, M.I.T., 1975.

Waugh, N. C., and Norman, D. A. Primary memory. *Psychological Review,* 1965, *72,* 89–104.

Young, R. M. *Seriation by children: An artificial intelligence analysis of a Piagetian task.* Basel, Switzerland: Birkhauser, 1976.

Young, R. M., and O'Shea, T. Errors in children's subtraction. *Cognitive Science,* 1981, *5,* 153–177.

6 Mechanisms of Cognitive Growth: Variation and Selection

Robert S. Siegler

[W] hen Bob Sternberg invited me to write a chapter about mechanisms of development, my first reaction was; "That's a really important issue. Too bad I don't know more about it." I started to write Bob a "thanks but no thanks' letter. While writing, however, I recalled that in a recent review article (Siegler, 1983), I had asserted that no one knew much about mechanisms of development, and that expanding our knowledge in this area should be given high priority. There seemed to be a chicken-and-egg problem, with lack of knowledge discouraging efforts to learn more, and lack of efforts to learn more preventing knowledge from accumulating. The circle could be broken only by efforts to accumulate knowledge, even if the initial attempts were not totally successful. Therefore, with some trepidation, I accepted the invitation.

Historically, understanding of scientific mechanisms has often benefited from analogies to domains in which mechanisms were better understood. For this reason, I started thinking about domains in which a sophisticated understanding of mechanisms had been attained, to see if they might suggest useful ideas about development. The first domain that came to mind was auto mechanics. Certainly, the mechanisms by which internal-combustion engines operate are well known. This analogy seemed unlikely to aid understanding of cognitive development, however. The problem was not so much the obvious differences between minds and engines as it was differences in our current understanding of the two types of devices. Understanding of internal-combustion engines rests on a firm structural base. We can understand such engines because we know what carburetors are and what they do, because we know what pistons are and what they do, because we know what spark plugs are and what they do, and so on. Unfortunately, we do not comprehend the structure of the mind in a way even remotely akin to our understanding of the structure of these engines. What seemed to be needed for a productive analogy, therefore, was a domain in which an understanding of mechanisms had been attained without a sophisticated understanding of underlying structure.

Evolutionary biology, at least the evolutionary biology of the nineteenth century, met this specification. When Darwin formulated

This research was supported by grants from the National Institute of Child Health and Human Development, from the Spencer Foundation, and from the National Institute of Education.

his theory of evolution, he knew almost nothing about the genetic structures on which evolution is based. Instead, the theory sprang from several macroscopic observations: variation among individuals, competition for scarce resources, extinction of previous species, relations among existing species, the passage of huge amounts of time in the earth's history, the introduction of new species, and so on. The qualitative nature of these observations, and Darwin's ignorance about the structural bases that gave rise to several of them, seem more comparable to our knowledge of cognition than does our knowledge of internal-combustion engines.

In this paper I will explore the usefulness of the evolutionary analogy for our understanding of mechanisms of psychological development. First, I will examine how the analogy has been used in psychology and in other social sciences. Next, I will argue that at least for understanding cognitive psychological development, a quite general level of analogy may be the most appropriate. Finally, I will describe research that illustrates the usefulness of the evolutionary analogy.

EVOLUTIONARY EXPLANATIONS IN THE SOCIAL SCIENCES

The questions that motivated Darwin's theory of biological evolution can be and have been extrapolated to cultural and societal development. What is the goal of evolution: is evolution striving for some optimal state, or is it merely a succession of local adaptations? What or who does the selecting? At what level does evolution operate: at the level of the individual, at the level of groups of individuals, or at some level within each individual? Is the variation mechanism independent of or dependent on the selection mechanism; in other words, is evolution blind or insightful? Finally, what is the role of an individual's worldly experience in the evolutionary process?

Although many social scientists have drawn evolutionary analogies, these analogies have been surprisingly limited. The main mechanisms of biological variation—mutation and recombination—are uncorrelated with the criteria along which selection occurs; however, few theories of economic, social, or behavioral evolution suggest that innovations are attempted without regard to their adaptiveness (Van Parijs, 1981). Biological selection is done at the level of individual reproduction; cultural selection is done at the level of group identification; cognitive evolution takes place at the level of concepts within individual minds. The time periods over which biological, social, and cognitive evolution occur obviously differ vastly. Even in aspects of the analogy that could be easily maintained, social scientists have often chosen different paths. Social scientists could have followed biologists in arguing that there is no goal of evolution, only a series of adjustments to changing environments. Simon's (1962/1981) concept of "satisficing" is one prominent case in which a social scientific approach did follow such a notion of "goal-less" evolution. In other well-known cases, however, social scientists have felt free to postulate specific evolutionary goals. For example, Piaget (1978) has argued that intellectual evolution is goal-directed, with the goal being "to increase the living organism's capacities" (p. 142). In economics, Leontiades (1980) has argued that firms have evolved toward a goal of the conglomerate form; this form is best adapted in an absolute sense because it allows maximum freedom to deploy capital and to weather business cycles.

Actually, only the broadest of analogies to biological evolution seems to be maintained in many social scientific theories that call themselves evolutionary: that there is a source of variation, that there is a source of selection, and that variation and selection together produce adaptation. It is possible that social science might benefit from tighter analogies to biological evolution. However, given the large number of economists (Hirshleifer, 1977; Leontiades, 1980; Nelson and Winter, 1978), sociologists and social psychologists (Campbell, 1975; Durkheim, 1912; Van Parijs, 1981), and philosophers, linguists, and cognitive psychologists (Dennett, 1978; Hockett, 1967; Popper, 1974) who have considered evolutionary analogies and eventually opted for relatively loose ones, the formulation of tight and revealing analogies seems unlikely. Instead, it may be most useful to adopt the global evolutionary analogy and, beyond this, to concentrate on what the mechanisms of variation and selection look like in particular domains. In the domain of cognitive development, feedback from the physical and social environments provide straightforward selection mechanisms. The means by which variations are produced are less clear, however. Therefore, in the remainder of this paper, I will consider how a variation mechanism might operate in the domain of children's conceptual development.

ENCODING AND COMBINATION AS SOURCES OF COGNITIVE VARIATION

Perhaps the simplest plausible model of cognitive variation involves two processes: encoding and combination. People could encode features of the world and combine subsets of them into conjunctive, disjunctive, prototypic, configural, or other relations. If existing rules generated inaccurate predictions, people would recombine the features into new relations. Such a model is implicit both in classical concept-formation theories (such as those of Haygood and Bourne,

1965; Levine, 1966) and in more recent featural theories (for example, those of Anderson, Kline, and Beasley, 1980; Smith, 1978).

These models of concept formation seem intuitively reasonable, but they may underestimate the complexity of the encoding process. The focus of the models is almost exclusively on combination; new concepts are equated with new combinations of a fixed set of features.[1] However, developmental studies of a variety of types attest that the world is not neatly divided into clear features a priori. Large changes occur, with age and experience, in the features that people use to represent objects and events. These changes influence the concepts that people can form. Thus, a comprehensive model of variation must focus on encoding as well as combination.

To appreciate the role of encoding, consider an anecdote from the history of art. Pablo Picasso painted a portrait of Gertrude Stein. An observer looked at the painting for several minutes and then commented that it did not look much like Stein. "No matter," Picasso is said to have answered. "It will."

Bransford (1979) has more directly described the role of encoding in concept formation:

> Imagine that a speaker says, "Notice the sepia," while pointing to a complex painting. Unless you know that sepia refers to a color (and more specifically, to a brownish color), you will have difficulty understanding what the speaker means. Wittgenstein argues that even learning by ostensive definition (for example, hearing "This is red" while seeing someone point to a red object) presupposes that one has some knowledge of what the ostensibly defined object is supposed to be an example of (in this case color). Knowledge that a word refers to the category "color" affects one's understanding of the objects of the pointing gesture, which in turn may increase one's understanding of what counts as red. (p. 222)

In many contexts, the term "encoding" is used interchangeably with "representation." In my usage, the terms are related but not synonymous. An encoding is the set of features by which a stimulus is described in a particular situation. A representation is the set of features by which a stimulus is described in long-term memory. The two are often not identical. Relevant information from long-term memory may be omitted from an encoding of a stimulus in a particular situation. For example, Sternberg (1977) presented the analogy problem

Washington:1 :: Lincoln:?,

for which possible answers are (a) 10 or (b) 5. This problem is difficult, not because the relevant information is absent from long-term-memory representations of Washington and Lincoln (whose faces are on $1 and $5 bills), but rather because the relevant information is not included in most people's encoding of the analogy problem. On the other hand, an encoding may contain features that are absent from long-term memory; such features may be created at the time the stimulus is presented. Illustratively, Pellegrino and Glaser (1982) presented college students with the analogy

$$15:19 \ :: \ 8:12 \ :: \ 5:?.$$

It seems unlikely that the students' long-term-memory representations of the number 19 included the property "is 4 more than 15" prior to the presentation of this problem. In the analogy test situation, however, 19 probably was encoded in this way.

Several artificial-intelligence investigators have recently suggested means by which changes in encoding might influence concept acquisition (Holland and Reitman, Note 1; Langley, 1981; Lenat, 1977). For example, Holland and Reitman illustrated how a process roughly analogous to biological evolution might operate. Their model of the learner's knowledge was a production system. Each production included a string of 1s and 0s on the condition side (the system's encoding of the environment), and another string of 1s and 0s on the action side (the response the system would make if the contents of short-term memory matched that encoding). Each production was also associated in varying "strengths" with attainment of the system's goal; these associations were strengthened when the production "fired" as part of a sequence that led to goal attainment. Periodically, two productions with different 1s and 0s on the condition side but with the same sequence on the action side were selected to be "parent productions."[2] For example, two parent productions were

$$1 \ 0 \ 1 \rightarrow 0 \ 1 \ 0 \quad \text{and} \quad 0 \ 0 \ 0 \rightarrow 0 \ 1 \ 0.$$

New productions were engendered by making an arbitrary cut in corresponding positions on the condition sides of the two parent productions, and then combining the symbols to the left of the cut in one production with the symbols to the right of the cut in the other. This created productions with new encodings of the environment. In the above two productions, making a cut between the second and third position on the condition side gave birth to the productions

$$0 \ 0 \ 1 \rightarrow 0 \ 1 \ 0 \quad \text{and} \quad 1 \ 0 \ 0 \rightarrow 0 \ 1 \ 0.$$

One of these newborn productions was chosen arbitrarily for inclusion in the production system and replaced a production that was weakly associated with goal attainment. Holland and Reitman reported that this mechanism for creating new encodings greatly increased the efficiency with which their model learned in an artificial environment. The mechanism also allowed the model to learn in a new environment in which it had no direct experience.

Cognitive psychological investigators also have used the encoding construct. Investigations of expertise in such areas as chess (Chase and Simon, 1973), the game Go (Reitman, 1976), physics (Larkin, McDermott, Simon, and Simon, 1980), and radiology (Lesgold, Feltovich, Glaser, and Wang, 1981) have indicated that the features that experts encode differ dramatically from those encoded by less knowledgeable individuals. In children's cognitive development, encoding skills may play an even larger role. The concepts of artists, radiologists, scientists, and chess and Go masters are well adapted to their domains of expertise. Such individuals have spent many years developing encodings that capture the useful features of their task environments. Young children, in contrast, frequently find themselves in task environments about which they know little or nothing. Tasks as mundane as learning to encode the first digit of school room numbers (for example, the 2 in Room 206) as communicating different information than the next two numbers; as learning to encode the words on street signs rather than the appearance of houses, in deciding where to turn off the main road on the walk home from school; and as learning to distinguish those typographic features that are of practical importance from those that serve only esthetic purposes; and so on. Thus, it seems essential to consider encoding as well as combination in thinking about cognitive variation.

A Framework for Considering Encoding and Combination

Figure 6-1 diagrams a simple framework that is useful in thinking about cognitive variation. Variation is divided into two parts: encoding and combination. Encoding is further divided into value-monitoring and feature-construction processes, whereas combination is divided into feature-selection, feature-integration, and rule-execution processes.

Each box at the lowest level of the framework corresponds to a specific function in the working of the variation mechanism. On the encoding side, *value monitoring* means keeping track of the values of features that are being encoded. *Feature construction* involves producing new features for use in mental representations. On the combination side, *feature selection* entails choosing which features, from among the set of all the encoded features, to incorporate into

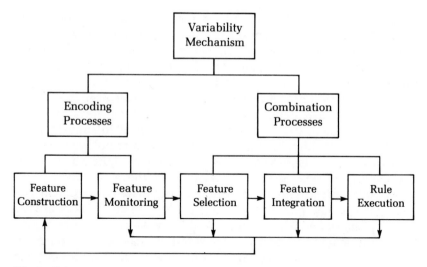

Figure 6-1
A framework for considering cognitive variation.

the rule that will produce behavior. *Feature integration* involves selecting among alternative organizations the features that will be used in the rule. Finally, in *rule execution*, people insert values of selected features into the organization they have chosen, to produce judgments, predictions, and other behaviors.

The part of this analysis that may be the most difficult to grasp intuitively is feature construction. Encoding of features is most often considered at an elementary level—at the level of horizontal, vertical, straight, and curved lines. Capacity to encode such features is almost certainly a biologically given property of humans; no construction is necessary. In the present context, however, the term "feature" is used to denote any component of a representation. When features are viewed in this way, it becomes apparent that features must often be built from more basic units before they can be encoded. For example, Shepard (1982) found that his most musical subjects based judgments of the similarity of two tones on such features as whether the tones were separated by a major fifth. In contrast, his least musical subjects did not view tones that were separated by a fifth as being at all similar. The ability to encode features such as "separated by a fifth" clearly is not a physiological given; such features must be assembled from more basic units.

I shall now describe several recent empirical studies within the framework of the proposed variation mechanism. In some ways, the presentation may seem like old wine in new bottles. Most of the empirical work has been reported previously (Siegler, 1976, 1981), and the experiments were not developed within any self-consciously evolutionary framework. The framework may be helpful, however, in placing the empirical findings in a richer context and in clarifying their theoretical implications. Since one of the purposes of thinking about mechanisms is to unify superficially diverse phenomena, it seems worthwhile to reconsider the experiments from the perspective of this new framework.

Value Monitoring.   The series of experiments that I will consider in greatest detail analyzed children's performance on a variant of Inhelder and Piaget's (1958) balance-scale task. The balance-scale apparatus that I used was a two-arm balance with several pegs located at equal intervals along each arm. Metal weights could be placed on any of these pegs. The child's task was to determine whether the arm would tip right, tip left, or remain level if a lever that held it motionless were released.

I found that the children solved the balance-scale problems by using one of four rules (Siegler, 1976). Children using Rule I considered only a single dimension: the amount of weight on each side. Those using Rule II proceeded similarly if the amount of weight differed on the two sides, but if the amount was the same they also considered distance from the fulcrum. A child using Rule III always considered both the amount of weight on each side and the distance of the weight from the fulcrum. If the values of either dimension or both were equal, the child performed the appropriate qualitative comparison. However, if one side had more weight and the other side had its weight farther from the fulcrum, the child muddled through or guessed. Finally, children who used Rule IV always answered correctly. When qualitative comparisons could yield a determinate answer, they solved problems in the same way as Rule III children. When one side had more weight and the other more distance from the fulcrum, they computed the torques on each side by multiplying the amount of weight by the weight's distance from the fulcrum, and then compared the torques on the two sides.

In the initial balance-scale experiment, 5-, 9-, 13-, and 17-year-olds were presented problems and asked to predict which side, if either, would go down (Siegler, 1976, Experiment 1). A rule-assessment method was used to determine the strategy that the children used to make their predictions. The results indicated that almost all the 5-year-olds used Rule I, in which they considered only the weight dimension in making their predictions; that the 9-year-olds most often used Rule II, in which they always considered weight and also distance when the weights were equal; and that the 13- and the 17-

year-olds usually used Rule III, in which they always considered weight and distance, solved problems correctly when the values of one or both dimensions were equal, and "muddled through" when one side had more weight and the other more distance. At no age was Rule IV, the torque rule, widely used. This rule sequence indicated that in making their predictions, the 5-year-olds relied on a single dimension, weight, and that the older children relied on both weight and distance.

The results might also have been interpreted as indicating that the Rule I users monitored only a single dimension, whereas the older children monitored two dimensions. This conclusion was indirectly challenged, however, in a second experiment reported in Siegler (1976). In this experiment, 5- and 8-year-olds who used Rule I on a pretest were chosen to participate. Then children of both ages were presented feedback problems in which the balance-scale lever was released after the children made their predictions. In this way, they could learn whether their predictions had been correct. The condition of greatest interest in the present context involved feedback problems whose solutions required a rule considerably more advanced than the children's existing approaches. Although most of the 8-year-olds who were given such problems advanced from Rule I to Rule III, not one of the 5-year-olds advanced beyond Rule I. This finding indirectly challenged the view that all children who used Rule I monitored only the weight dimension. Either the feedback problems caused the 8-year-olds to monitor distance from the fulcrum (or perhaps caused them to construct and then monitor it), or the older children had monitored distance from the outset, despite not using it in their predictive rule.

A direct measure of encoding helped in distinguishing between these possibilities. We presented 5- and 8-year-olds a balance-scale configuration of weights on pegs. Then the scale was hidden from sight and a second, identical scale was displayed. The task was to reproduce on the second scale the arrangement of weights on pegs that had been observed on the first. An advantage of this approach was that it allowed independent assessment of encoding of weight and distance from the fulcrum. A child could place the correct number of weights on each side of the fulcrum, could place the weights the correct distance from the fulcrum, could do both, or could do neither.

It was found that the 5-year-olds encoded only weight. They placed the correct number of weights on each side more than three times as often as they placed the weights the correct distance from the fulcrum. In contrast, the 8-year-olds' encoding of weight and distance was quite comparable; they encoded both features accurately. However, when children of both ages were presented the standard predictions test, both the 5- and the 8-year-olds predominantly used the weight rule.

Viewed within the Figure 6-1 framework, this finding indicated a clear difference between the features that the 8-year-olds had monitored (weight and distance from the fulcrum), and the features that they used in executing their performance rule (only weight). The results of the encoding assessment also indicated that the 8-year-olds did not need to construct a new feature in the course of the feedback problems, but rather that they entered the feedback session already monitoring both weight and distance. The 5-year-olds, on the other hand, appeared to monitor only a single feature and to use only that feature in their predictive rule. It was uncertain at this point whether they had constructed distance from the fulcrum as a feature and simply were not monitoring it, or whether they had not constructed it as a feature to which they could attend.

To determine whether they had constructed this feature, we told a new group of 5-year-olds that it was important to attend to two aspects of the balance scale: amount of weight and distance from the fulcrum. Then the children's encoding and predictive performance were assessed. Presumably, if children already had constructed distance from the fulcrum but were not monitoring it, this brief attention-directing statement would allow them to reproduce both features accurately. On the other hand, if they had not constructed distance from the fulcrum, the brief instructions would not teach them how to do so.

The instructions had little effect; again, the 5-year-olds failed to accurately encode distance from the fulcrum. The failure of these simple instructions to lead children to encode distance from the fulcrum suggested that they had not constructed this feature as one that they could monitor.

From this perspective, the 5-year-olds' earlier inability to learn from the feedback problems seemed less surprising than it had initially. To learn, 5-year-olds would need to construct distance from the fulcrum as a feature, to monitor it, to select it for inclusion in their performance rule, and to integrate it with weight to form a rule that they could execute. This analysis suggested that the 5-year-olds' ability to learn from feedback might be aided by a divide-and-conquer strategy. In situations in which a feature that is needed in a performance rule has not yet been constructed, it may often be valuable to help children construct the feature first, without any direct effort to help them integrate it into a performance rule. This may reduce the learning task to more manageable units.

Feature Construction.   To help 5-year-olds construct distance from
the fulcrum as a feature, explicit instruction in both what to encode
and how to encode seemed likely to be useful. Therefore, a new group
of 5-year-olds was selected. They were told first to count the disks
on the left side of the fulcrum, then to count the number of pegs
those disks were away from the fulcrum, then to rehearse the result
(for example, "three weights on the fourth peg"). They were next
told to repeat the procedure on the right side, to rehearse the combinations together (for example, "three weights on the second peg
and two weights on the third peg"), and then to produce the arrangements described by these statements. Finally, the children were
given the usual encoding and predictions tests.

    This procedure proved to be effective in helping the 5-year-olds
construct and monitor distance from the fulcrum. They were as accurate in placing the weights the correct distance from the fulcrum
as in selecting the correct number of weights; both features were
encoded as accurately as weight had been earlier. However, these
children, like peers who had not been taught to encode distance from
the fulcrum, used Rule I to predict the balance scale's behavior. The
finding underscored the necessity of distinguishing between which
features children monitor and which they use in performance rules.

    This set the stage for a direct test of our explanation of why 5-
year-olds had not benefited from the feedback problems. If their failure to learn stemmed from their not monitoring distance from the
fulcrum, and they now monitored it, they should now learn from
the feedback problems that previously had not helped their untu-
tored peers. Therefore, the 5-year-olds who had been taught to encode weight and distance from the fulcrum were brought back to the
experimental room two or three days later. They were presented the
same feedback problems that earlier had benefited 8-year-olds but
not 5-year-olds. Now, however, these feedback problems helped both
age groups. More than half of the children of each age adopted a
more advanced rule, compared to none in the initial sample. In short,
the 5-year-olds who had monitored distance from the fulcrum but
who had not used it in their performance rule could learn from the
feedback problems, just as had the 8-year-olds in that position. The
key to learning for the 5-year-olds was in getting help in constructing
and monitoring the feature in the first place.

    The finding raised the theoretical issue of how people construct
features. It seems likely that as a precondition, they need to already
possess all of the components that will be needed in the new feature.
For example, for a child to construct the feature "square," he or she
would need to already possess the features of lines, angles, and
closed figures. If this precondition is not met, the person would need

to descend recursively to a level at which all of the components of the next-more-complex feature were present, and to build upward from there.

Once all the components needed for the feature are present, the feature-construction process becomes the Figure 6-1 model minus the feature-construction process itself. That is, from among the features that are being monitored, the system chooses to include some subset, and then chooses an integration rule to combine them. Once constructed, they are added to the features that can be monitored. Thus, feature construction is both a cause and a product of cognitive growth.[3]

Feature Selection.   Encoding and combination interact in the process of feature selection. If useful features are not monitored, they cannot be chosen for inclusion in performance rules. Illustratively, the 5-year-olds' failure to construct and monitor distance from the fulcrum prevented them from advancing beyond the simple weight rule when they were given feedback problems. Even if useful features are monitored, however, people must choose which ones to include in their performance rules. A child might note that dentists' offices almost always have magazines, but might not include magazines in his or her rule for judging whether a room is a dentist's office.

On what basis might people choose features, from among those they monitor, to include in performance rules? Many investigators agree that correlations between the presence of a feature and the applicabiilty of concepts are one important factor used to select which features to include in the concepts (Gibson, 1969; Klahr and Wallance, 1976; Maratsos and Chalkley, 1981). For example, if the feature "four legs" is correlated with the applicability of the concept "dog," then having four legs is likely to become a part of the dog concept. There is less agreement concerning the nature of the correlation that is computed. For example, Smith, Rips, and Shoben's (1974) model suggests a zero-order correlation process, with each feature being considered independently. Langley's (1981) BACON model suggests a partial correlation process, with the critical determinant being the predictivity of the feature when values of other features are held constant. Rosch et al.'s (1976) model suggests a multiple-correlation process, with the combined predictivity of the features being critical. Neumann's (1977) finding that people can detect multiple central tendencies suggests that nonlinear as well as linear correlations exist. The most probable conclusion is that people can perform all of these correlational processes, and that their choice of which to use depends on the situation. In general, people appear to be highly competent at detecting correlations, so much so that any deviation from accurate detection is a matter of scientific interest (hence the literatures on illusory correlation and on superstitious behavior). Klahr's (this volume) description of the time line provides useful detail concerning the data base on which such correlations might be computed.

The types of correlations that people compute partially account for their choices of features to include in performance rules, but correlations are not the whole story. Weir's (1964) findings about probability learning illustrate why. No determinate solution existed on Weir's task, but a child could be correct on a high percentage of trials by choosing one response and not the other. Preschoolers consistently chose the most frequently successful response; older children entertained a variety of complex hypotheses, and were correct less often. From the present perspective, the older children did not integrate the simple response feature (for example, "the big one is usually right") into their performance rule, despite their likely monitoring of it and despite its having the highest correlation of any predictor with the outcome variable. Thus, to fully account for the selection of features to include in performance rules, we would need information about people's definitions of what qualities a performance rule should have in the situation, and probably also about the general knowledge that predisposes people to view some features as plausibly relevant and others as implausible.

The present research on the balance scale contrasts with Karmiloff-Smith and Inhelder's (1977) research on a different balance-scale task, and illustrates how people's general knowledge can influence the features they integrate in decision rules. In our version of the balance-scale task, children were asked: "Which side will go down, or will the balance stay like it is?" The 5- and 6-year-olds based their judgments solely on weight. Karmiloff-Smith and Inhelder presented symmetric and asymmetric blocks of wood and asked children to make the blocks "balance so that they do not fall." Their 5- and 6-year-olds either placed the block on the fulcrum at some arbitrarily chosen point, with no regard to the block's distribution of length or weight, or they placed it so that the block's geometric center was directly over the fulcrum. The children justified this latter choice with such explanations as "things always balance in the middle." In both experiments, the 5-year-olds focused on a single dimension, but in our version of the balance scale they attended exclusively to weight, whereas in Karmiloff-Smith and Inhelder's version they ignored weight altogether. Several possibilities exist for the difference in performance, but the form of the question seems the most likely explanation. Asking which side will "go down" encourages consideration of what types of things make other things go down. Heavy things become a prime candidate. In contrast, asking children to make the block balance encourages them to consider the circumstances under which things balance. As Karmiloff-Smith and Inhelder's subject stated, things tend to balance in the middle. Different wordings of a question may greatly influence which aspects of their knowledge children access, and thus which features they include in integration rules.[4,5]

Feature Integration.   Once people have determined relevant features to include in concepts, the choice of an integration rule can still be a formidable task. People presumably have a large number of integrative rules to draw on: conjunctive, disjunctive, prototypic, additive, multiplicative, configural, unidimensional, and so on. It seems unlikely that any one of these is the invariant form of concepts, or that any of them never appears.

The development of knowledge about balance scales illustrates just how difficult feature integration can be. Nine-year-olds use rules in which both of the relevant features, weight and distance from the fulcrum, are included. Yet even 17-year-olds typically do not know how to combine these dimensions so as to predict which side will go down. Given feedback problems, either of their own choice or of the experimenter's, most 17-year-olds still fail to induce the torque rule. Similar findings have been obtained with other tasks and other methods. I reported that performance on a projection-of-shadows task paralleled that on the balance scale; again, 9-year-olds knew the relevant dimensions, but even 17-year-olds did not know how to combine them (Siegler, 1981). Using the information-integration methodology, a number of investigators have identified tasks on which children consider all relevant dimensions but use additive rather than multiplicative rules (see, for example, Wilkening, Becker, and Trabasso, 1980).

Although people can use a variety of integration rules, they may consistently consider some before others. In artificial concept-learning tasks, adults have been found to try unidimensional rules before conjunctive ones, conjunctive rules before disjunctive ones, disjunctive rules before biconditional ones, and so on (Neisser and Weene, 1962). The order in which integration rules are tried may vary among problem domains. For example, quantitative functions might be the first ones considered by someone trying to solve physics problems, whereas prototypic organizations might be considered first in formation of historical concepts (for example, in characterizing a hero of the Wild West).

Developmental difference in choices of integrative rules may also exist. Numerous investigators have found that young children are more likely than older ones to adopt unidimensional rules. Case (Note 3), Piaget (1941/1952 and elsewhere), Strauss and Stavey (1982), and I (Siegler, 1981) have documented more than 30 cognitive and social congitive tasks on which older children and adults use rules that integrate multiple features, but on which 5-year-olds respond on the basis of a single feature. These developmental differences could be explained in at least four ways:

1. Young children are only capable of using unidimensional rules.

2. Young children can use the same rules as older children and adults, but consider them in a different order of preference.

3. Young children can use the same rules as older children and adults, and consider them in the same order of preference, but have a stronger preference for the favored rules relative to the unfavored ones. (For example, 5-year-olds and adults might both consider unidimensional rules first, but the adults might consider other rules after a small amount of negative feedback for their unidimensional rules, whereas the 5-year-olds might require a greater amount of negative feedback before they would consider other rules.)

4. Young children can use the same rules as older children and adults, consider them in the same order of preference, and have the same relative preference for them; but the young children have had less experience with many situations. This reduced experience results in fewer opportunities to have rejected the simple rules at the top of their (and older individuals') hierarchies of rule forms. (In other words, the feature-integration process is identical for young children and for older people, but the former have not learned the specifics of as many situations.)

A large body of evidence suggests that the third and fourth possibilities are the most likely. The first explanation is implausible because although 5-year-olds often use unidimensional rules, they certainly do not always do so. The repeated observation that 5-year-olds can solve variants of Piagetian concrete-operations tasks, and that they can be taught to solve the original forms of the problems, makes it clear that they can use multidimensional rules. The second explanation is unlikely because on artificial concept-learning tasks, adults, too, have been found to consider unidimensional rules first (Neisser and Weene, 1962). The fourth explanation seems likely to be one cause of the phenomenon, since both older and younger people often begin with unidimensional hypotheses, and older people would have encountered more disconfirming evidence on many tasks. However, this seems unlikely to be the sole explanation. Numerous Piagetian tasks were designed to be equally unfamiliar to both younger and older children, yet 5-year-olds typically use unidimensional rules on them, and older children multidimensional ones. It is not clear, for example, what experiences with balance scales would lead 9-year-olds but not 5-year-olds to consider both distance from the fulcrum and weight on the balance-scale task. (Both age groups appear to be familiar with seesaws.) The tenacity with which young children often cling to unidimensional rules even in the face of disconfirming feedback (Siegler and Liebert, 1972) is also difficult to explain from the point of view of the differing-content-knowledge explanation. Thus, both relatively limited content knowledge and relatively strong preferences are likely to be involved in 5-year-olds' frequent use of unidimensional rules.[6]

Rule Execution.   Even when children have encoded appropriate features, selected them for inclusion in performance rules, and integrated them into a combination formula, difficulties in executing the rules may obscure the children's knowledge and interfere with learning. Performance of children in a study of the fullness concept (Siegler and Vago, 1978, Experiment 1) has illustrated this phenomenon.

Vago and I presented children with two beakers, each containing some water. The experimenter asked the children to judge which beaker was more full. We were surprised when, in the initial experiment, fewer than 30 percent of the 10-year-olds used a discernible rule. Closer examination of the response patterns indicated that on all but two types of problems, the 10-year-olds consistently used a volume rule; they said (incorrectly) that whichever glass contained more water was fuller. On the other two types of problems, most children followed no obvious pattern. The attribute that distinguished these latter two problem-types was that in them, the two glasses contained equal volumes of water, despite having unequal heights and cross-sectional areas. Under these conditions, judging volume becomes difficult; even adults cannot judge accurately (Siegler, 1981). Given a new set of problems that did not include pairs of galsses with equal volumes of water, 10-year-olds consistently chose the glass with the greater liquid volume. Our conclusion was that the 10-year-olds had been encoding the heights and cross-sectional areas of filled space all along and had been trying to integrate the features in a multiplicative volume rule, but that difficulties in executing the rule prevented their behavior from consistently reflecting the fact in the first experiment.

The difficulties in rule execution that interfered with our efforts to assess children's knowledge may also interfere with children's efforts to learn. Suppose that we had been trying to teach children to accurately judge volume through presentation of feedback problems. Even if the children were using the correct volume rule, they would frequently be told that they were incorrect on problems with equal volumes. Without any simple way of discovering what was wrong with their approach, they might try a variety of other approaches in attempting to find one that yielded consistently correct performance (as in the Weir, 1964, probability-learning experiment). Thus, it may take longer to form concepts when rule execution is difficult than when it is straightforward.

CONCLUSIONS

The purpose of this paper was to examine whether an analogy to biological evolution might aid understanding of cognitive developmental mechanisms. Although several fairly specific analogies between biological and cultural evolution have been drawn, it seemed most useful to adopt a global approach that divided cognitive development into issues of selection and issues of variation. Within this division, we focused on how cognitive variations might be produced.

The analysis suggested that cognitive variations are produced by the following procedure. Under typical conditions, people monitor some features and use their values in the rule for operating in the situation, monitor other features but do not use their values in the operating rule, and do not monitor other potential features at all. As long as rules that make use of the first group of features lead to acceptable outcomes, people continue to use those rules. Even in this relatively steady state, however, the feature-construction process is always trying to synthesize new features that represent the environment more accurately and efficiently. Thus, the features that people monitor can change even while their behavior remains constant.

When existing performance rules yield unacceptable outcomes (for example, when they elicit frequent negative feedback—either explicit, as when another person says that some response is incorrect, or implicit, as when existing features of a musical composition fail to fall into a satisfying organization), all features that are being monitored are considered for inclusion in new rules. If these seem insufficient, other features that have been constructed and that are relevant to the situation but that have not been monitored may also begin to be monitored and considered for integration into new rules. Once features that correlate highly with the concept's applicability have been selected, the features are integrated in all of the ways that have been described by classical concept-learning theories and by more recent prototype and featural theories. The new rules that are generated are the ultimate products of the variation mechanism.

NOTES

[1] The degree to which this criticism applies to another approach to concept formation, prototype theories, is unclear. Illustratively, Rosch, Mervis, Gray, Johnson, and Boyes-Braem (1976) reported 12 experiments, all of which concerned the ways in which features are organized into basic-, subordinate-, and superordinate-level concepts. The very idea of a basic level, and its definition in terms of cue validities, implies that the component features are inherent demarcations of the world. Near the end of the article, however, Rosch et al. noted that the level that is basic, and the differentiation of features in the conceptual hierarchy, might vary with experience. This suggested a recognition that which features are encoded is not a given, and that the encoding process might influence which concepts are formed. In any case, encoding has not been the subject of much discussion in prototype theories.

[2] Unlike the situation in biological evolution, the more highly associated with goal attainment a production was, the more likely that it would be chosen as a parent production.

[3] This description of feature construction might create the impression that encoding can be reduced to combination—that the only difference is the level of concept that is being created. The monitoring process, however, remains apart from combination; the non-identity of the features that are monitored and those that are used in combination rules was documented in the Siegler (1976) experiments. In addition, it seems likely that with fairly simple features, the properties of specific sensory systems influence the features that are constructed, though little is known about how this occurs.

[4] The results of Karmiloff-Smith and Inhelder's experiment might be interpreted as indicating that 5-year-olds had constructed the distance-from-the-fulcrum feature. The children's placement of the board so that its middle made contact with the fulcrum does not necessarily imply that they had constructed the feature, however. Instead, they might simply have understood the concept "middle" as an isolated point, without understanding its status as a value in a continuous dimension.

[5] This interpretation implies that the wording of the question is crucial and that the apparatus is not. There exists a simple test for this claim. Children could be presented with the Karmiloff-Smith and Inhelder apparatus and, as in that experiment, asked to put boards on the fulcrum so that they would balance. Later, the experimenter could show children these arrangements mixed among other ones, and could ask the children whether the left side would go down, whether the right side would go down, or whether the board would balance if supports for it were removed. If the wording-of-instructions interpretation is correct, 5-year-olds should predict that the side with more weight will go down, even if they ignored the weight dimension earlier.

[6] In an earlier paper (Siegler, 1981), I advanced the idea of a "fallback" rule; this notion is closely related to the third interpretation in the present list. In both cases, the emphasis is on 5-year-olds using unidimensional rules when they do not have specific evidence to disconfirm them. On considering the fact that adults, also, may try such rules first when they lack specific disconfirming evidence, I was led to reconceptualize the phenomenon as reflecting the 5-year-olds' greater preference for unidimensional rules. Both they and older people may "fall back" on such rules, but the 5-year-olds may take longer to "get up" from them.

REFERENCES

Anderson, J. R., Kline, P. J., and Beasley, C. M., Jr. Complex learning processes. In R. E. Snow, P.-A. Federico, and W. E. Montague (Eds.), *Aptitude, learning, and instruction: Cognitive process analyses*, Vol. 1. Hillsdale, N.J.: Erlbaum, 1980.

Bransford, J. D. *Human cognition: Learning, understanding, and remembering.* Belmont, Calif.: Wadsworth, 1979.

Campbell, D. T. On the conflicts between biological and social evolution and between psychology and moral tradition. *American Psychologist*, 1975, *30*, 1103–1126.

Chase, W. G., and Simon, H. A. The mind's eye in chess. In W. G. Chase (Ed.), *Visual information processing*. New York: Academic Press, 1973.

Dennett, D. C. *Brainstorms: Philosophical essays on mind and psychology.* Montgomery, Vt.: Bradford Books, 1978.

Durkheim, E. *Les formes elementaires de la vie religieuse.* Paris: Presses Universitaires de France, 1912.

Gibson, E. J. *Principles of perceptual learning and development.* Englewood Cliffs, N.J.: Prentice-Hall, 1969.

Haygood, R. C., and Bourne, L. E., Jr. Attribute- and rule-learning aspects of conceptual behavior. *Psychological Review*, 1965, *72*, 175–195.

Hirshleifer, J. Economics from a biological point of view. *Journal of Law and Economics*, 1977, *20*, 1–52.

Hockett, C. F. The quantification of functional load. *Word*, 1967, *23*, 300–320.

Holland, J. H., and Reitman, J. S. *Cognitive systems based on adaptive algorithms*. Unpublished manuscript. Ann Arbor, MI, University of Michigan, 1981.

Inhelder, B., and Piaget, J. *The growth of logical thinking from childhood to adolescence*. New York: Basic Books, 1958.

Karmiloff-Smith, A., and Inhelder, B. If you want to get ahead, get a theory. *Cognition*, 1974–75, *3*(3), pp. 195–212.

Klahr, D., and Wallace, J. G. *Cognitive development: An information processing view*. Hillsdale, N.J.: Erlbaum, 1976.

Langley, P. Data-driven discovery of physical laws. *Cognitive Science*, 1981, *5*, 31–54.

Larkin, J. H., McDermott, J., Simon, D. P., and Simon, H. A. Models of competence in solving physics problems. *Cognitive Science*, 1980, *4*, 317–345.

Lenat, D. B. The ubiquity of discovery. *Artificial Intelligence*, 1977, *9*, 257–286.

Leontiades, M. *Strategies for diversification and change*. Boston: Little, Brown, 1980.

Lesgold, A. M., Feltovich, P. J., Glaser, R., and Wang, Y. *The acquisition of perceptual diagnostic skill in radiology* (Tech. rep.). Learning Research and Development Center, University of Pittsburgh, September 1981.

Levine, M. Hypothesis behavior by humans during discrimination learning. *Journal of Experimental Psychology*, 1966, *71*, 331–338.

Maratsos, M. P., and Chalkley, M. A. The internal language of children's syntax: The nature and ontogenesis of syntactic categories. In K. Nelson (Ed.), *Children's language*. New York: Gardner Press, 1981.

Neisser, U., and Weene, P. Hierarchies in concept attainment. *Journal of Experimental Psychology*, 1962, *64*, 640–645.

Nelson, R. R., and Winter, S. G. Forces generating and limiting concentration under Schumpterian competition. *Bell Journal of Economics*, 1978, *9*, 524–547.

Neumann, P. G. Visual prototype formation with discontinuous representation of dimensions of variability. *Memory & Cognition*, 1977, *5*, 187–197.

Pellegrino, J. W., and Glaser, R. Analyzing aptitudes for learning: Inductive reasoning. In R. Glaser (Eds.), *Advances in instructional psychology*. Hillsdale, N.J.: Erlbaum, 1982.

Piaget, J. *The child's conception of number.* New York: Humanities Press, (C. Gattegno and F. M. Hodgson, Trans.; original French edition, 1941.)

Piaget, J. *Behavior in evolution.* New York: Pantheon Books, 1978.

Popper, K. R. *Objective knowledge: An evolutionary approach.* London: Oxford University Press, 1974.

Reitman, J. S. Skilled perception in Go: Deducing memory structures from inter-response times. *Cognitive Psychology,* 1976, *8,* 336–356.

Rosch, E., Mervis, C. B., Gray, W. D., Johnson, D. M., and Boyes-Braem, P. Basic objects in natural categories. *Cognitive Psychology,* 1976, *8,* 382–439.

Shepard, R. N. Geometrical approximations to the structure of musical pitch. *Psychological Review,* 1982, *89,* 305–333.

Siegler, R. S. Three aspects of cognitive development. *Cognitive Psychology,* 1976, *8,* 481–520.

Siegler, R. S. Developmental sequences within and between concepts. *Monographs of the Society for Research in Child Development,* 1981, *46*(2, Serial no. 189).

Siegler, R. S. Information processing approaches to development. In P. Mussen (Ed.), Handbook of child psychology, Vol. 1: History, theory, and methods (W. Kessen (Volume Ed.), New York: Wiley, 1983.

Siegler, R. S., and Liebert, R. M. Effects of presenting relevant rules and complete feedback on the conservation of liquid quantity task. *Developmental Psychology,* 1972, *7,* 133–138.

Siegler, R. S., and Vago, S. The development of a proportionality concept: Judging relative fullness. *Journal of Experimental Child Psychology,* 1978, *25,* 371–395.

Simon, H. A. *The sciences of the artificial,* 2nd ed. Cambridge, Mass.: M.I.T. Press, 1981. (Original edition, 1962).

Smith, E. E. Theories of semantic memory. In W. K. Estes (Ed.), *Handbook of learning and cognitive processes.* Hillsdale, N.J.: Erlbaum, 1978.

Smith, E. E., Rips, L. J., and Shoben, E. J. Semantic memory and psychological semantics. In G. H. Bower (Ed.), *The psychology of learning and motivation.* New York: Academic press, 1974.

Sternberg, R. J. Component processes in analogical reasoning. *Psychological Review,* 1977, *84,* 353–378.

Strauss, S., and Stavey, R. *U-Shaped behavioral growth.* New York: Academic Press, 1982.

Van Parijs, P. *Evolutionary explanation in the social sciences.* Totowa, N.J.: Rowman and Littlefield, 1981.

Weir, M. W. Developmental changes in problem-solving stragegies. *Psychological Review,* 1964, *71,* 473–490.

Wilkening, F., Becker, J., and Trabasso, T. *Information integration by children.* Hillsdae, N.J.: Erlbaum, 1980.

7

MECHANISMS OF COGNITIVE DEVELOPMENT: A COMPONENTIAL APPROACH

Robert J. Sternberg

The question of "what develops" is probably the most central one in developmental psychology. Most theoretical and empirical works in developmental psychology attempt to deal with this question to a greater or lesser degree; indeed, the form a particular investigation takes is shaped in large part by the investigator's presuppositions as to the sources of intellectual development. Many aspects of behavior change with age, but only some of them help elucidate the basic mechanisms responsible for developmental change.

I propose in this article a set of mechanisms for addressing— although not, of course, for answering in full—the question of what develops in human intelligence. Using what I refer to as a "componential approach," I propose to account for intellectual development in terms of changes in the availability, accessibility, and ease of execution of a variety of kinds of information-processing components, and in terms of the increasing automatization of these components in task performance. Obviously, the proposed approach is only one of a number of alternative ones that provide frameworks for understanding how intelligence develops; like these other approaches, mine gives only a partial account of developmental mechanisms. Nevertheless, it seems to contribute one building block that may ultimately be combined with other building blocks to construct a more comprehensive theory of "what develops." My description of the proposed approach will begin with definitions of some constructs, continue with an account of how these constructs might interact, and proceed to a consideration of how the constructs become automatized. I will then provide a commentary on those facets of cognitive development that are most central to the development of intelligence, and conclude with a brief analysis of some loci of intellectual giftedness and retardation.

THE COMPONENTIAL FRAMEWORK[1]

The basic construct in the componential framework for understanding human intelligence is the *component*. A component is an elementary information process that operates upon internal representations of objects or symbols (Sternberg, 1977; see also Newell and

---

Preparation of this article was supported by a grant from the Spencer Foundation.

Simon, 1972). The component may translate a sensory input into a conceptual representation, transform one conceptual representation into another, or translate a conceptual representation into a motor output. What is considered to be "elementary" is viewed as a property of the level of theorizing one attempts, rather than as a property of the human mind. A given component may or may not be elementary, depending upon the theoretical context in which it is presented.

Each component has three important properties associated with it: duration, difficulty (that is, probability of being performed incorrectly), and probability of execution. In order to evaluate these properties of components, one needs to select appropriate dependent variables: examples are response latencies, for duration; error rates, for difficulty; and response-choice probabilities, for probability of execution.

Components are of three basic kinds: metacomponents, performance components, and knowledge-acquisition components. Each of the different kinds performs a different function. I will consider each kind of component in turn.

Metacomponents

Metacomponents are executive processes used in planning and decision making in task performance. I have identified nine metacomponents that I believe are particularly important in intellectual task performance; other writers (for example, Brown, 1978; Brown and DeLoache, 1978; Flavell, 1981; Markman, 1981) have suggested overlapping lists of executive processes. The metacomponents on my list are as follows:

1. *Recognition of just what the problem is that needs to be solved.*

2. *Selection of lower-order components for task performance* (selection of the components that actually execute the task).

3. *Selection of a strategy for combining lower-order components* (choice of a way of combining the components into a working algorithm for problem solving).

4. *Selection of one or more mental representations or organizations for information* (choice of a mental depiction of information upon which the components and strategy can operate).

5. *Allocation of componential resources* (deciding how to partition the available time for problem solving among the various kinds of components one can bring to bear upon the problem).

6. *Solution monitoring* (keeping track of what one has done, what one is doing, and what one still needs to do in problem solving).

7. *Understanding feedback* (correctly interpreting feedback regarding the effectiveness of one's task performance).

8. *Figuring out how to act upon feedback* (knowing what to do in response to the feedback as interpreted).

9. *Acting upon feedback* (doing something in response to one's knowledge about what one should do).

Consider an example of how metacomponential development can proceed; in particular, how strategy selection (process 3 above) changes with increasing age or expertise in problem solving. Converging evidence suggests two trends as children become older, and as novices gather expertise in a particular area of problem solving: (1) they become more nearly exhaustive in their processing of information presented in a problem, and consider all or almost all of the information presented rather than just a subset of it (Brown and DeLoache, 1978; Siegler, 1978; Sternberg and Nigro, 1980; Sternberg and Rifkin, 1979; Vurpillot, 1968); and (2) they spend relatively more time in planning how to go about solving a problem, and less time in actually solving it (Chi, Glaser, and Rees, 1982; Larkin, McDermott, Simon, and Simon, 1980; Sternberg, 1981). This latter finding is of particular interest because it suggests that in terms of general allocation of componential resources (process 5 above), more intellectually advanced individuals tend to spend relatively more time on higher-order metacomponential processing, and less time on lower-order componential processing.

Performance Components

Performance components are processes that are used in the execution of a task. Thus, the actual working through of the problem one has decided to solve, in the way one has decided to solve it, is done via a set of performance components. The number of possible performance components that can be brought to bear upon information-processing tasks is undoubtedly very large. However, certain components seem to be applicable to especially large domains of tasks, and thus to be of more psychological interest than those components that are relevant to only a small number of tasks. One set of performance components of particular interest is the set used in inductive reasoning; that is, reasoning that goes beyond the information given to come up with a solution. Various investigators (for example, Pellegrino and Glaser, 1980; Spearman, 1923; Sternberg, 1977; Whitely, 1980) have proposed somewhat different sets of components, or, in some cases, have given different names to what appear to be the same underlying processes.

We have identified performance components in three inductive-reasoning tasks—analogies, series completions, and classifications (Sternberg and Gardner, 1983). These components include:

1. *Encoding* of information (perceiving and storing information in working memory).

2. *Inference* of relations (recognizing the similarities and differences between two terms of a problem).

3. *Mapping* of higher-order relations (recognizing the similarities and differences between two lower-order relations).

4. *Application* of relations (carrying over a previously inferred relation to a new domain).

5. *Comparison* (comparing and contrasting any multiple answer options).

6. *Justification* (comparing the chosen answer option to one's perception of the ideal answer option, in order to determine whether the selected answer option is good enough).

7. *Response* (furnishing an answer to the given problem).

Consider an example of how performance-componential development can proceed—in particular, with respect to the mapping component (process 3 above). Mapping requires a person to link the first half of an induction item, such as an analogy, to the second half, by conceiving the higher-order relation between the two lower-order relations, one linking the first term of the analogy to the second, and the other linking the third term of the analogy to the fourth. The ability to conceive a second-order relation between relations is of particular interest to developmental theorists, because in Piaget's theory of intellectual development this ability marks the transition between concrete- and formal-operational thinking (Inhelder and Piaget, 1958). One might therefore expect concrete-operational children to have great difficulty in mapping higher-order relations, or to be unable to map at all. Indeed, several investigators have found this to be true (Gallagher and Wright, 1979; Levinson and Carpenter, 1974; Lunzer, 1965; Piaget with Montangero and Billeter, 1977; Sternberg and Rifkin, 1979). Thus, access to the mapping component appears to come later than access to inductive-reasoning components that deal only with lower- (first-) order relations.

Knowledge-Acquisition Components

Knowledge-acquisition components are used in acquiring new information. There may well be many ways in which new information can be acquired. I believe that three components of information processing, however, are particularly important in the acquisition of consequential information:

1. *Selective encoding* (sifting out relevant information from irrelevant information, in the stimulus environment, in order to select information for further processing).

2. *Selective combination* (combining selected information in such a way as to render it interpretable; that is, integrating it in some meaningful way).

3. *Selective comparison* (rendering newly encoded or combined information meaningful by perceiving its relations to old information previously stored).

According to this view, then, consequential knowledge acquisition (which does not include, for example, rote memorization of word lists) involves deciding what information is important to learn, putting that information together into a meaningful form so that it can be properly stored in long-term memory, and relating that information (where possible) to previously stored information so as to relate it to the already existing knowledge base.

Consider, for example, how the chess experts in the work of Chase and Simon (1973), Chi (1978), and others differ from chess players with equal experience but lesser expertise. What makes a better chess player (or someone who is more skilled in applying any kind of procedural or declarative knowledge) is the expert's better sense of, say, what moves have (and have not) been important for winning in the chess games the player has played or observed; the expert's adeptness at combining information about isolated moves into unitized information regarding which combinations of moves will win and which ones will not; and the expert's superior ability to relate this newly acquired knowledge to whatever knowledge he or she already had about the game, so that the new information does not remain in isolation from the player's previously acquired procedural and declarative knowledge. It may very well be true, as Chi and as Chase and Simon have claimed, that experts differ from novices in their superior knowledge base; but one might wonder how this difference came about, aside from differences in sheer amount of experience (which cannot possibly account for all differences, since most people never become experts no matter how much they play). I suggest that differential efficacy in use of knowledge-acquisition components can account for at least part of the difference between experts and novices.

COMPONENTIAL MECHANISMS FOR COGNITIVE DEVELOPMENT

Interrelations Among Kinds of Components

Consider first how the various kinds of components are interrelated, and next, how these interrelations contribute to cognitive development. The interrelations among the functionally different kinds of components are close and highly integrated. Four kinds of interrelations need to be considered:

1. *Direct activation* of one kind of component by another, or immediate passage of control from one kind to another. For example, in solving an analogy, the metacomponent of lower-order-component selection effectuates the use of a certain set of performance components (such as encoding, inference, mapping, and the like) for problem solving; the metacomponent for strategy selection effectuates a rule by which these components are combined.

2. *Indirect activation* of one kind of component by another, or mediated passage of control from one kind to another via a third kind. For example, if a metacomponent instructs a knowledge-acquisition component to select relevant information for solving an analogy, and this results indirectly in further encoding of information (via a performance component), the performance component was indirectly activated by the metacomponent via the knowledge-acquisition component of selective encoding.

3. *Direct feedback* from one kind of component to another, or immediate passage of information from one kind to another. For example, if inferring a rule between two terms of an analogy results in the realization that the terms refer to objects that are parallel in shape but not in color, and this information is used by a metacomponent as a basis for further decision making regarding what other attributes to look for in solving analogies, the information passed from the performance component to the metacomponent was direct feedback.

4. *Indirect feedback* from one kind of component to another, or mediated passage of information from one kind to another via a third kind. For example, if the information about shape and color in the analogy mentioned above results in one's learning that color is irrelevant for problem solving, the knowledge acquisition (learning) via selective encoding was a result of indirect feedback from the performance component to the knowledge-acquisition component via the metacomponent.

In the proposed system, only metacomponents can directly activate and receive feedback from each of the other kinds of components. Thus, all control in the system passes directly from the metacomponents, and all information from the system passes directly to them. The other two kinds of components can activate each other indirectly and receive information from each other indirectly; in every case, mediation must be supplied by the metacomponents. For example, acquisition of information affects further acquisition and the various kinds of transformations (performances) that follow upon that information, but only via the linkage of the knowledge-acquisition and performance components to the metacomponents. In sum, metacomponents serve as necessary conduits from which, to which, or through which all information passes.

Consider some examples of how the system might function in the solution of an analogy problem. As soon as one decides upon a certain tentative strategy for solving the analogy, activation of that strategy can pass directly from the metacomponent responsible for deciding upon a strategy to the performance component responsible for executing the first step of the strategy; subsequently, activation can pass to the successive performance components needed to execute the strategy. Feedback returning from the performance components will indicate how successful the strategy is turning out to be. If monitoring of this feedback indicates a lack of success, control may pass to the metacomponent that is "empowered" to select a new strategy; if no successful change in strategy can be realized, the solution-monitoring metacomponent may change the goal altogether (for example, by deciding to find an answer option that is a high associate of the last term in the stem, rather than one that is logically related to it in the same way that the second term was related to the first).

As a given strategy is being executed, new information may be acquired about how to solve analogies in general. This information is also fed back to the metacomponents, which may act upon it or ignore it. New information that seems useful is more likely to be directed back from the relevant metacomponents to the relevant acquisition components for storage in long-term memory. What is acquired does not directly influence what is retained, however, so that "practice" does not necessarily "make perfect": some people may be unable to profit from their experience because of inadequacies in metacomponential information processing. Similarly, what is retained does not directly influence what is later transferred. The chances of information being transferred to a later context will be largely dependent upon the form in which the information is encoded and then stored for later access. Also, as previously mentioned, acquired information does not *directly* affect transformations (performances) that follow upon that information. The results of the active knowledge-acquisition components must first be fed back into the metacomponents, which in effect decide what information will filter back indirectly from one type of component to another.

The metacomponents are able to process only a limited amount of information at a given time. In the performance of a difficult task, and especially a new and novel one, the amount of information being fed back to the metacomponents may exceed their capacity for acting upon it. In this case, the metacomponents become overloaded, and valuable information that cannot be processed may simply be wasted. The total information-handling capacity of the metacomponents of a given system will thus be an important limiting aspect of that system. Similarly, capacity for allocating attentional resources so as to minimize the probability of bottlenecks will be part of what determines the effective capacity of the system (see also Hunt, 1980).

I have not discussed interrelations among various individual members of each single kind of component. These interrelations can be easily described, however. Metacomponents are able to communicate directly with one another, and to activate one another directly. It seems likely that the solution-monitoring metacomponent controls intercommunication and interactivation among the other metacomponents, and there is a certain sense in which this particular metacomponent might be viewed as a "metametacomponent." Again, other kinds of components are not able to communicate with one another directly or to activate one another directly. But components of a given kind can communicate indirectly with other components of the same kind, and can activate them indirectly. Indirect communication and activation proceed through the metacomponents.

Componential Interrelations and Intellectual Development

The system of interrelations among kinds of components described above implicitly contains several bases for intellectual change. In this section, at least some of these bases for change will be explicit.

First, the components of knowledge acquisition provide the mechanisms for a steadily developing knowledge base. Increments in the knowledge base in turn allow for more sophisticated forms of later acquisition, and possibly for greater ease in the execution of performance components. For example, knowledge-acquisition components facilitate learning of vocabulary. Increased vocabulary facilitates later operation of these knowledge-acquisition components (Sternberg and Powell, 1983). As the base of old knowledge becomes deeper and broader, the possibilities for relating new knowledge to old knowledge—and consequently for incorporating that new knowledge into the existing knowledge base—increase. There is thus the possibility of an unending feedback loop: the components lead to an increased knowledge base, which leads to more effective use of the components, which leads to further increases in the knowledge base, and so on. This set of mechanisms is believed to be largely responsible for differences between experts and novices in a variety of domains, as in the chess domain discussed earlier.

Second, the self-monitoring metacomponents can, in effect, learn from their own mistakes. Early on, allocation of metacomponential resources to varying tasks or kinds of components may be less than optimal, with resulting loss of valuable feedback information. Self-monitoring should eventually result in improved allocation of metacomponential resources—including to the self-monitoring of the metacomponents. Thus, self-monitoring by the metacomponents results in improved allocation of metacomponential resources to the self-monitoring of the metacomponents, which in turn leads to improved self-monitoring, and so on and so forth. Here, as above, there exists the possibility of an unending feedback loop, one that is internal to the metacomponents themselves.

Finally, indirect feedback from kinds of components other than metacomponents to one another and direct feedback to the metacomponents should result in improved performance. Acquisition components, for example, can provide valuable information to performance components (via the metacomponents) concerning how to perform a task; and the performance components in turn can provide feedback to the acquisition components (via the metacomponents) concerning what else needs to be learned in order to perform the task optimally. Thus, the two other kinds of components can generate unending feedback loops in which performance improves as a result of interactions between these kinds of components, or among multiple components of the same kind.

There can be no doubt that in the present conceptual scheme, the metacomponents form the major basis for the development of intelligence. All activation and feedback are filtered through these elements, and if they do not perform their function well, then it will not matter very much what the other kinds of components do. It is for this reason that the metacomponents are viewed as truly central in understanding the nature and development of intelligence.

To summarize, part of cognitive development is understood here in terms of the result of repeated interactive functioning in a componential subsystem. Iterative activation by and feedback to metacomponents results in the accumulation of both declarative and procedural knowledge. Increasing expertise in task performance is, in part, a function of the success of the various types of interactions of components in relevant componential subsystems.

COMPONENTIAL AUTOMATIZATION IN COGNITIVE DEVELOPMENT

Cognitive development arises not only from improved performance resulting from repeated activation and feedback within a given componential subsystem, but also from automatization of the functioning of such a subsystem. In particular, the functioning of a given componential subsystem for a particular task domain proceeds from "controlled" to "automatic." *Controlled* information processing is hierarchical in nature, with the executive metacomponents consciously directing the nonexecutive performance and knowledge-acquisition components. Controlled processing is also of strictly limited capacity, primarily serial; but it has unlimited ability to call upon all of an individual's stored knowledge base. *Automatic* information processing is preconscious and is thus not under the voluntary direction of the individual; in automatic processing there is no functional distinction between executive and nonexecutive processing. This type of processing is in the mode of a production system, where all kinds of components function at a single level of analysis. The system has almost unlimited parallel capacity; but it is strictly limited in the portion of the knowledge base stored in long-term memory upon which it can draw (as will be discussed later).

The distinction between controlled and automatic processes (Schneider and Shiffrin, 1977; Shiffrin and Schneider, 1977) is related to the distinction between executive and nonexecutive processes. Whether executive and nonexecutive processes are hierarchically ordered or not depends upon whether information processing is controlled or automatic. In controlled processing, the metacomponents are strictly higher-order with respect to the other kinds of components. This is the typical situation considered in the preceding part of this chapter. But in automatic processing, metacomponents, performance components, and knowledge-acquisition components become of a single order. There is no hierarchical distinction between higher-order executive and lower-order nonexecutive processes.

In processing information from new domains (and especially nonentrenched ones; see Sternberg, 1981) or domains in which one does not have much expertise, the individual relies primarily upon controlled, global processing. A central executive consisting of a set of metacomponents directly activates nonexecutive components (performance and knowledge-acquisition components), and receives direct feedback from them. Information processing is of strictly limited capacity, and attention is focused upon the task at hand. The total knowledge base stored in long-term memory is available for access by the knowledge-acquisition components utilized in a given task situation. A critical point is that higher-order metacomponents activate individual lower-order components.

In processing information from old domains or domains in which one has acquired considerable expertise, the individual relies primarily upon automatic, local processing. Metacomponents in a central executive subsystem initially activate a subsystem consisting of locally applicable processes and a locally applicable knowledge base. Multiple local subsystems can operate in parallel. Performance in these multiple local subsystems is automatic and of almost unlimited capacity; attention is not focused upon the task at hand. Only knowledge that has been transferred to the local knowledge base is available for access by the knowledge-acquisition components utilized in a given task situation. Activation is by metacomponents in the global subsystem to the local subsystem as a whole. The metacomponents can instantiate themselves as part of this local subsystem; when used in this instantiation, they do not differ functionally from components of any other kind.

In domains in which a person has little expertise, processing is largely focused in the global processing and knowledge subsystem. As expertise develops, greater and greater proportions of processing are transferred to (or packed into) a given local processing subsystem. The advantage of using the local subsystem is that activation is of the subsystem as a whole rather than of individual components within the subsystem, so that the amount of attention that needs to be devoted to use of the domain is much less than it is under global control. Indeed, attention allocation for a whole local subsystem is comparable to that for a single lower-order component activated by the global subsystem as part of the global subsystem's functioning. The disadvantage of using the local subsystem is that it is able to call upon only a limited knowledge base and limited processes: the knowledge base and processes that have been packed into it. Experts are able to handle a wide variety of situations through the use of the local subsystem because they have packed tremendous amounts of information into it. Novices can use local subsystems hardly at all because these subsystems have as yet acquired relatively few processes and little knowledge.

Control passes to a local processing subsystem when a metacomponent recognizes a given situation as one for which a local subsystem is potentially relevant. The local subsystem, presumed to be of the nature of a production system, has a set of productions ready to act upon the problem at hand. The productions comprise functions that are metacomponential in nature as well as functions that are not. But all of these functions are integrated into a single, nonhierarchical subsystem. Control is passed back to the global processing subsystem during task performance when none of the productions in a subsystem is able to satisfy a given presented condition. When the bottom of the production list is reached and no given condition is satisfied, global processing is necessary to decide how to handle the new situation. Once this situation is successfully handled, acquisition components can pack what has been learned from global processing of the new experience into a given local processing subsystem, so that the next time such a situation is encountered there will be no need to exit from the local processing subsystem. Control never passes directly between two automated subsystems, but rather passes first from a local automated subsystem to the global controlled subsystem and then to another local automated subsystem.

In this scheme, the extent to which one develops expertise in a given domain depends in large part upon the ability of acquisition components to pack new information in a usable way into a given local processing subsystem. Experts are at an advantage in their domain of expertise, because their ability to stay for longer amounts of time in the better-developed local processing subsystem enables them to free global processing resources for what, to them, are new situations. Novices are overwhelmed with new information, and must engage global resources so frequently that most of the new information that is encountered is quickly lost. Experts are thus better able to handle familiar tasks within the domain of expertise, and also to learn new tasks, since global processing resources are more freely available for the intricacies of the situation confronted. In essence, a loop is set up whereby packing more information and processes into the local subsystems enables people to automate more processing and thus to have global resources more available for what is new in a given situation. Experts are also able to perform more different kinds of tasks simultaneously, because whereas the global processing subsystem is conscious and serial in its processing, multiple local processing subsystems can operate in parallel. For example, driving a car consumes almost all of a novice's available global resources. In contrast, driving a car consumes an expert's local resources and leaves central resources available for other tasks, unless the driver is confronted by an unfamiliar situation (such as a road block) that requires redirection of control to the global resources.

To summarize, my view is that information processing is hierarchical and controlled in a global processing mode, and nonhierarchical and automatic in local processing modes. Expertise develops largely from the successively greater assumption of information processing by local resources. When these local resources are engaged, parallel processing of multiple kinds of tasks becomes possible. Global resources, however, are serial and are of very limited capacity in problem solving.

CRITICAL FACETS OF COGNITIVE DEVELOPMENT

Although I believe that the mechanisms presented in the preceding sections of this chapter apply equally to all aspects of cognitive development, they are probably more important in some facets of development than in others. In particular, they appear to be most critical in the development of human intellectual functioning. Just what facets of development are involved here?

I view a task as measuring "intelligence" to the extent that it requires either or both of two skills: the ability to deal with novel kinds of task and situational demands, and the ability to automatize information processing. I will consider each of these facets in turn.

The Ability to Deal with Novel Task and Situational Demands

The ability to deal with novelty can be applied both to tasks and to situations.

Novel Tasks. The idea that intelligence involves the ability to deal with novel task demands is certainly far from novel. Indeed, I have previously suggested that intelligence is best measured by tasks that are "nonentrenched," in the sense that they require information processing of kinds that are outside people's ordinary experience. A task may be nonentrenched in the kinds of operations it requires, or in the concepts it requires the subject to utilize. It is important to note that the usefulness of a task in measuring intelligence is not a linear function of task novelty. If the task is too novel, then the individual will not have any cognitive structures to bring to bear upon it, and as a result the task will simply be outside of the individual's range of comprehension. Calculus, for example, would be a highly novel field of endeavor for most 5-year-olds. But calculus tasks would be so far outside their range of experience that such tasks would be worthless for the assessment of 5-year-olds' intelligence. In Piagetian terms, the task should require accommodation primarily, but it must require some assimilation as well.

Implicit in the above discussion is the notion that novelty can be of two kinds, either or both of which may be involved in task performance. The two kinds of novelty might be characterized as involving (1) comprehension of the task, and (2) acting upon one's comprehension of the task.

Novelty in "comprehension of the task" emphasizes the actual understanding of the problem. Once one understands the task, acting upon it may or may not be challenging. Consider, for example, the "conceptual projection" task I used in a recent study (Sternberg, 1981, 1982). Subjects were presented with elaborate scenarios regarding objects that changed their properties over time and space. In one scenario, certain objects changed colors in the year 2000 and others did not. The subjects were required to learn how to make judgments regarding what colors particular objects would be in 2000. In another scenario, some objects changed consistency (from liquid to solid, or vice versa) when they were transported from one side of the equator of a distant planet to the other side; again, other objects did not change. And again, subjects had to learn how to make judgments regarding what had happened to the consistencies of objects that had been transported, in this case in space as well as in time. Learning how to perform the task was quite difficult and took the subjects a fair amount of time. But once they had learned how to do it, their error rates were quite low, generally under 5 percent. In this particular task, difficulty due to task novelty seemed to inhere primarily in learning the nature of the task and in the rather bizarre concepts it employed. Once subjects succeeded in this learning, however, their performance was almost error-free.

Novelty in "acting upon one's comprehension of the task" emphasizes the actual solution of a problem, rather than learning about the problem or learning how to solve it. Consider, for example, the insight problems used in some of our investigations of novel task performance. A typical insight problem was as follows: "Water lilies double in area every 24 hours. At the beginning of the summer there is one water lily on a lake. It takes 60 days for the lake to become covered with water lilies. On what day is the lake half covered?" (Sternberg and Davidson, 1983).

Janet Davidson and I found that people generally had little difficulty in comprehending what problems such as this one were saying. Indeed, they had encountered many superficially similar problems in their school careers. But people often had considerable difficulty in coming up with the insights needed to solve the problems. Thus, their difficulty was in acting upon their understanding of the problems rather than in understanding the problems themselves. In the present instance, they had to infer that the fact that the water lilies double in area every 24 hours implies that 24 hours before the lake became fully covered on the 60th day, it was half covered. The answer to the problem is thus "the 59th day." In this particular kind of task, subjects were able to solve only about two-fifths of the problems correctly.

It is possible, of course, to formulate problems involving novelty in both comprehension and execution of a particular kind of task, and problems involving novelty in neither comprehension nor execution. Problems of these two kinds might be less satisfactory measures of intelligence than problems involving novelty in either comprehension or execution, but not both. The reason for this is that the former problems might be too novel, whereas the latter problems might not be novel enough to provide optimal measurement of intelligence.

Novel Situations.   The notion that intelligence is particularly aptly measured in situations that require adaptation to new and challenging environmental demands has been a common one since the times of Binet. Almost everyone knows someone (perhaps oneself) who performs well when confronted with tasks that are presented in a familiar milieu, but who falls apart when presented with similar or even identical tasks that are presented in an unfamiliar milieu. For example, a person who performs well in his or her everyday environment may find it difficult to function in a foreign country, even if the new environment is similar in many respects to the home environment.

The Ability to Automatize Information Processing

The proposal being made here is that complex information-processing tasks can feasibly be executed only because many of the operations involved in their performance have been automatized (in accordance with the mechanisms described earlier in the chapter). Failure to automatize such operations, whether fully or in part, results in a breakdown of information processing and hence in impaired intelligent task performance. Intellectual operations that can be performed smoothly and automatically by more intelligent individuals are performed only haltingly by less intelligent individuals, who must exercise conscious control.

As in the case of novelty, automatization can occur in task comprehension, in task execution, or in both; and it can be specific to certain situations. I will consider how each of these kinds of automatization operates in various kinds of tasks.

The standard synonyms test used to measure vocabulary is highly familiar to most middle-class students at or above the secondary-school level. Indeed, when confronted with a multiple-choice synonyms test, about the only things the students need to attend to are whether the test is in fact one of synonyms (as opposed to, say, antonyms), and whether there is a penalty for guessing. Examinees can usually read the directions to such a test cursorily, and can probably skip them altogether if they are just told the name of the task. Comprehension of what is required is essentially automatic. But solution of individual test items may be far from automatic. Students may find that they have to give a fair amount of thought to the individual items, whether because they need to discriminate relatively fine shades of meaning, or because they are unsure of particular words' meanings and have to employ strategies to guess the best answers. In the standard synonyms task, then, comprehension of task instructions is essentially automatic (or nearly so), but solution of test items (beyond the simplest ones) probably is not.

In contrast, the experimental tasks used in the cognitive psychologist's laboratory seem to present the opposite situation, at least in one respect. Tasks such as the Posner–Mitchell letter-matching task are unfamiliar to most subjects when they enter the cognitive psychologist's laboratory. The subjects do not automatically know what is expected of them, and have to listen reasonably carefully to the instructions. But after the task is explained and the subjects have had some practice in performing it, task performance usually becomes rapidly automatized. The individual tasks come to be executed almost effortlessly and with little conscious thought.

Very little is known about how situations affect automatization of task performance. Clearly, investigators ought to provide as much practice as possible, and to use a fixed-set rather than a varied-set mode of presentation (Shiffrin and Schneider, 1977). Presumably, it is desirable to minimize distractions in order to allow the individual to concentrate on learning the task and eventually automatizing it.

The Relationship Between the Abilities to Deal with Novelty and to Automatize Processing

For many kinds of tasks, the ability to deal with novelty may occur along an experiential continuum with automatization of information processing. When people first encounter a task or a particular kind of situation, the ability to deal with novelty comes into play. The more intelligent people will be more rapidly and fully able to cope with the novel demands being made upon them. As experience with the task or kind of situation increases, novelty decreases, and the task or situation will become less apt in its measurement of intelligence from the standpoint of processing of novelty. However, after some amount of practice with the task or in the situation, automatization skill may come into play, in which case the task will start to become a more apt measure of automatization skill. Thus, a given task or situation may continue to provide apt measurement of intelligence over practice, but in different ways at different points in time: early on in the person's experience, the ability to deal with novelty is assessed; later, the ability to automatize information processing is assessed. Having a large number of tasks automatized frees processing resources for handling new, novel tasks.

INTELLECTUAL GIFTEDNESS AND RETARDATION

Assessing intelligence with a unidimensional measure such as IQ typically leads to the view that giftedness and retardation are on opposite ends of a single scale. In some quantitative sense, this may be true. But I doubt that the attributes that distinguish the intellectually gifted are truly the same as those in which the retarded show impaired development. Rather, the gifted are probably above average, but not necessarily exceptional, in those attributes that distinguish the retarded from the normal. At exceptional levels of talent, the abilities that start to matter are qualitatively different from those that distinguish normal from retarded performance. In particular, giftedness appears to derive largely from an unusual ability to deal with novel kinds of tasks and situations, whereas retardation appears to derive largely from the inadequate functioning of componential subsystems, the inadequate automatization of componential subsystems, or both.

Giftedness

Janet Davidson and I (Sternberg and Davidson, 1983) have proposed that intellectual giftedness can be understood in terms of the ability of the gifted to think in novel ways, and particularly to think insightfully. Significant and exceptional intellectual accomplishments—for example, major scientific discoveries, important inventions, and new understandings of major literary and philosophical works—almost always involve major intellectual insights. The thinkers' gifts seem to lie directly in their insight abilities, rather than simply in their IQ-test-type abilities or in their abilities to process information rapidly. Although the gifted do seem to differ quantitatively from others in measures of IQ, speed of information processing, ideational fluency (as measured by standard creativity tests), and the like, they also seem to differ qualitatively from others in their insight abilities. Whereas the truly gifted may have several or even many major intellectual insights in their lifetimes, the nongifted will probably have none, although they may well have the relatively more minor kinds of insights that form the bases for term papers, everyday decision making, and the like. The gifted can interpret genuinely novel situations, whereas typical individuals often have difficulty in even comprehending the nature of such situations.

Exactly what processes are involved in such insightful thinking? Davidson and I have proposed that they are the three knowledge-acquisition components—selective encoding, selective combination, and selective comparison—applied in unconventional ways to novel materials. For example, Alexander Fleming's discovery of penicillin may be seen in part as an extraordinary application of selective encoding: in looking at a Petri dish containing a culture that had become moldy, Fleming noticed that bacteria in the vicinity of the mold had been destroyed, presumably by the mold; in essence, Fleming encoded the information in his visual field in a highly selective way, zeroing in on that part of the field that was relevant to the discovery of the antibiotic. A famous example of selective combination is Darwin's formulation of the theory of evolution. It is well known that Darwin had available to him for many years the facts he needed to form the theory of natural selection. What eluded him during these years was a way to combine these facts into a coherent package. His putting together these facts constitutes an insight of selective combination. And finally, a famous example of an insight deriving from selective comparison is Friedrich Kekulé's discovery of a fundamental chemical structure. Kekulé dreamed of a snake curling back on itself and catching its tail. When he woke up, he realized that the image of the snake catching its tail was a metaphor for the structure of the benzene ring.

In sum, our proposition is that the truly intellectually gifted are not merely better in the IQ-test-type tasks employed in standard psychometric instruments, and, occasionally, in laboratory experiments. Rather, the gifted are able to have insights that differ, in their striking originality and consequentiality, from those of ordinary individuals. Moreover, these insights can be understood in terms of the three components of knowledge acquisition described earlier in the chapter. Knowledge acquisition becomes insight when it is applied to novel or nonentrenched domains in an original and consequential way.

Retardation

Retardation is not meaningfully understood in terms of the relative absence of striking insights. People of normal intelligence rarely or never have such insights either. Rather, as mentioned earlier, retardation may be understood in terms of the inadequate functioning of componential subsystems, the inadequate automatization of componential subsystems, or both. The degree of impairment will depend upon the range of task domains to which the impairment extends. The range will in turn depend on things such as the individual's motivation (or lack thereof) in different task domains; the kind and extent of organic damage, if any; the compatibility of teaching methods with the individual's particular set of abilities; and the quantity, quality, and timing of exposure to materials in the various task domains.

I will now consider the loci of retardation suggested by the model, and show how these can be applied to understanding deficient performance on a typical IQ test.

1. *Impaired activation of metacomponents and other kinds of components by metacomponents.* Retarded persons have all the procedural and declarative knowledge necessary to solving a problem, but they are unable to bring this knowledge to bear upon the problem. There is a gap in communication between the metacomponents that "know" what to do and (say) the performance components that would actually do it. This kind of impairment seems closely analogous to what Flavell and Wohlwill (1969) have referred to as a "performance deficit," in contrast to a "mediation deficit." If, for example, a child knows how to solve a certain kind of reasoning problem but is unable to come up with solutions to problems of this kind, impaired activation of performance components by metacomponents might be a source of difficulty.

2. *Impaired feedback to metacomponents from other metacomponents and other kinds of components.* Retarded persons are unable to use information acquired during the course of information processing to alter their performance. For example, if a person reads an algebra word problem and encodes the information that a certain item costs a certain amount, but the person is then unable to feed this information into his or her decision-making processes to determine how the problem should be solved or further analyzed, an impairment in feedback might be indicated. This situation is, in a sense, the reverse of the one described immediately above. In the above (activation) case, communication from metacomponents to other kinds of components was impaired; in this (feedback) case,

communication to metacomponents from other kinds of components is impaired.

3. *Impaired functioning of components of one or more kinds, either through (1) unavailability of components, (2) inaccessibility of components, (3) slowness of component execution, or (4) inaccuracy in the results of component execution.* Retarded persons either lack certain components needed for task performance, fail to access these components (although they are available), or use these components in an inefficacious way. For example, a young child may be unable to map second-order relations because the component is unavailable; or the child may be able to encode information but only incompletely or sloppily.

4. *Impaired automatization of componential subsystems.* Retarded persons cannot make the transition from controlled to automatic processing in a task; or can make this transition only very slowly. For example, the reading skills of slow or otherwise disabled readers are often characterized by excessive amounts of controlled processing and by nonautomatization of bottom-up (low-level) processes that peers would have automatized long ago (Sternberg and Wagner, 1982).

5. *Impaired coordination between controlled and automated componential subsystems, so that control of processing does not pass readily between the two kinds of subsystems.* Retarded persons are unable to effect a smooth transition between controlled and automated information processing in a task. For example, in reading, it is often necessary to move back and forth quickly between relatively well automatized bottom-up processing (such as recognizing phonemes) and relatively controlled top-down processing (such as recognizing the main idea of a paragraph). A person who is unable to transit smoothly between controlled and automated processing is at a disadvantage in reading material of any complexity.

Something ought to be said about acceleration as opposed to retardation of these sources of development. Clearly, acceleration of these processes will result in more rapid cognitive development, and, presumably, in higher scores on IQ tests and the like. Thus, in one sense, high intelligence is the mirror image of low intelligence. But like many other writers, I do not see high intelligence as sufficient for intellectual giftedness. As I have mentioned, the gifted are likely to be above average, but not necessarily outstanding, in these loci of cognitive development: what distinguishes the gifted is their ability to deal with novel domains, rather than merely their ability to solve standard kinds of problems particularly well.

To conclude, I have proposed a componential approach to understanding mental mechanisms in cognitive development, and have suggested how this view might be applied to the understanding of gifted and retarded performance. The proposed view certainly does not account for all of cognitive development, and it is both vague and speculative in its formulations, but it seems to provide a useful start toward understanding at least some aspects of how transitions in cognitive development take place.

NOTES

[1] The framework presented here represents an elaboration but also a modification of views presented in Sternberg (1980).

REFERENCES

Brown, A. L. Knowing when, where, and how to remember: A problem of metacognition. In R. Glaser (Ed.), *Advances in instructional psychology*, Vol. 1. Hillsdale, N.J.: Erlbaum, 1978.

Brown, A. L., and DeLoache, J. S. Skills, plans and self-regulation. In R. Siegler (Ed.), *Children's thinking: What develops?* Hillsdale, N.J.: Erlbaum, 1978.

Chase, W. G., and Simon, H. A. The mind's eye in chess. In W. G. Chase (Ed.), *Visual information processing*. New York: Academic Press, 1973.

Chi, M. T. H. Knowledge structures and memory development. In R. Siegler (Ed.), *Children's thinking: What develops?* Hillsdale, N.J.: Erlbaum, 1978.

Chi, M. T. H., Glaser, R., and Rees, E. Expertise in problem solving. In R. J. Sternberg (Ed.), *Advances in the psychology of human intelligence*, Vol. 1. Hillsdale, N.J.: Erlbaum, 1982.

Flavell, J. H. Cognitive monitoring. In W. P. Dickson (Ed.), *Children's oral communication skills*. New York: Academic Press, 1981.

Flavell, J. H., and Wohlwill, J. F. Formal and functional aspects of cognitive development. In D. Elkind and J. H. Flavell (Eds.), *Studies in cognitive development: Essays in honor of Jean Piaget*. New York: Oxford University Press, 1969.

Gallagher, J. M., and Wright, R. J. Piaget and the study of analogy: Structural analysis of items. In J. Magary (Ed.), *Piaget and the helping professions*, Vol. 8. Los Angeles: University of Southern California, 1979.

Hunt, E. B. Intelligence as an information-processing concept. *British Journal of Psychology*, 1980, 71, 449–474.

Inhelder, B., and Piaget, J. *The growth of logical thinking from childhood to adolescence*. New York: Basic Books, 1958.

Larkin, J. H., McDermott, J., Simon, D. P., and Simon, H. A. Expert and novice performance in solving physics problems. *Science*, 1980, *208*, 1335–1342.

Levinson, P. J., and Carpenter, R. L. An analysis of analogical reasoning in children. *Child Development*, 1974, *45*, 857–861.

Lunzer, E. A. Problems of formal reasoning in test situations. In P. H. Mussen (Ed.), European research in cognitive development. *Monographs of the Society for Research in Child Development*, 1965, *30*(2, Serial No. 100), 19–46.

Markman, E. M. Comprehension monitoring. In W. P. Dickson (Ed.), *Children's oral communication skills*. New York: Academic Press, 1981.

Newell, A., and Simon, H. A. *Human problem solving*. Englewood Cliffs, N.J.: Prentice-Hall, 1972.

Pellegrino, J. W., and Glaser, R. Components of inductive reasoning. In R. E. Snow, P.-A. Federico, and W. E. Montague (Eds.), *Aptitude, learning, and instruction: Cognitive process analyses of aptitude*, Vol. 1. Hillsdale, N.J.: Erlbaum, 1980.

Piaget, J., with J. Montangero and J. Billeter. Les correlats. *L'Abstraction réflèchissante*. Paris: Presses Universitaires de France, 1977.

Schneider, W., and Shiffrin, R. M. Controlled and automatic human information processing: I. Detection, search, and attention. *Psychological Review*, 1977, *84*, 1–66.

Shiffrin, R. M., and Schneider, W. Controlled and automatic human information processing, II: Perceptual learning, automatic attending, and a general theory. *Psychological Review*, 1977, *84*, 127–190.

Siegler, R. S. The origins of scientific reasoning. In R. S. Siegler (Ed.), *Children's thinking: What develops?* Hillsdale, N.J.: Erlbaum, 1978.

Spearman, C. *The nature of "intelligence" and the principles of cognition*. London: Macmillan, 1923.

Sternberg, R. J. *Intelligence, information processing, and analogical reasoning: The componential analysis of human abilities*. Hillsdale, N.J.: Erlbaum, 1977.

Sternberg, R. J. Sketch of a componential subtheory of human intelligence. *Behavioral and Brain Sciences*, 1980 *3*, 573–584.

Sternberg, R. J. Intelligence and nonentrenchment. *Journal of Educational Psychology*, 1981, *73*, 1–16.

Sternberg, R. J. Natural, unnatural, and supernatural concepts. *Cognitive Psychology*, 1982, *14*, 451–488.

Sternberg, R. J., and Davidson, J. E. Insight in the gifted. *Educational Psychologist*, 1983, *18*, 52–58.

Sternberg, R. J., and Gardner, M. K. A componential interpretation of the general factor in human intelligence. In H. Eysenck (Ed.), *A model for intelligence*. Heidelberg: Springer-Verlag, 1982.

Sternberg, R. J., and Gardner, M. K. Unities in inductive reasoning. *Journal of Experimental Psychology: General*, 1983, *112*, 80–116.

Sternberg, R. J., and Nigro, G. Developmental patterns in the solution of verbal analogies. *Child Development*, 1980, *51*, 27–38.

Sternberg, R. J., and Powell, J. S. Comprehending verbal comprehension. *American Psychologist*, 1983, *38*, 878–893.

Sternberg, R. J., and Rifkin, B. The development of analogical reasoning processes. *Journal of Experimental Child Psychology*, 1979, *27*, 195–232.

Sternberg, R. J., and Wagner, R. K. Automatization failure in learning disabilities. *Topics in Learning and Learning Disabilities*, 1982, *2*, 1–11.

Vurpillot, E. The development of scanning strategies and their relation to visual differentiation. *Journal of Experimental Child Psychology*, 1968, *6*, 632–650.

Whitely, S. E. Multicomponent latent trait models for ability tests. *Psychometrika*, 1980, *45*, 479–494.

8 Discussion

John H. Flavell

[I]n this chapter I begin by presenting some historical background and context for the theories presented in the preceding chapters. Next I compare these theories to previous theories and to one another, and suggest what some of their implications for future theorizing might be. Then I discuss each of the six theories briefly and conclude with a few general comments.

BACKGROUND

All the authors in this volume agree that the "mechanisms question" is a crucial one—perhaps *the* crucial one for students of cognitive development to address. Why is it considered so important? One answer is that mechanisms of cognitive development constitute one-half of the developmental story:

> Any account of development, cognitive or otherwise, must speak to two interdependent aspects of the developmental process: formal and functional. The formal aspect has to do with the "morphology" of the process: the sorts of cognitive entities that make up the successive outputs of development and how these entities are causally, temporally, and otherwise interrelated. . . . The other aspect . . . has to do with function and mechanism: the activities and processes of the organism somehow specified in relation to environmental inputs, by which it in fact makes the cognitive progress that has been formally characterized. (Flavell and Wohlwill, 1969, pp. 67–68)

Furthermore, mechanisms are considered by many to be the more important half of the story. One could argue that *what* gets acquired in human cognitive development is to some extent contingent on the nature of the person and of the person's childhood experiences. In contrast, *how* whatever gets acquired is acquired—that is, how the basic development-making mechanisms or processes do the job—may be largely invariant across human development. Moreover, the mechanisms half appears to be the explanation half (the "how" versus the "what" of development), and explanation is the ultimate objective of any science.

As the above quotation suggests (" . . . two *interdependent* aspects . . ."), one's ideas about mechanism are likely to influence and be influenced by the rest of one's ideas about cognitive development. These ideas include beliefs about the basic nature of the creature that does the developing, about what the most important things are that get acquired or changed during its development, and about the overall character of the developmental course (for example, stage-like or not). Accordingly, it is apparent in this volume that each author's views about mechanisms are to a greater or lesser extent organically related to that author's views about cognizers, cognition, and cognitive development. That fact provides those of us who read these chapters with some unexpected but important fringe benefits: namely, some interesting insights and suggestions about other, non-mechanism aspects of human cognitive growth.

Needless to say, these psychologists are not the first to propose mechanisms or processes of cognitive development. Piaget, Werner, E. J. Gibson, and others (including Flavell, 1972, 1977) have suggested various processes or principles:

> Two major classes of these processes or principles seem to be distinguishable. One class generates distinctions within cognitive entities. The other relates one cognitive entity to one or more others. The first class of processes is almost always called *differentiation*. There is no satisfactory generic name for the second, because more than one kind of relationship among entities can be postulated. For example, the terms used to characterize various kinds of relationships among cognitive entities include *integration*, *hierarchic integration*, *subordination*, *coordination*, *regulation*, *conflict*, and *equilibration*. (Flavell, 1977, pp. 240–241)

Not surprisingly, some of the present authors describe processes of cognitive growth that are reminiscent of these; see, for example, Fischer's transformation rules of *compounding*, *intercoordination*, and *differentiation*. It is also no surprise to see that Piaget's ideas about mechanisms and other aspects of cognitive development have had an important influence on many of the proposals made in these chapters.

This bit of history notwithstanding, serious theorizing about basic mechanisms of cognitive growth has actually never been a popular pastime, now or in the past. It is rare indeed to encounter a substantive treatment of the problem in the annual flood of articles, chapters, and books on cognitive development. The reason is not hard to find: good theorizing about mechanisms is very, very hard to do. As Furth notes (1981, p. 253), it took Piaget almost 50 years to produce the final version of his equilibration model (Piaget, 1975). Yet despite all that talent and time, the final version seems to me much less clear and specific than a good theory of the developmental process should be. The ideal theory would propose specific, clearly defined mechanisms, with their modes of operation characterized precisely and in great detail. It may be asking too much to insist that the theory actually be falsifiable by experimental test. However, the theory should at least suggest empirical studies that would, depending upon how they turned out, enhance or reduce its plausibility as an account of how cognitive development proceeds. Above all, it should also suggest studies that would yield new factual knowledge and new insights concerning anything cognitive developmental, mechanisms or other. Like Piaget's, the present theories surely fall short of this ideal. (Whenever one sees six different theories supposedly trying to explain the same thing, one should suspect that Truth is not yet at hand!) But also like Piaget's, they are interesting, insightful efforts to crack the toughest conundrum in the field: how the mind of the child develops.

COMPARISONS AMONG THE THEORIES

It may be revealing to compare and contrast the six theories with respect to: (1) their relationships to other theories or approaches, (2) their ideas about how the nature and development of cognition might be constrained, and (3) their general content and their implications for future theorizing about mechanisms.

Relationships to Other Theories or Approaches

It is a sign of the times that all six theories show the influence of Piaget's theory, the information-processing movement, or—in most cases—both. Other theories or approaches have also had their effects.

Case is, in his own words (p. 20), a neo-Piagetian theorist. Like that of most other neo-Piagetians (Pascual-Leone, Halford), his theory represents a sort of marriage between Piagetian-like stage theory and information-processing psychology (see also Case, 1984).

Fischer and Pipp's theory (henceforth "Fischer's," for short) has a more complex ancestry. It clearly owes a great deal to Piaget, but also more than a little to Bruner, Werner, Skinner, information-processing psychology, and the study of skill learning (Fischer, 1980, pp. 477–478). The theories of Case and Fischer share fundamental commonalities, and seem more similar to one another than either does to any of the other four theories.

Keil's theory owes much to the thinking of Chomsky and Fodor (see Keil, 1981). Although neither a neo-Piagetian nor an information-processing theory, it incorporates a little Piaget (the developmental role of inconsistencies and contradictions) and more than a little information-processing psychology (for example, the importance of domain-specific knowledge structures).

Klahr is well known for his efforts to use self-modifying production systems and other concepts from information-processing psychology to explain cognitive developmental acquisitions (Klahr and Wallace, 1976). However, the acquisitions explained are often Piagetian ones, such as conservation, and Piagetian concepts like reflective abstraction play a role in his theory as well. Klahr's colleague, Siegler is also an information-processing psychologist who often studies Piagetian or Piagetian-like developments, frequently using a special rule-assessment method (for example, see Siegler, 1981). Klahr and Siegler are more similar in their basic views about what cognitive development is like and how it can be profitably studied than their chapters in this book might suggest (Klahr and Siegler, 1978).

Sternberg's theory, too, is clearly of the information-processing genre. However, his views about the nature and development of cognition have been significantly influenced, not so much by Piagetian psychology, but by work in the area of human abilities (the nature of intelligence and related topics), an area in which he has done important research (for example, see Sternberg, 1977).

Ideas About Constraints

The term "constraints" is owed to Keil. However, the present use of it, while including Keil's meaning, is broader. A distinction can be made among *domain-related constraints* (Keil's meaning), *age-related constraints*, and *expertise-related constraints*.

Domain-Related Constraints. Keil introduces the notion of domain-related constraints in the following way:

> The notion of constrained faculties views humans less as all-purpose learning machines and more as biological organisms that have, through the course of evolution, developed specialized "mental organs" that are used to deal with different aspects of their physical and mental worlds (cf. Fodor, 1972). Each organ imposes its own set of constraints on the types of knowledge structures it uses, such that we have different domains of cognition with different formal properties (p. 122).

I think Keil's ideas about domain-related constraints have interesting implications. The subject of all the mechanisms-of-cognitive-development stories told in this book is of course the human child. But exactly what kind of cognitive creature or device is that subject implicitly or explicitly taken to be in each story?

In Keil's story (see also Keil, 1981), the subject is explicitly represented as an immature member of a particular biological species. As such, the child is viewed as prepared by evolution to think and learn in characteristic, species-specific ways, and to find some things easier and more "natural" to develop or learn than others. There are a priori, biologically given constraints on the nature and development of cognition in these natural domains. Children and adults can also think and learn in other, nonnatural domains, making use of more general, all-purpose cognitive and learning procedures. Although Keil does not say this, it can be assumed that these all-purpose procedures have also evolved, perhaps helping to make us the versatile thinkers and learners our species reputes itself to be. Thus, Keil favors "a compromise view: that humans have a relatively small number of specialized cognitive faculties as well as some more general learning procedures and forms of representations" (p. 125).

No other theorist in this volume explicitly represents the subject of human cognitive development as a biological organism that has evolved the capability and disposition to acquire some things differently, and with more native talent or special aptitude, than other things. Siegler describes the subject's cognitive development in analogy with biological evolution, but does not characterize the subject itself in biological-evolutionary terms. Whatever position on the matter the other theorists may take privately, their chapters certainly portray a child that is more "all-purpose learning machine" than, à la Keil, all-purpose machine plus "specialized 'mental organs.'" If Keil's view is even roughly correct (and I, for one, strongly suspect that it is), it would seem to follow logically that the other theories are at present too monolithic, too undifferentiated over cognitive domains, to explain adequately all of human cognitive development.

Age-Related Constraints.   Like Pascual-Leone (1970) before them, Case and Fischer argue that there are age-related constraints or limitations on the child's cognitive and learning capabilities. At any given age, there will be a processing limit on the mental computations the child can perform and, therefore, on what the child can learn or acquire. As the child grows older, these constraints are progressively reduced and the child's cognitive and learning capabilities increase. For Case, the constraint is due to a limitation in the size of the child's short-term storage space. For Fischer, it is characterized as an "optimal level," or upper limit on the complexity of skills that the child can construct and control. Both speculate that biological-maturational factors may be at least partly responsible for these age-dependent limitations. Thus, Case and Fischer are stage theorists who believe that processing limitations, yoked to the child's age and therefore probably to the child's neurological development, constrain the rate of childhood cognitive development. In both theories the content and rate of cognitive developmental acquisitions are also seen as highly dependent upon specific experiences and opportunities to learn; more consideration and emphasis is given to environmental factors in these theories than in Piaget's—an improvement on Piaget's theory, in my judgment. However, any "heterogeneity" (Flavell, 1982) or unevenness in the child's cognitive level due to intra-individual variation in domain-specific aptitudes or experiences is constrained by a built-in, age-dependent, domain-independent "homogeneity" in processing capacity.

The other four theorists do not assume any such endogenous governors for the rate of childhood cognitive growth. Even Keil, otherwise the most "biological" of all the authors, makes no such assumptions. Quite the contrary: his biological-evolutionary view undoubtedly rules out the possibility of much if any age-dependent, domain-independent limitation on cognition and learning. Just as one would not expect the heart and the liver to be on the "same" developmental level (whatever that might mean) at each point in embryogenesis, so would one not expect homogeneity of level or processing capacity across developing mental organs—or between any mental organ and Keil's general, domain-independent procedures—at each point in cognitive ontogenesis. Of course, Keil might believe that each "natural," domain-specific development is to some degree age-locked, but he makes no such claim in his chapter.

What would be the consequences of not assuming any biological-maturational, age-dependent constraints on the rate of cognitive development, or, more strongly, of explicitly asserting that there are none? I think that there would be two significant effects.

The first is that the rapidity of cognitive development during childhood would be limited only by the availability of developmentally formative inputs and experiences. To add " . . . and by the child's ability to process them," as all of us would doubtless want to do, means putting assumptions about rate of development into the developmental story. To add further, " . . . and convert them into cognitive progress," as we might also all want to do, implies the need for still more assumptions about rate.

The second consequence of this assumption is that the process of cognitive development could continue unabated until death. (I want to say something startling like, " . . . could career along at the same dizzying rate until it hurtles into the river Styx," to underscore this point.) With apologies to the life-span developmental psychologists, I have the strong sense that "cognitive development of the prototypical, childhood variety" (which I shall not further define) does not continue past late adolescence or young adulthood. Fischer (Table 3-1) and Case (see Case, 1984) explicitly set its upper limit in this age period. Although they are less explicit than Case and Fischer on this point, Keil, Klahr, Siegler, and Sternberg also seem to construe cognitive development as "childhood cognitive development," and to propose mechanisms designed to explain the latter. Certainly none of them is known as a student of cognitive changes during adulthood. Nevertheless, there appears to me to be nothing in their theories that characterizes childhood and adulthood cognitive changes as different in any way, or as requiring different mechanisms for their explanation.

I believe, therefore, that Keil, Klahr, Siegler, and Sternberg should try to take more explicit account in their theories of the fact that cognitive growth in normal individuals proceeds within the range of rates that it does—neither a great deal faster nor a great deal slower—and of the probability that it does not continue to any significant extent after late adolescence or early adulthood. Adding the idea of possible domain-related constraints to possible age-related ones, I would urge Klahr, Siegler, and Sternberg to be more precise in locating the subject of their theories in phylogenetic and ontogenetic space. That is, I think they should identify the subject as a biologically evolved, partly specialized "creature" rather than (perhaps more by default than by design) as a nonbiological, all-purpose "device", one that is undergoing a special, nonarbitrary course of cognitive change constrained in both rate and time of life.

Expertise-Related Constraints.   Before Piagetian psychology became widely known, cognitive development was regarded by most psychologists as the mere accumulation of knowledge. As one grew older one learned more. Big deal! Question: why study such a dull process? Answer: for no good reason; and most psychologists didn't. Then Piaget portrayed cognitive development as a stage-wise sequential acquisition of fundamental, broadly generalizable structures of cognitive actions (for example, systems of tightly related, reversible operations), and that made the process seem far more interesting. Now cognitive development is once again being described as the growth of knowledge. However, there are at least two reasons why this should not portend a regression to the bad old days. First, the process is not seen as one of knowledge "accumulation." Rather, it is conceived of as the building up of richly organized conceptual networks or structures of declarative and procedural knowledge. Second, there is nothing "mere" about this process, because the construction of such extensive, complex networks of knowledge in a domain makes possible efficient, skillful, and otherwise very mature-looking cognitive functioning in that domain. How it does so is nicely described in Sternberg's chapter. To put it the other way around, the absence of sufficient organized knowledge or expertise in a domain can profoundly constrain cognitive functioning in that domain. Hence the notion of expertise-related constraints.

I suspect that most, if not all, of the six theorists do believe that at least a good deal of human cognitive development can be profitably conceptualized in terms of the acquisition of domain-specific expertise and of the high-quality cognitive functioning that expertise brings with it. The belief is perhaps most explicit in the chapters by Keil and Sternberg, although the two authors discuss it in somewhat different contexts. Even those theorists who do not argue for domain-related and/or age-related constraints (Klahr, Siegler, and Sternberg) certainly believe that insufficient procedural or declarative knowledge in any area can severely constrain the child's cognitive functioning in that area.

A Brief Summary of the Theories and Their Implications

What is the acutal content of each of the six theories, and what implications or prescriptions do they suggest for future theorizing about mechanisms? Table 8-1 summarizes some of the main points of each theory. "Cognitive units" are the core theoretical entites that constitute, within each theory, major sources, loci, and outcomes of cognitive development. Some of the descriptions of mechanisms given in the table are virtually copied from the chapters (for example, Fischer and Pipp's); others necessitated some interpretation on my part (for example, Keil's). The last column cites additional features of interest.

Following are some of the things that future theorists might be advised to try to do, based upon what one or more of the present theorists have attempted:

1. Try to get clues about mechanisms of cognitive development by looking at mechanisms postulated for other kinds of development. Siegler looks to evolutionary theory for clues. Keil has found the Chomskyan view of language development useful in thinking about development in other "natural" cognitive domains. I think we might examine still other kinds of "development" for whatever hints they might provide. Examples that come to mind are intellectual history (especially history of science), embryogenesis of organ systems (recall Chomsky's "mental organs" metaphor), neuropsychological de-

Table 1
Major Constituents of Each Theory

Theorist	Cognitive units	Mechanisms of cognitive development	Other features
Case	Executive control structures	Processes: problem solving, exploration, imitation, and mutual regulation; also differentiation and hierarchical integration of executive control structures to form more complex ones	Stages and substages
		Subprocesses within each process: goal setting, novel-sequence generation, utility evaluation, executive restructuring, and consolidation	
		Increase in short term storage space with age	
Fisher and Pipp	Skill structures	Transformation rules: substitution, focusing, compounding, differentiation, and intercoordination	Stages and substages
		Increase in the structural complexity of skills children can construct and control (optimal level) with age	Treatment of individual differences

Keil	Knowledge structures, especially in "natural" conceptual domains	Increase in knowledge within domains, leading to: differentiation of knowledge, resulting in awareness of interdomain relations; detection of, and response to, internal inconsistencies or contradictions; and avoidance of violations of universal constraints	Nature of mechanisms depends upon domain
Klahr	Self-modifying production systems	Analysis of a stored record of previous behavior and its results (the time line) leads to: detection of regularities, elimination of redundancies, and activation of such self-modification mechanisms as conflict-resolution rules, discrimination, generalization, and composition	Treatment of individual differences
Siegler	Rules	Variability mechanism consisting of: encoding processes (feature construction and value monitoring) and combination processes (feature selection, feature integration, and rule execution)	Cognitive development analogous to evolution
Sternberg	Components (elementary information processes)	Interactions within and between three major classes of components (metacomponents, performance components, and knowledge-acquisition components), making endless feedback loops possible Automatization of components	Treatment of individual differences

velopment of the visual system (nowadays replete with critical periods and other interesting developmental phenomena), physical growth, and motor learning and development.

2. Whether or not you actually believe the assumption, assume provisionally that cognitive development is equivalent to "learning," broadly construed. Then see how many principles, mechanisms, or processes that have been worked out over decades of research on learning and instruction might prove useful in explaining cognitive development. Considerable attention is given in these chapters to learning through imitation, perceptual learning (feature encoding and so forth), automatization through practice, use of corrective feedback, discrimination, generalization, and other processes from the field(s) of learning. Learning principles that do not prove useful in explaining a particular segment of cognitive growth can of course be abandoned (for that segment). This strategy for theory construction is essentially the same as the one above: when trying to explain something, first see what you can use from previous attempts to explain similar things.

3. As Klahr points out: "Unambiguous theories of knowledge states are a necessary prerequisite for theories of transition, because a transition theory can be no better than a theory of what it is that is undergoing that transition" (p. 138). He says that we need a conceptualization of the child's knowledge representation; that is, "descriptive formalisms for characterizing the structures and processes in which children's knowledge is embedded" (p. 137). Thus, future theories of transition will need to specify carefully and in clear detail the "cognitive units" (Table 8-1) that constitute their starting points.

4. As present and previous theorists have done, pay attention to the imaginable, conceivable ways that knowledge and cognition can change. Then provisionally assume that such changes really do commonly occur in human cognitive development. That is, assume that for cognitive entities, differentiation, coordination, integration (hierarchical or otherwise), and so on represent important categories of developmental change. Processes like Piaget's equilibration (for example, resolution of conflicts, inconsistencies, and contradictions) should be given serious consideration (although I personally doubt if they account for as much of the variance in cognitive growth as Piaget thought they did).

5. In keeping with the general Zeitgeist in psychology, assume that children "develop themselves" more than they "get developed." All of the present authors presuppose, in the Piagetian spirit, that children are active, self-directing cognitive entrepreneurs who develop their minds through a great many spontaneously generated

information-processing activities. Each theorist has his own pre-
ferred list of such activities, and some of the lists are quite long (for
example, Sternberg's). There is some overlap in the lists at the surface
level, and probably a great deal more beneath the surface. That is,
an information-processing activity that is given a name in one theory
may often be an unnamed, covert constituent of a differently named
activity in aother theory; or it may simply be an activity that the
other theorist would not object to but did not highlight. This would
make microscopic, point-by-point comparisons of the six theories
difficult, and, I believe, ultimately more misleading than helpful.
Activities of an executive sort are given prominent play in several
theories. Case, for example, speaks of planning, goal setting, strategy
selection, and executive restructuring. Executive processes are emphasized even more strongly in Sternberg's theory, with its sovereign
metacomponents.

6. Give theoretical consideration to cognitive changes that proceed without any present input or feedback from the external environment. These presumably occur through operations on internal
stored representations of past actions or other data. Klahr's concept
of the time line and Piaget's equilibration model attempt to take
account of these "underground" cognitive changes. Obviously, the
child develops in the course of processing external data; everyone's
theory addresses change of that kind. However, I think that changes
of this other, completely internal variety may ultimately be proven
to be at least as important.

7. Also give theoretical consideration to changes in the data children notice and use in their thinking and problem solving: that is,
changes in what they attend to, encode, represent, accommodate to,
assimilate, and the like. Siegler's theory in particular emphasizes the
importance of encoding processes (the construction, monitoring, selection, and integration of features) in the child's acquisition and
use of cognitive rules. Sternberg also describes changes in what is
noticed and used in his description of knowledge-acquisition components.

8. Take account of and try to explain the fact that older children
usually appear to have something akin to a greater working-memory
capacity than do younger children. Whether this increased capacity
must ultimately be explained by appealing to maturational factors
(Case, Fischer) or whether it can be explained in other ways is a
highly controversial issue in developmental psychology at present.
Case's exciting recent research may help to resolve the issue.

9. Try to account for both big and little cognitive developmental
changes, either by the same mechanisms or by different ones. In the

last version of his equilibration theory, Piaget described three types of equilibration or cognitive balances (Furth, 1981; Piaget, 1975): (1) an assimilation–accommodation balance (a balance between subject and object), (2) a balance involving coordinations among schemes or subschemes (for example, the mutual or reciprocal assimilation of two schemes), and (3) a balance involving the integration of schemes into higher-order totalities. If I have understood the theory correctly, the achievement of these balances could be interpreted as entailing cognitive changes of small scope (1), medium scope (2), and large scope (3). Fischer distinguishes between mechanisms that produce small or medium-sized (within level) cognitive advances and mechanisms that produce large (between-level) cognitive advances: substitution, focusing, compounding, and differentiation for the former; intercoordination for the latter. Case and Keil also distinguish between smaller, more continuous changes and larger, more qualitative ones. In contrast, Klahr believes that the same mechanisms that produce minor advances can also explain major ones.

10. Finally, attempt to explain individual differences in cognitive growth. In this volume, some of the chapters deal with individual differences in the rate or the final level of cognitive growth— differences that are a factor in various forms of retarded versus precocious development (Fischer, Sternberg). Differences in developmental paths or routes to particular cognitive achievements are also discussed (Case, Fischer, Klahr).

COMMENTS ON INDIVIDUAL THEORIES

I will now mention briefly what seem to be to me some of the most noteworthy positive and negative features of each theory.

Case

Although Case's theory is certainly highly interesting and thought-provoking, it seems unclear and not very carefully thought through in places (at least in its present exposition—but cf. Case, 1984). He distinguishes between "functions that do not vary in human development" (p. 37) and "capabilities that are not present at birth" (p. 46). This sort of distinction is an interesting and important one. However, some of the functions he places in the former category do in fact vary in human cognitive development. For instance, it can be argued that "the capability for setting goals" (p. 37) is actually absent at birth, and there can be no doubt but that it changes with age. Conversely, Case surely did not mean to claim that short-term storage space (the only "capability" he discusses in this chapter) is not present at birth.

Probably the most interesting and controversial part of Case's theory is his claim that the child's ability to assemble executive control structures for solving problems is constrained by age-dependent limitations on working memory. In one section of his chapter ("The Role of Short-Term Storage Space"), he tries to show how the integration of two executive structures into a more complex structure (all concerning the scale-balance problem) would require the same working-memory capacity whether this were accomplished via problem solving, exploration, imitation, or mutual regulation. In his analysis, each of the four acquisition routes requires of the child the capacity to allot either operating space or storage space to two cognitive events called "enumeration" and "weight estimation." However, the events subsumed under "enumeration" are not the same from route to route, and I believe they must be in order for Case's reasoning here to be convincing. Enumeration uses operating space in the problem-solving and mutual-regulation routes. It is described as "applying the enumeration structure" for problem solving, and as "processing the demonstration"—that is, listening to or watching another's demonstration of how to compare weights via enumeration—"and attempting it oneself" in mutual regulation. In the exploration and imitation routes, enumeration uses storage space. It is described as "storing some record of the result of the enumeration structure's application a second earlier" in exploration, and as "remembering that the enumeration structure was applied a second or two earlier" in limitation.

It seems most unlikely *prima facie* that these four mental events, or even the two events within each pair, make even roughly equal demands on the child's working memory. More generally, I think it is a very hazardous and uncertain undertaking to try to infer, rather than measure, the quantitative processing demands of a particular problem-solving or learning experience. How can one be sure how much processing demand each component operation makes, or even exactly what all the component operations are? It may very well be that Case deals with such concerns adequately in his new book (Case, 1984), but he does not do so here.

These objections to "memory-slot counting" are not meant to suggest that Case must therefore be wrong in his basic belief in age-dependent—rather than simply expertise-dependent—processing-capacity constraints. In fact, he and his coworkers have recently gathered some highly interesting experimental data that appear to support his belief. If his belief does eventually prove to be right, it should make possible, at long last, a workable stage theory of cognitive development, one with the intuitively right (to me) mix of, at any given age, centrifugal "heterogeneity" (Flavell, 1982) of mind due to inter-individual and intra-individual differences in aptitudes, experiences, and so on, and centripetal "homogeneity" of mind due to age-dependent processing-capacity constraints. The result might be a highly plausible theoretical account of what has so far eluded us: exactly how younger and older children differ cognitively.

Fischer and Pipp

Like Case but perhaps to an even greater extent, Fischer and his colleagues make a large number of bold and imaginative claims about a wide variety of cognitive developmental phenomena, and also try to test their claims experimentally. Both theorists try to see "the big picture" (Fischer, 1980, p. 520) in this broad and complex area, and that is very laudable. However, bold and imaginative claims are likely to elicit skepticism as well as admiration in most of us. I wonder how easy and straightforward a task it is to assign unambiguously a skill-structure description, and hence a cognitive level, to a cognitive performance in any area. My reaction here is somewhat similar to my reaction to Case's slot counting. Fischer's level assignments for pretend play seem quite clear and unambiguous, to be sure, but I wonder if they would be equally so in other areas. I am just not sure I understand the precise, domain-invariant, essential meaning of "system of representational systems, equivalent to a single abstract set" (Table 3-1), and the like.

Similarly, the five transformation rules are certainly interesting, and together with the system of levels they have generated some good, innovative research on developmental sequences. But again I wonder if, say, "intercoordination" (p. 79) has a single, uniform meaning in all its uses, a meaning that is clearly distinguishable from "compounding" (p. 78). For example, at the level of "mappings," intercoordination can mean getting doctor and patient dolls to interact with one another in role-appropriate ways, rather than acting in these ways alone, nonsocially. At the level of "system," it can mean getting one doll to act in two roles at once; for example, as both doctor and father. Why would both of these types of activities be described with the term "intercoordination"? Is the core meaning of intercoordination—the meaning that holds across all uses of the term—that of "linking together," and if so, how is that clearly distinguishable from the "linking together" meaning of compounding? As with Case's theory, I wonder if things given the same name in Fischer's theory always refer to the same cognitive entities or processes. Of course, this does not necessarily mean that the theory is wrong, but I do believe that it needs further specification and clarification.

I am also presently skeptical about the research method and research evidence Fischer and Pipp use to document the existence of growth spurts at specific ages (Figure 3-3 and accompanying text). Perhaps the more detailed treatment of growth spurts in the forthcoming Fischer, Pipp, and Bullock chapter (in press) will be more convincing. I am also somewhat dubious about their suggestions concerning the loci of differences between bright and retarded children (similar optimal levels, different skill-acquisition proficiencies), although I find them intriguing. Finally, Fischer and Pipp say that "the growing efficiency [of a rise in optimal level] comes not from an increase in the number of items that can be held in working memory, but from a change in the type of structure that can be controlled" (p. 88). This claim distinguishes Fischer's theory from Case's, but leaves me wondering what undergirds the change in the type of structure that can be controlled, if it is not something like an age-dependent increase in working-memory capacity. The possibility of an age-related constraint that is not ascribed to attentional or memory limitations is certainly interesting, however, and reminiscent of pre-neo-Piagetian Piagetian theory.

Keil

As must have been apparent in my previous section on domain-related constraints, I found Keil's chapter to be highly stimulating reading. I think that its biological emphasis is basically right-minded, and that its proposed distinction between domain-specific and all-purpose cognitive skills is both novel and quite plausible. Further elaboration of these positive points would be redundant with that section.

At the same time, the writing tends to be vague and overly abstract, with the result that one often simply does not understand exactly what Keil is proposing. In contrast to the preceding two chapters, it seems to present more of a theoretical agenda than an explicit, worked-out theory. Keil does not specify exactly which domains are and are not "natural" ones, nor exactly what the constraints in the natural domains consist of (except in the case of the M-constraint), nor exactly what his favored transition mechanisms are. On this last point, he gives us "four examples of apparently discontinuous changes in cognitive development" in a section entitled "Some Examples of Structure-Dependent Transition Mechanisms," but he does not clearly spell out what mechanisms are responsible for each change.

Klahr

In his review of Klahr and Wallace's (1976) book, Trabasso commended their approach for its explicit, detailed nature "in a field where explicitness is generally in short supply" (Trabasso, 1977, p. 492). I find the present chapter even clearer and more explicit than that book and many of Klahr's subsequent writings. Klahr's approach to the description and explanation of cognitive growth continues to progress and show promise for still more progress, as Klahr, Anderson, Neches, and others continue to work out effective change mechanisms in self-modifying production systems. Klahr is probably justified in saying, "to the best of my knowledge, there are not other equally specific proposals for how self-modification might come about" (p. 159). I like his idea about developmental tractability, his mechanisms for self-modification, and, especially, his time-line concept. I look forward to reading his and his colleagues' most recent, detailed accounts of exactly how the time line and the associated processes work (see note 12, p. 169 of this volume). The addition of the strength mechanism addresses the problem of the seemingly all-or-none, nonprobabilistic character of productions. I also believe that Klahr makes a reasonable defense against the objection that self-modifying production systems can account for learning but not for the "essence" of development.

What of possible criticisms? As with Siegler's and Sternberg's theories, I wish it had some biology in it. On the other hand, there is no reason to think that Klahr's approach could not be adapted to constrained as well as unconstrained developments. Trabasso (1977) objected that the psychological validity of the model remained to be proven on empirical grounds. I believe that subsequent work by Klahr and his coworkers (for example, Klahr and Robinson, 1981) has reduced the force of that objection somewhat, although not wholly. Finally, I think that the approach has been better at explaining developments discovered by others (such as number-conservation development) than at suggesting new, previously unstudied developments. Fischer's theory, for example, appears to have been more productive thus far than Klahr's in generating novel developmental sequences for empirical test. On the other hand, it should be added that one of Klahr's explicit objectives has been to apply his approach to developmental progressions that we already know something about.

Siegler

As Siegler indicates (p. 172), his account of how cognitive development proceeds was partly created for the occasion of this book.

More than Fischer's, for example, it could be described as "computed" rather than "retrieved from storage." It also does not have, as helpful context and support, the architecture of an already worked out "big-picture" theory of cognitive development, as do, say, Case and Fischer. On the other hand, it does grow out of Siegler's previous theorizing and research, and makes some very nice points about the roles of the encoding and combination of features in the generation of cognitive change. For example, the chapter contains an insightful discussion of why young children might be as predisposed as they are to use unidimensional rules. It appears that Siegler and Case (and also perhaps Fischer) would differ in their favored explanation for this predisposition. Also very interesting is Siegler's suggestion that the feature-construction process continues to synthesize and monitor new features even while the child continues to use only old ones for old rules; thus, when the old rules prove unsatisfactory, new features lie ready at hand for the construction of new rules. My impression is that Siegler's theory is more aptly described as limited in scope than as unclear or off-track in what it proposes. As such, one could imagine it profitably being incorporated into or combined with other theoretical approaches.

Sternberg

Sternberg provides a generally plausible-seeming account of how cognitive development might proceed, drawing upon his elegant componential theory of intelligence. I found a number of ideas in his chapter interesting and insightful: Metacomponents are regarded as truly central to understanding both the nature and development of intelligence (I am biased in favor of "meta-" type cognition and knowledge). Cognitive development proceeds in part by a bootstrapping, reciprocal-mediation-type interactive process in which progress in knowledge or component A makes for progress in B, which in turn leads to further progress in A, and so on and on through a succession of possibly endless feedback loops. The proposed interplay between activation of and feedback from various components is likewise very plausible. Automatization of functioning is also identified as a potent source of cognitive growth, and that seems right. Finally, Sternberg's ideas about how gifted, high-intelligence, and retarded individuals differ from one another within his theoretical framework are very thought-provoking. They represent a good example of how hard thinking about one topic (mechanisms of cognitive development in normal children) can often lead to insights about related topics (giftedness, retardation).

I do have several questions concerning Sternberg's theory. Are the various components as distinct and different from one another as his chapter would lead one to think? For example, are there still-more-elementary information processes that several, or even all, of his different components share in common? In other words, do the different components have common subcomponents? When do we get ever-continuing cognitive progress ("unending feedback loops") and when don't we? That is, under what conditions does cognitive progress in a domain slow down, temporarily stall, or even cease for good? Is Sternberg's theoretical system better able to explain some cognitive acquisitions than others? For example, are the cognitive advances that we make in the early months of life mediated by the nine metacomponents described in this chapter? This is a question that can be raised, in one form or another, about all six theories, as I will show in the last section.

FINAL COMMENTS

I believe, finally, that there is more variety and complexity in cognitive development than is suggested by these six theories (cf. Flavell, 1982, pp. 24–25). There is more variety in *what* gets developed and also more variety in *how* these varied developments get accomplished.

As to the "what," the theories of the future will have to account for the development, not only of the skill and knowledge structures, rules, and other cognitive units cited in these chapters, but also of a diverse assortment of other, possibly very different "units." Examples include tacit or explicit theories, beliefs, attitudes, fantasies, and feelings about self, others, causality, morality, friendship, politics, and myriad other objects, events, and relations in our social and nonsocial worlds. How well could the present theories explain the development of such oddments as the capacity to use symbols, a "theory of mind," self schemata, social-comparison processes, story grammars, the appearance-reality distinction, a sense of self-efficacy, and good judgment or wisdom? Would all of these theories be able to explain such "nonprototypical" developments naturally and easily? Indeed, would *any* of them be able to do so? Moreover, there are undoubtedly other important cognitive developmental outcomes that we have not yet unearthed. Given all those that the field has identified and studied over the past few decades, who would bet that the "what" of cognitive growth has now been completely charted? Recall Klahr's statement about theories of transition being no better than theories of what undergoes transition (p. 138).

As to "how," the authors of these chapters have for the most part described general mechanisms that can apply at any point or period of ontogenesis. That is, of course, a sensible strategy early on in a theoretical enterprise (and we are all certainly very early on in this theoretical enterprise). However, at some point we will have to face the likelihood that part of what mechanisms of cognitive development generate is other mechanisms of cognitive development. This implies that some of the agents (activities, knowledge, skills, or other mechanisms or processes) of our cognitive growth are not age-independent functional invariants. Rather, requiring development themselves, they would become available to help generate further growth only after a certain age or developmental level. I am, of course, talking about processes that are more specific than general processing capacity or the like. For example, I believe that the capacity to manipulate symbols is both a product of development and a mechanism of subsequent development. The same is arguably true for such diverse ensembles of processes as imitation, social-perspective taking, comprehension monitoring, and the use of memory strategies. They are part of the "what" of development, but, once developed, they also become part of the "how." In this respect, cognitive development is a little like technological development (yet another model for cognitive development?). Technological innovations make possible new products, some of which in turn engender further technological innovations.

One implication of the idea that developmental mechanisms generate other developmental mechanisms is that the acquisition of any X by two children—one older and one younger—may not be mediated by exactly the same mechanisms (and also, for that reason, may not even be exactly the same X). For example, perhaps a younger and an older novice do not achieve expertise in some or in many domains via identical mechanisms, because the older one may use learning strategies or other metacognitive skills that the younger one has not yet acquired.

This emphasis on variety and diversity in the what and how of cognitive ontogenesis may seem counterproductive in some ways. First let us find some plausible-looking mechanisms for some developments, one might argue, and leave the explanation of other developments until later. Reasonable enough, but keeping all this heterogeneity in mind while doing that may alert us to a disturbing but real possibility: namely, that there simply cannot be any single theory that would be capable of explaining—adequately, in detail—everything that we shall want to explain concerning cognitive developmental mechanisms. As in other areas of psychology, we may be obliged to devise specific theories for specific transitions, because different transitions may be accomplished in quite different ways. I am not convinced that things will turn out this way, and I certainly hope they do not. But I wouldn't be greatly surprised if they did.

REFERENCES

Case, R. Intellectual development: A systematic reinterpretation. New York: Academic Press, 1984.

Fischer, K. W. A theory of cognitive development: The control and construction of hierarchies of skills. Psychological Review, 1980, 87, 477–531.

Fischer, K. W., Pipp, S. L., and Bullock, D. Detecting developmental discontinuities: Method and measurement. In R. Harmon and R. N. Emde (Eds.), Continuities and discontinuities in development. New York: Plenum Press, in press.

Flavell, J. H. An analysis of cognitive-developmental sequences. Genetic Psychology Monographs, 1972, 86, 279–350.

Flavell, J. H. Cognitive development. Englewood Cliffs, N.J.: Prentice-Hall, 1977.

Flavell, J. H. Structures, stages and sequences in cognitive development. Minnesota Symposium on Child Psychology, 1982, 15, 1–28.

Flavell, J. H., and Wohlwill, J. F. Formal and functional aspects of cognitive development. In D. Elkind and J. H. Flavell (Eds.), Studies in cognitive development: Essays in honor of Jean Piaget. New York: Oxford University Press, 1969.

Fodor, J. Some reflections on L. S. Vygotsky's Thought and Language. Cognition, 1972, 1, 83–95.

Furth, H. G. Piaget and knowledge: Theoretical foundations, 2nd ed. Chicago: University of Chicago Press, 1981.

Keil, F. C. Constraints on knowledge and cognitive development. Psychological Review, 1981, 88, 197–227.

Klahr, D., and Robinson, M. Formal assessment of problem solving and planning processes in preschool children. Cognitive Psychology, 1981, 13, 113–148.

Klahr, D., and Siegler, R. S. The representation of children's knowledge. In H W. Reese and L. P. Lipsitt (Eds.), Advances in child development, Vol. 12. New York: Academic Press, 1978.

Klahr, D., and Wallace, J. G. Cognitive development: An information processing view. Hillsdale, N.J.: Erlbaum, 1976.

Pascual-Leone, J. A mathematical model for the transition rule in Piaget's developmental stages. Acta Psychologica, 1970, 32, 301–345.

Piaget, J. L'équilibration des structures cognitives: Problème central du développement. Paris: Presses Universitaires de France, 1975.

Siegler, R. S. Developmental sequences within and between concepts. Monographs of the Society for Research in Child Development, 1981, 46, (2, Serial no. 189).

Sternberg, R. J. Intelligence, information processing, and analogical reasoning: The componential analysis of human abilities. Hillsdale, N.J.: Erlbaum, 1977.

Trabasso, T. Review of Klahr and Wallace's Cognitive development: An information processing view. Contemporary Psychology, 1977, 22, 492–494.

Index

Adults, subitizing in, 112–114
Affiliation domains, 11–12
Age-related constraints, 192–194
Aitken, A. C., 92–93
Angott-Kwan, T., 49
Anderson, J. R., 91, 125, 127, 128, 145, 204
Anzai, Y., 128, 131
Asche, S. E., 84

Baldwin, J. M., 3, 8, 11, 38
Batterman, N., 89
Baylor, G. W., 104, 106
Beasley, C. M., Jr., 125, 128, 145
Becker, J., 155
Beilin, H., 130
Berman, M., 2
Bertenthal, B. I., 64
Bever, T. G., 88, 91
Biemiller, A. J., 30
Biggs, J., 49, 68
Billeter, J., 167
Binet, A., 178
Biological correlates of optimal level, 57–58
Biological theory, see Evolution theory
Blake, W., 2
Borys, S. V., 103
Boundary conditions, influence of, in structure-dependent transitions, 87–89
Bourne, L. E., Jr., 144–145
Bower, G. H., 104
Bower, T. G. R., 85, 86
Bransford, J. D., 145
Briga, J., 111, 116
Bronfenbrenner, U., 14
Brown, A. L., 69, 82, 103, 165, 166

Bruner, J. S., 26, 190
Bryant, P. E., 22
Bullock, D., 47, 54, 60, 64, 65, 69, 72, 203
Bullock, M., 115–116
Burke, D., 53, 70

Caharack, G., 72
Campbell, D. T., 144
Carey, S., 89
Carnap, R., 14
Carpenter, R. L., 167
Carroll, J. B., 89
Case, R., 19–44, 49, 53, 70, 103, 190, 192–194, 196, 199–203, 205
Chalkley, M. A., 153
Characteristic-to-defining shift in structure-dependent transitions, 89–90
Chase, W. G., 91, 93, 114, 147, 167
Chi, M. T. H., 38, 70, 80, 103, 112, 166, 168
Chomsky, N., 9, 14, 59, 91, 190, 195
Cognitive-development mechanisms, overview of, 187–209
    comparisons among theories, 190–200
    final comments on, 206–208
    historical background to, 188–190
    individual theories of, 200–206
    See also Development; Theory
Cole, M., 9
Collis, K., 49, 68
Combination, encoding and, see Variation
Componential approach, 163–186
    automatization in, see Componential automatization

component, defined, 164–165
as critical in intellectual functioning,
    176–180
framework for, see Componential
    framework
to giftedness, 180–181
mechanisms in, see Componential
    mechanisms
to novel situations, 178
to novel tasks, 176–178
and relationship between dealing
    with novelty and automatization,
    179–180
to retardation, 182–184
as theory, 191, 193–200, 205–207
Componential automatization, 173–176
information processing and, 178–179
relationship between dealing with
    novelty and, 179–180
Componential framework
knowledge-acquisition components
    of, 167–168
metacomponents of, 165–166
performance components of, 166–167
Componential mechanisms, 169–173
intellectual development and
    componential interrelations in,
    171–173
interrelations among components in,
    169–171
Composition in self-modifying system,
    127–128
Conflict resolution rules, 125–126
Conservation of number, 108–112, 117–
    125
applying "the" conservation rule in,
    110–112
construction of internal quantitative
    representation in, 108–109
elaboration of transformational
    classes in, 123–125
encoding type of transformation in,
    110
generalization over time-line
    sequences in, 118–120
individual variation in acquisition of,
    121–123
inferring external equivalence from
    internal equality in, 109–110
rule formation via redundancy
    elimination in, 120–121
self-modifying systems and
    acquisition of, 129–130
time line in, 117–118
Contradictions, resolution of, in
    structure-dependent transitions,
    85–87

Constrained mechanisms, 8–9
as theory, 191–195
Cooper, R. G., Jr., 115
Corrigan, R., 47, 49, 57, 65, 68
Counting, 116–117
Cowan, R., 120
Curtis, L. E., 103, 115

Daneman, M., 39, 40
Darwin, C., 3, 9, 10, 15, 16, 142, 143,
    181
Davidson, J. E., 177, 180, 181
Davison, M. L., 55
Day, M. C., 60
DeLoache, J. S., 165, 166
Dempster, F. N., 38, 70
Dennett, D. C., 144
Development, 1–17
history, context, and essential
    messiness in psychology of, 14–15
overview of ends of, 4–15
as progress, 2–4
segmented into domains, 10–14
See also Cognitive-development
    mechanisms, overview of; Theory
Dewey, J., 9
Directive mechanisms, 7–8
Discrimination in self-modifying
    system, 126–127
Domain-related constraints, 191–192
Domain specificity of knowledge
    structures, 93–95
Domains
of application of self-modifying
    systems, 128–129
development segmented into, 10–14
    see also Development
Downing, C. J., 84, 85
Durkheim, E., 144

Eggleston, V. H., 110, 115
Emde, R., 57, 58
Encoding and combination, see
    Variation
Encoding type of transformation in
    number conservation, 110
Environmental conditions for detecting
    levels of skill acquisition, 55–57
Epigenetic transition, problems of, 8–9
Epstein, H. T., 58, 68
Ericsson, K. A., 93
Estes, K. W., 116
Ethical choice, role of, 14–16
Evolution theory (biological theory)
in child development, 3, 4
as productive analogy, 142–143

in social sciences, 143–144
  See also Variation
Executive control structures, 19–44
  and capabilities not present from
    birth, 33–34
  defined, 21
  functional invariance in, 27–33
  operational efficiency in short-term
    storage space, 37–39
  operational practice in short-term
    storage space, 39–40
  problems in, 21–27
  short-term storage space in, 34–40
  as theory, 190, 192–202, 206–207
Expertise-related constraints, 194–195

Falcon, S., 93
Feature construction in encoding and
    combination framework, 147, 148,
    152–153
Feature integration in encoding and
    combination framework, 147, 148,
    155–157
Feature selection in encoding and
    combination framework, 147, 153–
    155
Feigenbaum, E. A., 131
Feltovich, P. J., 147
Feyerabend, P., 14
Fischer, K. W., 45–79, 103, 122, 131,
    189, 190, 192–196, 199, 200, 202–
    205
Flavell, J. H., 25, 64, 65, 67, 97, 165,
    182, 187–209
Fleming, A., 181
Fodor, J. A., 91, 94, 190, 191
Forgy, C. L., 125
Fot, C., 26
Freud, S., 11
Functional invariance and executive
    control structure, 27–33
Furth, H. G., 189, 200

Gaensbauer, T., 57, 58
Gallagher, J. M., 167
Gallistel, C. R., 115, 116
Gardner, M. K., 167
Garrett, M. F., 91
Gascon, J., 104, 106
Gelman, R., 103, 111, 115–116, 121,
    123
Generalization in self-modifying
    system, 127
Gentner, D., 103
Gesell, A., 8
Gibson, E. J., 153, 189

Gibson, R. O., 57, 68
Giftedness, componential approach to,
    180–181
Gladwin, T., 96
Glaser, R., 146, 147, 166
Glass, A., 91
Glenn, C. G., 103
Goals, overview of, of development, 4–
    15
Goethe, J. von, 2
Goldberg, J., 37, 39, 70
Goldstein, G. I., 69
Goodman, G. S., 66
Gottlieb, D. E., 61
Gould, S. J., 4
Greeno, J. G., 116
Gregg, L. W., 131

Haeckel, E. H. P. A., 3
Haith, M. M., 103, 106
Halford, G. S., 26, 123, 190
Hall, G. S., 3
Hand, H. H., 49, 52, 55–56, 61, 68, 69
Harmon, R., 57, 58
Harris, D., 10
Harter, S., 52, 61
Haygood, R. C., 144–145
Hayes, J. R., 92
Higher-order relations, appearance of
    new, in structure-dependent
    transitions, 83–85
Hirshleifer, J., 144
Hirst, W., 72
History, overview of role of, 13–15
Hockett, C. F., 144
Hogan, A. E., 69
Holland, J. H., 146, 147
Holyoak, K. J., 91
Horn, J. L., 65, 68, 69
Hull, C. L., 14
Huttenlocher, J., 53, 70
Hunt, E. B., 104, 171
Hunter, I. M. L., 93

Infants, subitizing in, 114–116
Information-processing movement,
    influence of, 190–191
Inhelder, B., 149, 154, 155, 167
Internal equality, inferring external
    equivalence from, in number
    conservation, 109–110
Internal inconsistencies (or
    contradictions), resolution of, in
    structure-dependent transitions,
    85–87

Internal quantitative representation in number conservation, 108–109
Intellectual functioning
  componential approach as critical in, 176–180
  See also Componential approach
Intelligence, individual differences in, affecting optimal level and skill acquisition, 676–69
Isaac, D. J., 57, 58

Jaques, E., 57, 68
James, W., 9, 11
Jennings, S., 49
John, E. R., 58

Kagan, J., 58, 69
Kaplan, B., 4
Karmiloff-Smith, A., 154, 155
Keil, F. C., 81–99, 190–196, 200, 203
Kekulé, Friedrich, 181
Kendler, T. S., 57, 68
Kenny, S. R., 55, 57, 58
Kessen, W., 1–17, 82
Kessel, F., 13
King, P. M., 55
Kipling, R., 2
Kitchener, K. S., 55, 68
Klahr, D., 38, 46, 66, 101–139, 153, 154, 191, 194–196, 198–200, 204, 206
Kline, P. J., 125, 127, 128, 145
Knowledge-acquisition components in componential framework, 167–168
Knowledge states, transition process and, 102–107
  knowledge states, 103–106
  theoretical criteria, 107
  transition, 106
Knowledge structures, 83–99
  domain specificity of, 93–95
  and structure-dependent transitions, see Structure-dependent transition mechanisms
  structure/process dilemma and, 90–93
  as theory, 190–203, 206–207
Koffka, K., 11
Kohlberg, L., 15
Kuhn, D., 65
Kurland, D. M., 37, 39, 40, 70

Lancy, D. F., 69
Langedoen, D. T., 88
Langley, P., 106, 125–128, 146, 153
Larkin, J. H., 147, 166
Lasnik, H., 91

Lawler, R. W., 65
Lears, J., 2
Lecours, A. R., 40
Lehrer, A., 84
Lenat, D. B., 146
Leonard, E., 57, 68
Leontiades, M., 144
Lesgold, A. M., 147
Levine, M., 145
Levinson, P. J., 167
Lewontin, R. C., 4, 16
Liebert, R., 157
Lincoln, A., 145, 146
Liu, P., 21
Local adaptation, as open mechanism, 9
Logan, G. D., 39
Lovell, K., 69
Luchins, A. S., 128
Lunzer, E. A., 167

McCall, R. B., 57, 67, 68
McCosh, J., 15
McDermott, J., 147, 166
McLaughlin, J. A., 116
MacWhinney, B., 66
Mandelbaum, M., 2
Mandler, J. M., 103
Maratsos, M. P., 153
Markman, E. M., 165
Martarano, S. C., 69
Martin, L. M. W., 121, 122
Matousek, M., 58
Maturation, as basis for explanation, 7–8
Meltzoff, A., 31
Memory limitations in skill acquisition, 70–73
Metacomponents in componential framework, 165–166
Method domains, overview of, 11
Montangero, J., 167
Montesquieu, C. L., 15
Moral choice, role of, 14–16
Motivation, 10
Mundy, P. C., 69

Natural kinds
  and historical change, 13
  theory of, 12–13
Neches, R., 128, 129, 131, 204
Neisser, U., 72, 95, 130, 155, 156
Nelson, K., 103
Nelson, R. R., 144
Nerlove, H., 84
Neumann, P. G., 153
Neves, D. M., 128

Newell, A., 82, 91, 92, 125, 164–165
Newman, D., 121, 122
Nigro, G., 166
Noelting, G., 22, 24
Norman, D., 82, 104
Novel situations
  componential approach to, 178
  relationship between automatization
    and dealing with, 179–180
Novel tasks, componential approach to,
  176–178

O'Brien, D. P., 57
Open mechanisms, 9–10
Operational efficiency and short-term
  storage space, 37–39
Operational practice and short-term
  storage space, 39–40
Optimal level, 47–60
  biological correlates of, 57–58
  defined, 47
  and environmental conditions for
    detecting levels, 55–57
  functioning of, 58–60
  individual differences in intelligence
    affecting, 67–69
  limits transformations, 66–67
  memory limitations on, 70–73
  spurts in performance at, 53–55
  and ten levels of development, 48–53
O'Shea, T., 103
Overton, W. F., 57

Palmer, S., 114
Parker, C. A., 55
Pascual-Leone, J., 38, 53, 70, 104, 190,
  192
Pellegrino, J. W., 146, 166
Performance components in
  componential framework, 166–167
Peters, A. M., 57, 68
Petersen, I., 58
Phelps, E., 65
Piaget, J., 11, 28, 102, 149, 156
  and children counting equal
    collections, 109–110
  contradiction as impetus in theory of,
    86
  and environmental influences, 47
  epigenetic proposal of, 8
  evolutionary concepts of child
    development in work of, 3, 4
  and formal-operational reasoning, 122
  goal-direction as viewed by, 144
  influences of theories of, 189–191,
    193, 194, 198–200, 203

learning distinguished from
    development by, 46
  neo-Piagetian distinguished from, 20,
    40–42
  reflective abstraction and, 117
  second-order relations and, 167
  and single path for development, 64
  skill theory compared with theory of,
    59
  and term "functional invariant," 27
  transition from 4 to 6 in theory of,
    25–26
  two-process model and, 69
  weak-form goal system of, 5
Picasso, P., 145
Pipp, S. L., 45–79, 190, 195, 196, 202–
  203
Politics, role of, 13
Popper, K. R., 144
Posner-Mitchell letter-matching task,
  179
Pound, E., 2
Powell, J. S., 171
Preschoolers, subitizing in, 114–116
Production-system state descriptions,
  104–106
Pseudomechanisms, 7

Quantitative development
  counting in, 116–117
  subitizing in, see Subitizing
  as theory, 191, 193–200, 204, 206–
    207
  See also Conservation of number;
    Knowledge states; Self-modifying
    systems

Reaves, C. C., 72
Redundancy elimination, rule formation
  via, in number conservation, 120–
  121
Rees, E., 166
Reinforcement-contingency model of
  change, 9
Reitman, J. S., 146, 147
Retardation, componential approach to,
  182–184
Riel, M., 121, 122
Rifkin, B., 166, 167
Riley, M. S., 116
Rips, L. J., 91, 153
Ritter, L., 89
Roberts, R. J., Jr., 69
Robinson, M., 22, 103, 116, 123, 204
Rosch, E., 153
Rose, A. P., 125

Ruderman, A., 61
Rule execution in encoding and combination framework, 157–158
Rumelhart, D. E., 82
Russell, S., 52, 55–56, 68, 69

Sameroff, A., 46
Saxe, G. B., 22
Schaeffer, B., 110, 115
Schneider, W., 173, 179
Scott, J. L., 110, 115
Scribner, S., 9
Seibert, J. M., 69
Self-modifying systems, 125–132
    composition in, 127–128
    and conflict resolution rules, 125–126
    and conservation acquisition, 129–130
    discrimination in, 126–127
    and distinction between learning and development, 130–132
    domains of application of, 128–129
    generalization in, 127
Selman, R. L., 57
Shepard, R. N., 148
Shepard-Metzler block configurations, 114
Shields, J. B., 69
Shiffrin, R. M., 173, 179
Shoben, E. J., 91, 153
Short-term storage space (STSS), 34–40
    operational efficiency in, 37–39
    operational practice in, 39–40
Siegel, A., 13
Siegel, L. S., 116
Siegler, R. S., 22, 24, 26, 64, 103, 104, 106, 116, 120, 123, 125, 141–162, 166, 191, 192, 194–196, 199, 204–205
Silverman, I. W., 111, 116, 125
Simon, D. P., 147, 166
Simon, H. A., 82, 91, 92, 128, 131, 144, 147, 166, 167
Skill acquisition, 60–67
    defined, 47
    development sequence illustrating transformations in, 61–64
    individual differences in intelligence affecting, 67–69
    memory limitations on, 70–73
    optimal level limits transformations in, 66–67; see also Optimal level
    paths for transformations in, 64–66
Skill theory, 46–47
    conclusions on, 73–74
    as theory, 59, 180, 192–200, 202–203, 206–207

See also Optimal level; Skill acquisition
Skinner, B. F., 9, 46, 190
Smith, E. E., 91, 145, 153
Sommers, F., 88
Spearman, C., 166
Spelke, E. S., 72, 115, 116
Spencer, H., 3, 15
Spitz, H. H., 103
Starkey, P., 115, 116
Stavey, R., 156
Stein, G., 145
Stein, N. L., 103
Stern, D., 28, 32
Sternberg, R. J., 4, 11, 65, 66, 69, 84, 85, 103, 142, 145, 163–186, 194–196, 200, 204–206
Stone, C. A., 60
Strauss, M. S., 103, 115
Strauss, S., 156
Structure-dependent transition mechanisms, examples of, 83–90
    characteristic-to-defining shift, 89–90
    influence of boundary conditions, 87–89
    new higher order relations appearing, 83–85
    resolution of internal inconsistencies or contradictions, 85–87
    summary of examples, 90
Structure/process dilemma, 90–93
STSS, see Short-term storage space
Subitizing, 112–116
    in adults, 112–114
    in preschoolers and infants, 114–116

Tabor, L. E., 57, 68
Taine, H. A., 9
Taylor, S. E., 61
Theory
    and essential messiness, 14
    evolution, see Evolution theory
    overview of domains of, 11–13
    See also Cognitive-development mechanisms, overview of; Development
Time line in number conservation, 117–120
    generalizations over sequences in, 118–120
Trabasso, T., 155, 204
Transformation rules, skill acquisition, see Skill acquisition
Transition mechanisms, overview of, 6–10
Tucker, J. L., 49
Tucker, M. F., 115

Vago, S., 157
Value monitoring in encoding and
    combination framework, 149–151
Van Oeffelen, M. P., 114
Van Parijs, P., 143, 144
Van Parys, M., 49
Variation, encoding and combination as
    sources of cognitive, 144–159
  conclusions on, 158–159
  encoding and combination
    framework, 147–158
  feature construction in framework,
    147, 148, 152–153
  feature integration in framework, 147,
    148, 155–157
  feature selection in framework, 147,
    153–155
  rule execution in framework, 147,
    148, 157–158
  value monitoring in framework, 147,
    149–151
  as theory, 191, 193–200, 204–207
Vos, P. G., 114
Vurpillot, E., 166
Vygotsky, L. S., 6, 8, 55, 89

Wagner, R. K., 183
Wallace, J. G., 46, 66, 104, 114, 153,
    191, 204

Wang, Y., 147
Washington, G., 145, 146
Waterman, D., 106
Watson, J. B., 5, 6
Watson, M. W., 49, 52, 55, 61
Waugh, N. C., 104
Webb, R. A., 69
Weene, P., 155, 156
Weir, M. W., 154, 158
Werner, H., 11, 63, 189, 190
Westerman, M. A., 49
White, B., 33
White, M. G., 2
White, S. H., 15, 58
Whitely, S. E., 166
Wilkening, F., 155
Willy, R., 2
Winter, S. G., 144
Wittgenstein, L., 145
Wohlwill, J. F., 67, 182, 188
Wright, R. J., 167
Wundt, W. M., 11

Yakovlev, P., 40
Young, R. M., 103, 104

Zaidel, E., 57, 68
Zelazo, P. R., 57, 68

D M